*Beasts and Birds of the Middle Ages*

University of Pennsylvania Press
MIDDLE AGES SERIES
*Edited by Edward Peters*
Henry Charles Lea Professor
of Medieval History
University of Pennsylvania

A complete listing of the books in this series
appears at the back of this volume

# Beasts and Birds of the Middle Ages

The Bestiary and Its Legacy

edited by Willene B. Clark
and Meradith T. McMunn

University of Pennsylvania Press
*Philadelphia*

*Frontispiece:* Ashmole Bestiary: Adam Naming the Animals (Oxford, Bodleian Lib. MS Ashmole 1511, fol. 9). (Photo: Conway Library, Courtauld Institute of Art)

Copyright © 1989 by the University of Pennsylvania Press
All rights reserved
Printed in the United States of America

Library of Congress Cataloging-in-Publication Data

Beasts and birds of the Middle Ages: the bestiary and its legacy /
    edited by Willene B. Clark and Meradith T. McMunn.
        p.   cm. — (Middle Ages series)
    Bibliography: p.
    Includes index.
    ISBN 0-8122-8147-0
        1. Bestiaries—History and criticism.   2. Didactic literature,
    Latin (Medieval and modern)—History and criticism.   3. Literature,
    Medieval—History and criticism.   4. Animals, Mythical, in
    literature.   5. Animals in literature.   I. Clark, Willene B.
    II. McMunn, Meradith T.   III. Series.
    PA8275.B4Z55   1989
    809'.9336—dc20                                              89-4915
                                                                   CIP

*We dedicate this collection of essays to the memory of*

FLORENCE McCULLOCH

*Professor of French at Wellesley College, who, through her own research and through her generous encouragement of others, stimulated the current renewal of interest in this important medieval genre*

# Contents

# Acknowledgments

Many individuals, libraries, and institutions have assisted the authors of the essays in this collection and are acknowledged in the notes. In addition, the editors wish to express their gratitude to the Samuel H. Kress Foundation for a grant to support the illustration of the volume, to Marlboro College and Rhode Island College for financial and clerical assistance, and to Wellesley College, Florence McCulloch's institution, for support and encouragement from the inception to the completion of this project.

# Introduction

The animals with which we humans share the earth have always fascinated us. We admire their physical beauty, or oddity, or strength, or grace, and we attribute to them all manner of human social and spiritual qualities. They inform our myths, rituals, and narratives. In antiquity and the Middle Ages, each animal species had its place and function in the cosmos, but with the rise of modern zoology in the eighteenth and nineteenth centuries, humans tended to take an empirical rather than anthropomorphic view of animals. Nevertheless, the interconnectedness of all creatures of the earth is still a central tenet of the ecology movement, which is our modern analogue of earlier cosmologies.

The bestiaries, or books of beasts, are collections of animal descriptions and lore, both real and fantastic, which are interpreted as spiritual or moral lessons and often provided with illustrations. Topoi originating in or popularized by the bestiaries are found in diverse media from the Middle Ages to the present day. Both text and picture were frequent sources for exempla and iconography in the literature and art of the Middle Ages. "For every virtue and for every sin there is an example drawn from bestiaries, and animals exemplify the human world."[1] An ecclesiastical image such as the pelican reviving her young, and the quotation of bestiary chapters in a medieval romance or in instructional texts such as Jacques de Vitry's *Exempla,* illustrate the breadth of bestiary influence, touching both the sacred and the secular worlds. Given the bestiary's widespread and enduring authority, it is surprising that until recently only a few scholars had seriously examined its traditions and their effects.

This volume is designed not only to collect some recent bestiary scholarship for the convenience of specialists, but also to give students and non-specialists a summary of the development of the generic entity known as the bestiary, especially in its European permutations. The specialist essays that follow demonstrate the vitality of contemporary bestiary studies, as well as ways in which various versions of the bestiary, bestiary manuscripts, and bestiary iconography can be studied, and how animal lore which is not itself from the bestiary can be useful in understanding the larger context in which the bestiaries were compiled and were understood in the Middle Ages. A selected bibliography of works on bestiaries and related lore published since 1962 and a list of Western European bestiary manuscripts are also provided.

## History of the Bestiary

The bestiary derives from an important text of late antique animal literature, the *Physiologus* (*The Naturalist*), which dates probably from the second century A.D. and which may have originated in Alexandria.[2] The *Physiologus* exists in a number of versions and is composed of animal lore, disposed in some twenty to fifty chapters. Each chapter treats a different creature—animal, bird, serpent, or insect—and describes characteristics drawn from direct observation, traditional lore, fable, and myth, to which the author-compiler or a slightly later writer added Christian moralizations. Michael Curley notes that the moralizer finds purely moral lessons in the world of animals, "but more often aims at making manifest the nature of God himself by unveiling the vestiges of the Creator in creation."[3] In the moral sense, just as the antelope snags its horns in a bush and is slain by the hunter, so the Christian, trusting in the two horns of the Old and New Testaments, must avoid the snares of slander, pleasure, desire, and worldly pomp. In the spiritual sense, the eagle, perceiving its eyes to grow dim with age, flies up to the sun to burn away the dimness, then bathes in a fountain and is made new; so the dimness of the eyes of the heart is healed by the spiritual fountain of the Lord, who is the sun of justice. With its lively animal tales and compelling lessons, the *Physiologus* became a popular source of exempla and a favorite school-text in the Middle Ages.[4] Although surviving illustrated copies of the *Physiologus* are rare, the earliest—the famous Bern *Physiologus* (Bürgerbibliothek MS 318) from the ninth century—provides stylistic evidence that a program of illustrations was invented for the work in late antiquity.[5] A number of the Bern designs can be traced in the bestiaries of the high and late Middle Ages. The original Greek *Physiologus* was translated into numerous languages—Coptic, Ethiopic, Armenian, Syrian, Arabic, German, Old English, Icelandic, French, Italian, and Latin—in verse as well as prose.[6] However, it is from the Latin versions of the *Physiologus* that the various medieval bestiaries descend.

The structure and character of the bestiary are essentially the same as those of the *Physiologus*. The point at which the *Physiologus* becomes a bestiary is not clear, a confusion which is reflected in the titles used in its manuscripts as well as on medieval book inventories and school-text lists. When significant numbers of new chapters and new animals are added to the traditional *Physiologus* chapters, and when material is interpolated into existing chapters from sources such as St. Ambrose's *Hexameron* and Isidore's *Etymologies,* the resulting compilation can safely be considered a bestiary.[7] As Nikolaus Henkel points out, even the earliest *Physiologus* manuscripts contain texts which have additions from other sources; it is the number and extent of these additions which for him finally establishes the bestiary as a separate work.[8] The earliest known bestiaries are the version, dating as early as the tenth century, that Florence McCulloch called B-Isidore (B-Is), because it combines a B-version *Physiologus* text with passages from Isidore of Seville's *Etymologies,* and the so-called Dicta Chrysostomi version, probably from the eleventh century, which adds material to the *Physiologus* but differs from it principally in chapter order.[9] Most bestiaries, however, were compiled in the twelfth and thirteenth centuries. The modern choice between the terms "Physiologus" or "bestiary" depends, as it did in the Middle Ages, on the view of the writer. Here we consider the bestiary to be any work deriving from the Latin *Physiologus* which departs, by means of additions and interpolations, from the Latin *Physiologus* versions known as Y, C, and B.

The medieval bestiary, regardless of its demarcation from the *Physiologus,* exists in versions written in Latin and a number of the European languages. It consists of chapters, passages, and paraphrases from the *Physiologus,* to which are added animal lore from Near Eastern and classical sources, from folklore, and from various Christian writers, especially the *Etymologies* of Isidore of Seville. The most widely copied versions, as reflected in extant manuscripts, are the Latin ones, especially the so-called Dicta Chrysostomi and Second Family Bestiaries.[10] The various European vernacular versions descend from the Latin bestiary versions. Each of these vernacular versions is a unique compilation from the existing bestiary materials together with its own modifications and interpolations.[11]

As a result of these textual changes, the bestiary differs in tone and emphasis from the *Physiologus.* The animal interpretations in the *Physiologus* tend to be more theological, that is, "mystical," while the bestiary expands the moral-ethical content considerably, making the work more obviously didactic than its predecessor.[12] The bestiary, like the *Physiologus,* became a popular source for sermon writers. Another likely bestiary use was as a monastic teaching text,[13] and where early provenance is known, it is usually monastic. The bestiary's varied appeal is reflected in the Second Family version, produced mainly in England beginning probably in the twelfth century,[14] where there are lessons in ethical behavior and Christian spirituality for both religious and lay audiences. The stag that crosses dangerous seas to a new pasture is the Christian, who leaves this world for the religious life. The dove, so gentle and reserved, is a lesson to widows to remain chaste. The author of the thirteenth-century *Bestiaire divin* adds to the traditional bestiary material an extended passage portraying the evils of wealth. Resonances of the essentially ethical nature of the bestiary occur in Richard de Fournival's choice of form and subject matter in the *Bestiaire d'amour,* where bestiary animal traits are used to create a satiric commentary on the courtly ethic. Only two known bestiaries omit all the didactic allegory.[15]

## Bestiary Illustration

The majority of bestiaries are illustrated, or have spaces left for illustrations, especially, as Florence McCulloch observed, the vernacular versions.[16] This apparent reversal of the practice in the *Physiologus,* where illustrations are rare, may only reflect the considerable increase in manuscript illustration in the twelfth century in general. This increase was the result of the new monasticism and new learning which produced not only more texts suited to illustration, but also an impetus to decorate older texts.[17] On the other hand, it may have been a response to the use of beast-moral literature as an instructional tool for those who were not functionally literate, such as lay-brothers in the monasteries, who would remember the lessons more easily with the aid of pictures.[18] Despite frequent visual references to an earlier *Physiologus* program as represented in the Bern copy—for example, in the fox and caladrius designs—each bestiary version has certain characteristic designs of its own, such as those noted by Xenia Muratova for the Second Family Bestiary and by Willene Clark for the H-version in their essays in this volume. These matters are currently under investigation.

## Continuing Popularity

Production of Latin bestiary manuscripts was at its peak in the late twelfth and thirteenth centuries.[19] Vernacular versions continued in popularity into the early fifteenth century. With the advent of printing in the fifteenth century, there was a resurgence of interest in animal genres including fables and other edifying literature with popular appeal. One explanation of the revival of this literature in the late fifteenth century is that the growing middle classes, while literate, were not necessarily intellectual. Women in particular wanted easily understood books for their own improvement and for teaching their children.[20] Medieval bestiary texts were not simply set into print, however, but instead new compilations were made which combined bestiary lore with material from other sources, both theological and secular, and with an increasing amount of scientific observation.[21] These printed versions are illustrated with woodcut pictures which bear little or no relation to the designs in either the *Physiologus* or the bestiary traditions. Thus, new versions of the bestiary have continued to evolve into our own time. Recent examples, all using the word "bestiary" in their titles, include a collection of animal subjects in American art, an analysis of animal symbolism in the life and writings of St. Jerome, a fancifully illustrated book on the real and imaginary animals in the fiction of J. R. R. Tolkien, and an essay on natural history by a well-known scientist.[22]

## Bestiary Research

As we have seen, the development of the material which was compiled in the bestiaries can be traced back to late antiquity. It is surprising, therefore, that modern research on the history of the bestiary scarcely predates the twentieth century and precise details of bestiary influence have seldom been analyzed. Montague Rhodes James's *The Bestiary* (1928) and Florence McCulloch's *Mediaeval Latin and French Bestiaries* (1960; revised 1962) are the foundations of current research on the bestiary tradition.[23] In the periods before and between these two seminal works, few bestiary studies appeared.

Perhaps the reason for the neglect of such a rich visual and verbal tradition lies partly in a too close, and misleading, identification of the bestiary with either science or pseudo-science. In fact, the medieval bestiary, in its descent from Eastern fables, Eastern and Western animal lore, and the early Christian *Physiologus*, follows a line quite distinct from that deriving from the ancient sciences. In Augustine's *De doctrina christiana*, Creation was a mirror of the Creator, a means of revealing his nature and his intentions for the life and salvation of the Christian believer. It is this view which informs the bestiary, whose prime function was clearly to present Christian teachings in an easily comprehended, indeed appealing manner to a broad audience. As Nikolaus Henkel has shown, even medieval readers did not take the animal descriptions too seriously or believe them to be natural history.[24] One proof of the essentially moral-ethical character of the bestiary is its transformation by Richard de Fournival into a form of social satire in the *Bestiaire d'amour*. If medieval natural history can be inferred from various versions and copies of the bestiary, it must be done in the fundamentally allegorical context of the work.

The publication of Florence McCulloch's *Mediaeval Latin and French Bestiaries* in a well-known, accessible scholarly series provided a systematic presentation and comparison of the complex bestiary versions. With a solid foundation for further research thus established, interest in bestiary studies increased steadily with the appearance of bestiary facsimiles and translations, studies in a wide variety of related materials (see bibliography), a new journal devoted to beast epic, fable, and fabliau, including material on the bestiary, and conferences on bestiary lore. This activity is, in turn, generating new excitement and stimulating investigations of the bestiary tradition and its dissemination in art history and literature.

The field of bestiary studies offers a number of challenging issues. Current research centers on studies of the verbal and visual iconography of individual animals in various media, translations of several bestiary versions with complementary investigations of sources and manuscripts, studies of bestiary material in medieval sermons, bestiary patronage, and the relationship between text and image in the tradition of a given bestiary version. Yet much remains to be done. Most bestiary versions have been edited, but some still need modern critical editions.[25] There is a need for comparative catalogs of the illustrations in the many bestiary versions and of bestiary images in other media. Moreover, despite its non-scientific character, the bestiary can yield interesting and useful data to the historian of science who understands the work and its essential purpose. The relationship between the bestiaries and the medieval encyclopedias, with the latter's greater emphasis on empirical fact, needs to be more closely defined. Specifics of bestiary influences on non-bestiary genres need to be worked out. The very difficult questions of audience and patrons need considerable work. While both McCulloch and Henkel provide summaries of the geographic distribution of versions, more detailed study of this question would furnish helpful information.

In addition to these specific questions for study of the bestiary, there is a need for application of broader interpretive methods, including theological and literary critical analysis. Most attention is still directed to iconography, texts, sources, and influences. It is time to turn some attention to problems of theoretical frameworks and critical strategies, which may in turn shed new light on the results of the more narrowly or traditionally defined investigations.

## The Present Volume

Each essay in this volume serves three functions: (1) it presents new material on the bestiary and related issues, (2) it addresses current questions in medieval scholarship in the context of literature, art, history, and manuscript studies, and (3) it serves as a methodological paradigm for future bestiary research. The studies fall naturally into four general categories: a study of the use of the bestiary (Rowland), studies of bestiary manuscripts (Clark, Muratova), studies of individual bestiary animal iconography (Beer, Mermier, Pfeffer), and studies of the influence of the bestiary on other medieval genres (Curley, Friedman, Joslin, McMunn, Randall).

In the first category, Beryl Rowland examines the relation of the bestiary to the art of memory in the classical and medieval periods. She concludes that one function of the word and picture relationship in the bestiary was to aid recall of the lessons in the text.

The essays by Willene Clark and Xenia Muratova illustrate two different approaches to style and physical structure in bestiaries, in both instances by the comparison of important manuscripts. Each takes the opportunity to use bestiary evidence to make wider claims about changes from Romanesque to Gothic, and about the production of manuscripts and the relation of a manuscript to its model.

The third group of essays concentrates on a particular bestiary animal or bird to explore thematic or iconographic developments. Guy Mermier uses variants in the tradition of the Greek, Latin, and French descriptions of the phoenix to suggest a model for the symbolic world of the bestiary and how its animal symbolism functioned. This study includes examples of literature from the beginning to the end of the Middle Ages, although it is focused in the earlier centuries of the period. Wendy Pfeffer offers a more general survey of the imagery associated with another bird, the nightingale, in both Eastern and Western literature. She shows that the nightingale is most familiar as a secular symbol, particularly in the courtly literature of the high Middle Ages. Jeanette Beer explores the transformation of the bestiary into a work with secular symbolism in the *Bestiaire d'amour* and *Réponse de la Dame* of Richard de Fournival, using the cock to illustrate her arguments.

In the fourth group the authors demonstrate bestiary influence on other genres. Lilian Randall explains the complex meanings of bestiary animals in a thirteenth-century Psalter and demonstrates their secular context. Both Meradith McMunn and Michael Curley study the extension of bestiary influence to secular medieval genres. McMunn documents two types of use of bestiary material in the romance: quotation and allusion. Curley surveys the use of animal symbolism, including some from the bestiary, in the development of the most enduring of medieval legends, that of King Arthur. Mary Joslin explores the use of animals in the *Histoire ancienne jusqu'à César*. John Friedman discusses the use of animal exempla in Marcus of Orvieto's *Liber de moralitatibus* and provides an edition of the text.

These essays represent current work in bestiary studies, but by no means all areas of bestiary research in the late 1980s. The growth in variety of investigations in the field has been rapid and reflects the variety in the bestiary itself, with its several functions, its many versions and traditions, and its enduring capacity to fascinate its readers.

*Notes*

1. Umberto Eco, *The Name of the Rose* (San Diego, New York, London: Harcourt Brace Jovanovich, 1983), p. 79.
2. Florence McCulloch, *Mediaeval Latin and French Bestiaries,* University of North Carolina Studies in the Romance Languages and Literatures 33 (Chapel Hill: University of North Carolina Press, 1960; rev. 1962), p. 17; Nikolaus Henkel, *Studien zum Physiologus im Mittelalter* (Tübingen: Max Niemeyer, 1976), pp. 14–15; Michael J. Curley, trans., *Physiologus* (Austin and London: University of Texas Press, 1979), pp. xvi–xvii. Curley translates the Latin versions Y and B.
3. Curley, *Physiologus,* p. xv.
4. Günther Glauche, *Schullektüre im Mittelalter* (Munich: Arbeo-Gesellschaft, 1970), p. 70. Two other famous compendia of animal lore from the classical age, Aelian's *On the Characteristics of Animals* and Solinus's *Polyhistoria,* also appear on the school-text lists. See Klaus Grubmüller, *Meister Esopus: Untersuchungen zu Geschichte und Funktion der Fabel im Mittelalter* (Munich: Artemis, 1977), p. 49; Pierre Riché, *Les Ecoles et l'enseignement dans l'occident chrétien de la fin du v<sup>e</sup> siècle au milieu du xi<sup>e</sup> siècle* (Paris: Aubier Montaigne, 1979), p. 228; and E. R. Curtius, *European Literature and the Latin Middle Ages* (New York: Bollingen, 1953), p. 49.
5. Bern, Bürgerbibliothek MS Bongarsiansis 318, a Latin version; see *Physiologus*

*Bernensis,* facsimile, ed. Christoph von Steiger and Otto Homburger (Basel: Alkuin-Verlag, 1964), and Helen Woodruf, "The Physiologus of Bern," *Art Bulletin,* 12 (1930), 226–253, who describes the classical properties of the miniatures. Among the often repeated visual motifs are the designs for the antelope with horns caught in bushes and the fox feigning death to catch birds, the unicorn with its head in a virgin's lap, and the caladrius predicting life or death for a sick man.

6. The history of the *Physiologus* and of scholarship on the subject is reviewed by McCulloch, *Mediaeval Bestiaries,* chs. 1–2; Henkel, *Studien,* passim, on the Latin and German versions, with lists of editions, pp. 207–208; Curley, *Physiologus,* introduction.

7. The various modifications producing the medieval bestiary are described by McCulloch, *Mediaeval Bestiaries,* pp. 28–44, who does not, however, address the terminology issue directly. The Dicta Chrysostomi and Theobald versions present some of the most difficult problems of terminology. As Henkel notes, *Studien,* p. 24, it does not appear that the manuscript evidence, both internal and external, will ever permit a clear distinction between *Physiologus* and bestiary in some versions.

8. Henkel, *Studien,* p. 24 and ch. 6.

9. For the B-Is version, McCulloch, *Mediaeval Bestiaries,* pp. 28–30. The Dicta Chrysostomi version takes its name from an erroneous attribution to St. John Chrysostom; see McCulloch, pp. 41–44; Henkel, *Studien,* pp. 29–34.

10. For summaries of the Latin versions, see McCulloch, *Mediaeval Bestiaries,* ch. 2, pp. 28–44; Henkel, *Studien,* pp. 29–34. Most European versions derive from the *Physiologus* version B, for which see McCulloch, p. 25, and Henkel, p. 27.

11. The French versions are reviewed by McCulloch, *Mediaeval Bestiaries,* ch. 3; the German versions by Henkel, *Studien,* ch. 4.

12. Kenneth McKenzie, "Unpublished Manuscripts of Italian Bestiaries," *PMLA,* 20 n.s. 13 (1905), 380–409, draws too strictly the distinctions between the "mystical" *Physiologus* and the "moral" bestiary (pp. 381–382). The bestiary differs not so much in kind from its model as in amount, and the amount of moral teaching is obviously increased in the bestiary.

13. On the bestiary as a source of sermon exempla, Fr. John Morson, "The English Cistercians and the Bestiary," *Bulletin of the John Rylands Library,* 39 (1956), 146–170; and as a teaching text for monastic lay-brothers, Willene B. Clark, "The Illustrated Medieval Aviary and the Lay-Brotherhood," *Gesta,* 21 (1982), pp. 70–71, and the essay by Beryl Rowland in the present volume.

14. McCulloch, *Mediaeval Bestiaries,* pp. 34–38.

15. The Cambrai Bestiary (Cambrai, Bibl. Mun. MS 370) and a Provençal version entitled *Aiso son las naturas d'alcus auzels e d'alcunas bestias;* McCulloch, *Mediaeval Bestiaries,* pp. 46–47.

16. McCulloch, *Mediaeval Bestiaries,* p. 70.

17. On the twelfth-century increase in numbers of illuminated manuscripts, Otto Pächt, *The Rise of Pictorial Narrative in Twelfth-Century England* (Oxford: Clarendon Press, 1962), ch. 2, and Walter Cahn, *Romanesque Bible Illumination* (Ithaca: Cornell University Press, 1982), p. 121.

18. See n. 13 above. The lay-brothers, who may have been taught spiritual lessons

from the bestiary, were usually illiterate. Among the upper classes, which may have been the principal audience for vernacular bestiaries, literacy was growing but was scarcely widespread. On the illiterate audience in the Middle Ages, see Franz H. Bäuml, "Varieties and Consequences of Medieval Literacy and Illiteracy," *Speculum*, 55 (1980), 237–265, and with reference to art, pp. 259–265; Michael Camille, "Seeing and Reading: Some Visual Implications of Medieval Literacy," *Art History*, 8 (1985), 26–49; and Brian Stock, *The Implications of Literacy: Written Language and Models of Interpretation in the Eleventh and Twelfth Centuries* (Princeton: Princeton University Press, 1983).

19. A reason for the decline in production late in the thirteenth century is suggested by Clark, "The Illustrated Medieval Aviary," p. 71.

20. E. P. Goldschmidt, *The Printed Book of the Renaissance* (Amsterdam: Gerard Th. van Heusden, 1966), p. 48.

21. Konrad von Meganberg's *Buch der Natur* (Augsburg: Johann Bämler, 1475, 1478), and Konrad Gesner's *Historia animalium* (Zurich: C. Forschover, 1551–1558); also Edward Topsell, *History of Foure-Footed Beastes* (London: W. Iaggard, 1607, rpt. New York: Da Cappo Press, 1973), based largely on Gesner. The more traditional bestiary mode is retained in Maynus de Mayneriis, *Dyalogus creaturarum moralizatus* (Gouda: Gheraert Leeu, 1480), which, however, interpolates numerous fables and folktales (facsimile of the Stockholm edition of 1483, Stockholm: Michaelisgillet/Bokförlaget Bra Böker, 1983). For a printed German version, Henkel, *Studien*, pp. 110–112. For a summary review see Luisa Cogliati Arano, "Bestiari ed erbari dal manoscritto alla stampa," in Henri Zerner, *Le stampe e la diffusione della imagini e degli stili* (Atti del XXIV Congr. C.I.H.A., Bologna, 1979; Bologna: CLUEB, 1983), pp. 17–22.

22. Mary Sayre Haverstock, *An American Bestiary* (New York: Abrams, 1979); Herbert Friedmann, *A Bestiary for St. Jerome: Animal Symbolism in European Religious Art* (Washington: Smithsonian Institution Press, 1980); David Day, *A Tolkien Bestiary* (New York: Ballantine Books, 1979); Stephen Jay Gould, *Illuminations: A Bestiary*, with photographs by Rosamond Wolff Purcell (New York: Norton, 1987).

23. M. R. James, *The Bestiary* (Oxford: The Roxburghe Club, 1928); for McCulloch, see n. 2 above.

24. On the differences between the Augustinian and Aristotelian traditions in writings about animals, Michel de Boüard, "Encyclopédies médiévales: Sur la 'connaissance de la nature et du monde' au moyen âge," *Revue des Questions Historiques*, series 3, 16 (1930), 258–304. See also Gabriel Bianciotto, *Bestiaires du Moyen Age* (Paris: Stock, 1980), especially pp. 12–14; Mia I. Gerhardt, "Zoologie médiévale: préoccupations et procédés," in *Methoden in Wissenschaft und Kunst des Mittelalters* (*Miscellenea Mediaevalia* 7), ed. Albert Zimmermann (Berlin: W. de Gruyter, 1970), pp. 231–248; Gudrun Schleusener-Eichholz, "Naturwissenschaft und Allegorese: Der 'Tractatus de occulo morali' des Petrus von Limoges," *Frühmittelalterliche Studien*, 12 (1978), 258–309, who notes that some of the more scientific works were moralized by later writers (pp. 277–278). The mix of science and myth in encyclopedias is discussed in D. C. Gretham, "The Concept of Nature in Bartholomaeus Anglicus (Fl. 1230)," *Journal of the History of Ideas*, 41 (1980), 577–663.

25. References to editions can be found in McCulloch, *Mediaeval Bestiaries,* passim, and Henkel, *Studien,* pp. 207–208. Even more recent editions are noted in this volume's bibliography. Modern editions of the Second Family Bestiary, the Old English Bestiary, and the long form of Pierre de Beauvais' bestiary are in progress.

# Beryl Rowland

## I. *The Art of Memory and the Bestiary*

Remarking on the extraordinary popularity of the bestiary, as evinced by its frequent appearance in medieval libraries in England and on the Continent, Florence McCulloch suggested that its appeal lay in "the concrete descriptive element, easily retainable because of its very lack of subtlety, which then recalled the Christian dogma or moral exhortation that the reader was summoned to heed."[1] Professor McCulloch's statement went to the heart of the matter. The bestiary was concerned with memory, with providing moral instruction in such a way that it could be remembered by the reader or auditor. "Memoire est tresoriere de toutes choses," observed Brunetto Latini at the beginning of *Li Livres dou tresor*, a moralized account of fish, serpents, birds, and beasts. He thereby repeated Cicero's famous phrase:[2] "Rerum omnium Thesaurus memoria est." The bestiary's function was similar to that of the medieval sermon: it was to teach the Christian ethic in such a manner that would fix itself indelibly on the mind and, like the sermons of such preachers as John Ridevall and Robert Holcot,[3] its form and style appear to have been indebted to a technique of Greek and Roman rhetoricians which, in many modified forms, has continued to be practiced until the present century.[4]

The attention that has been paid to this art in recent decades is sufficient to allow me to give here only the points essential to my immediate subject. The fullest account of this system occurs in *Rhetorica ad Herennium* (c. 86–82 B.C.), a work that in medieval times was believed to have been written by Cicero and was, indeed, supplemented by Cicero's *De oratore* (55 B.C.) and by Quintilian's *Institutio oratoria* (c. A.D. 95).[5] The system depended on a carefully ordered series of places (*loci* or *loca*) and representations (*imagines*). For places the practitioner might select a large building such as a Roman house or, in medieval times, a cathedral or monastery. He then placed in imagination in the chambers (*camerae*), arches, pillars, niches, ornaments and the like, images of items that he wanted to memorize—ideas, actions, people, words, sentences, or even whole narratives.[6]

Once fixed in their *loci*, these images could be easily recalled and used in proper sequence, especially if they were *imagines agentes*, corporeal figures engaged in some conspicuous action or possessing striking characteristics. Even abstractions were visualized. Strength was represented by a picture of Samson, Wisdom by Solomon.[7] "To represent bitterness," said Bishop Bradwardine, "place someone eating something bitter and at once foully vomiting it. For fetidness, however, put something rotten in front of someone who with one hand closes his nostrils as though for the smell, and with the other puts aside the material with contempt."[8] Bradwardine, like many scholars in the medieval period, wrote a formal *ars memorativa* which largely adhered to the classical rules. Other earlier and more influential practitioners, such as Thomas Aquinas and Albertus Magnus, introduced further subtleties from Aristotle's *De memoria et reminiscentia* and reformulated the art, treating it as part of Prudence and making its use a moral duty.[9] Others again, such as John of Garland,[10] appear to have misinterpreted the system, and still others were imaginative and experimental in their adaptation of the classical rules: even the squares of a chessboard might serve as *loci* and chessmen as *imagines* in a work intended as *regimen principum*.[11] Some such treatments show that a tremendous modification of the rhetorical tradition had taken place. They illustrate Frances Yates's contention that in the Middle Ages "the artificial memory has moved over from *rhetoric* to *ethics*."[12]

Contingent upon this shift, and of great importance to our consideration of the bestiary, was a remarkable endeavor to adapt the system and accommodate it to the laity. The main practitioners of the cultivated memory were, of course, the learned. They read or were read to and they stocked their memories according to the recognized classical precepts. To them, books were, indeed, "the key to remembrance," and the artificial memory compensated for their limited availability. As a direct result of their training, many writers of sermons and didactic treatises developed an arresting style that offered elaborate images, ingenious similitudes, and complex mnemonic schemes, as well as traditional but powerful representations of the Redemption story that the listener was exhorted to visualize. Their intention, however, was not simply to retain the material in their own memories and be able to deliver it with ease when the occasion arose, but to implant it ineffaceably in the minds of those whose memories were untrained. To fix in the memory the lesson that was to be recalled, they often externalized the art of memory process: they produced real *imagines* for the laity to regard *cum oculis carnis*. The method most commonly used reflected the often repeated observation of St. Gregory that "Ymagines et picturae sanctorum, et precipue crucis Christi, sunt libri laicorum."[13] Probably the more extreme measure of provoking what Owst called "holy terror of earthly vanities" by suddenly flashing a skull from beneath priestly robes was a rarity.[14] "Ymages and payntours ben lewde menys bokys," stated John Mirk, "and I say boldyly þer ben mony þousaund of pepul þat couþ not ymagen in her hert how Christ was don on þe rood, but as þai lerne hit be syȝt of ymages and payntours."[15] "Regard as models of deport-ment the graven images of the churches," said John of Garland, "which you should carry in your minds as living and indelible pictures."[16] The laity thus acquired its knowledge of the Christian dogma by looking at ecclesiastical images, as well as by listening to the preacher. Whereas the building recommended by the ancients for the establishing of *loci* could be real or imaginary, the memory house now became the actual church through which the laity walked every Sunday, and the memory figures were an *immutable series,* each image fixed in its niche, in its assigned locus, each summoning to mind the particular lesson to be associated with it. Even the Lollards admitted the "ymages ben bokis of lewid men."[17] The laity performed physically what Quintilian had described as a mental exer-cise: "As soon as the memory of the facts requires to be revived," said Quintilian, "all these places are visited in turn and the various deposits are demanded from their custodians, as the sight of each recalls the respective details. Consequently, however large the number of these which it is re-quired to remember, all are linked, one to the other, like dancers hand-in-hand and there can be no mistake since they join what precedes to what follows."[18]

While the sermon shows most clearly the attempt to persuade laymen to use external images and convert them into mental pictures for the purpose of remembering the Christian lesson, some memory treatises themselves seem to have been intended for the same audience. The Dominican Bar-tolomeo da San Concordio in *Ammaestramenti degli antichi,* writing in the vulgar tongue early in the fourteenth century, described memory tech-niques largely from Aquinas with specifications for places, corporeal si-militudes, and order from *Rhetorica ad Herennium,* and recommended them to the laity as a devotional exercise. The writer of an Italian work, *Rosaio della vita,* gave the memory rules for the purpose of remembering the Virtues and Vices and concluded, "Now that we have provided the book to be read, it remains to hold it in the memory."[19] An anonymous Vienna manuscript of the fifteenth century combines verbal descriptions

with external representations serving as examples for invisible memory images to be used in practical mnemonics. Here crude drawings of the Virtues and Vices demonstrate the type of mental pictures that the student
must form and retain in order to remember admonitions concerning the
roads to heaven and hell, and the last figure in the series bears the inscription "Ex locis et imaginibus ars memorativa constat Tullius ait."[20] Not surprisingly, the visual representation often closely resembled the corporeal
similitude that existed solely in the mind. Indeed, the figures portrayed in
the graphic arts had their counterparts described in the memory treatises.
For example, the personifications of the cardinal virtues whose attributes
were established in Carolingean times[21] are found both in descriptions in
the *ars memoriae artificialis* and in painting, sculpture, and ivory and wood
carving. Made visible, their postures suggest the animation of true *imagines
agentes:* Justitia with her balance, Prudence with her snake and scroll,
Temperantia with her vessel and spray of blossoms seem designed to im-
press upon the viewer the exemplary qualities that are to be remembered
and practiced.[22] Fortitudo, in an *ars memorativa* of 1425, is described as
"Virgo amata leonem calcat et os eius dilacerat," and thus she appears in a
miniature of the same date.[23]

Of even more significance to us because of their combined use of word
and picture are those secular compilations of exempla that proved so popular that they were among the earliest texts printed. In these didactic texts,
every moral lesson was accompanied by an illustration: the assault was
made through both the ear and the eye. Such works provided words and
visual images that could readily be translated into figures to be retained in
the memory according to the classical principles. The reader or auditor
was expected to glimpse the moral double meaning in the text as soon as
he or she embarked on the description or narrative, and some elements of
the allegory were usually reinforced by what was perceived to be taking
place in the accompanying illustrations. In *Destructiorum vitiorum,* for example, the text tells us that the siren luring man to his doom symbolizes
earthly delights that destroy man's soul. The woodcut reinforces the lesson,
supplying the corporeal representations that, as mental images, might be
retained in the memory: a drowning man despairingly stretches out his
arms to a smiling, bare-breasted young woman, who, with a pointedly
hands-off gesture, nonchalantly applies a large currycomb to her tail-
length hair.[24] Here the figure conveys something about *quid agas* even
without the text because of the associations already acquired from the classical story. A similar moral lesson is offered by the siren of the bestiary,

whether she is plucking an instrument, attacking a boatload of sleeping sailors, tearing off a man's clothes, or simply suckling her child while an ape performs headstands nearby.[25]

The illustrated bestiary itself seems to have been one of the earliest popular texts in which moral lessons and doctrinal mysteries were taught through an appeal to both the eye and the ear. Ranked with the Psalter and the Apocalypse as one of the leading picture books in twelfth- and thirteenth-century England,[26] it may be seen as an attempt to instruct the laity in the Christian life by impressing relevant images on the memory. It provides the verbal descriptions and moralization with pictures which, as McCulloch observed, are of immense aid "in revealing common or curious interpretations of the text."[27]

Such illustrations ultimately derive from two traditions in the Greek *Physiologus*.[28] The first is reflected in the ninth-century Bern MS 318, in which framed illustrations alternate with the text and achieve a spatial effect with the animals set in some kind of landscape. The second is assumed to derive from another cycle of illustrations of the Greek *Physiologus,* and in contrast to the illusionist techniques evident in the Bern manuscript, it has unframed line drawings accompanied by human figures that portray the allegorical meaning. A relatively early example is the tenth-century manuscript at Brussels, MS 10066-7. Evidence of the way these traditions developed in the eleventh century is lacking, but the enormous production of bestiaries associated with the flowering of the Anglo-Norman culture in the twelfth century enables us to follow the transformation. In the carefully painted miniatures of deluxe editions the designs become more elaborate and exuberant, generously employing strong colors for pink wolves, green oxen, and blue manticores, goats, and camels, all highlighted in gold. Such productions call into question the recent view of one scholar that bestiary illustrations "are never symbolic, nor do they address the moral life of man. They amount to picture book comprehension in terms of natural history alone."[29] Even in illustrations which seem to depict Isidore's etymology, the viewer is likely to perceive more than a pseudo-zoological trait, because the alleged derivation is the starting point for narrative and allegory. The bear licking her cubs into shape is a reminder not only that, according to Isidore, *ursus* is connected with *orsus* and is so named because she fashions her dead brood with her mouth (*ore*), but also of God restoring his Son to life;[30] the panther, a variegated creature breathing upon an assortment of transfixed sheep, reindeer, bears, and the like, not only illustrates the etymology *panthera* and the Aristotelian idea that this animal exhaled a sweet odor in order to catch other beasts but also symbolizes Christ drawing all men to him.[31] In some illustrations the dragon, representing the Devil, is cowering at his feet or flying away in terror. Even more emphatic is the message given by the dog-like animal with a broad tail, the beaver: Latin *castor,* said to derive from *castrando*— "castrating." This creature, emasculating itself in full view of hunters who are pursuing it for the medicine in its testicles, teaches that those who wish to live chastely must cut off their sins and throw them in the face of the Devil.[32] Some illustrations, like that of the pelican, sometimes depict a fuller allegory. In the first compartment in several manuscripts, the young pelicans attack the parent, in the second the parent kills her young, and in the third the pelican pierces her side, bathes her young in her blood, and revives them. These representations signify in turn: Christ wounded by mankind, God sacrificing his Son, and Christ saving mankind by shedding his blood.[33] The allegorical function is stressed by Philippe de Thaon, the author of the first verse bestiary in the vernacular. In all three manuscripts extant, the pictures are mentioned in various places of the poem in such comments as "Tel est sa nature / Ceo est cette peinture" or "Iceste nature / Mustre ceste figure." In addition there are Latin rubrics which indicate the figurative use. Of the lion that catches animals within a circle made by its tail, the rubric states: "Hic leo pingitur et quomodo capit animalia per circulum." The word *pingere* appears to be used in both the direct and the figurative sense, as for example: "Hic assida pingitur et allegorice intellegitur" (223).

The essential quality of these pictures is their animation. The animals are presented with such vivacity and vigor that they are oddly compelling, pulsating with life even when grotesque. In one manuscript, the domestic scene of the woman milking her cow not only aptly illustrates the fecundity and love which, according to the moralist, the reader must take as an example, but strikingly conveys the bustle of the farmyard and the hum of everyday activity. The woman's hand is poised at the udder, while the milk pours down into a coopered wooden tub, and the cow's full protruding tongue purposefully licks her calf, who rewards her with a grateful smile.[34] Of the fifty-four illuminations that McCulloch selected as being typical of the bestiary,[35] only the yale, sitting with crossed forepaws, is static, and even this creature, with its flexible horns, illustrates a point in the text and in some bestiaries is seen executing a vigorous leap.[36]

The dynamic character of the externalized visual representations accompanying the text lends support to the view that they are intended as aids to the creation of the invisible pictures in memory. Willene Clark points out in her study of Hugh of Fouilloy's *De avibus* that the basic purpose of the bestiary appears to have been similar to that of the *Aviary,* a work which it resembles in both literary structure and popular appeal.[37] Hugh of Fouilloy's *De avibus,* written sometime after 1132, was a teaching text for monastic lay-brothers, using birds as the subject of moral allegory, and the illuminations that are found in twenty-seven manuscripts were a means of instructing the "lewede."[38] "I have decided," wrote this Benedictine prior, "to paint the dove with silver wings and back of pale gold, and by a picture enlighten the minds of the uneducated . . . and what the ear could hardly perceive, the eye might take in. I wish not only to paint the dove by modeling it, but also to outline it by words, so that through writing I may set off the picture."[39] The mnemonic purpose is further underlined in the more diagrammatic pictures with texts and captions on borders of cross-pieces. Clark has suggested that both the illustrated Aviary and bestiary may have been used to instruct illiterate lay brothers whose attention might be held "by the pictures, while their teachers translated and explained, in whatever the local dialect, the simplified lessons contained in the text."[40]

Of course, the milieu of the bestiary varied but the overall function of the illustrations probably remained unaltered. In a noble household, the wealthy patron and his ladies would remember the Christian story by studying the brilliant illuminations while the text was read aloud; in various theological schools that possessed bestiaries, in the Augustinian priory that received the Morgan Bestiary *ad edificationem fratrum* or in the priory where Hugh composed the *Aviary,* the illustrations would assist in the moral and spiritual edification of lay brothers or provide preachers with easily remembered allegories for their sermons.

A more explicit explanation than Hugh's on the function of text and illustration, one that elaborates on Hugh's concern with the use of eye and ear, occurs in Richard de Fournival's *Le Bestiaire d'amour,* a popular work composed in the mid-thirteenth century, of which fourteen fully illustrated manuscripts survive.[41] While Richard no doubt drew much of his material from the longer bestiary of Pierre de Beauvais and made full use of the allegorical conventions of animals, the conception and treatment are highly original. The basic theme of the *Physiologus* concerns the Incarnation, Death, and Resurrection of Christ; that of *Le Bestiaire d'amour* has to do with the Death and Resurrection of the secular lover, who purports to be Richard himself, the "I" of the narrative.[42] The image of the redeemed sinner joining Christ in glory is replaced by the lover's dream of being united with his lady for eternity, and while the traditional animal characteristics are retained, the allegories are skillfully transformed. Thus the image of the lion cub, infant pelican, or weasel being resuscitated by its parent, which serves in the bestiary proper as a metaphor for Christ emerging from the tomb, becomes the symbol of the lover being revived by his lady. At the same time the subtlety and sophistication of the treatment seems to parody the naively transmitted message of the traditional bestiary.

In the accompanying miniatures, the animal or bird often appears with the lady or lover acting out of the message. In the Oxford Bodley manuscript Douce 308, most of the sixty-eight illustrations with gold, rose, or blue backgrounds are familiar to us from other bestiaries, but the caladrius perching on a sick man's bed,[43] the pelican feeding its young with its blood,[44] and the unicorn kneeling with its head in a virgin's lap[45] are no longer symbols of Christ, and their actions carry no doctrinal lesson; they are devices to encourage the lady to remember the message of the text: she is the caladrius who will cause the lover to die if she turns away from him, the pelican who alone can revive him; he is the unicorn enslaved by love. Important to our argument are Richard's observations on the overall function of such illustrations. In the preface he describes the way in which words and external images are inculcated in the memory. The accompanying picture shows a reader looking at knights of romance as though they were physically present: [46]

> And God, who loves man so that he wishes to provide him with everything that is necessary, gave him a virtue of strength of soul which is called the memory. This memory has two doors, to see and to hear, and there is a path by which one can go to each of these two doors. The paths are painting and speech.
>
> Painting serves for the eye, speech for the ear. And the way one can repair to the house of memory by painting and by speech is thus made clear: memory which is the guardian of the treasures acquired by man's senses through the excellence of his imagination makes what is past seem as if it were present. And one arrives at these things by painting and speech. For when one sees painted a history, whether of Troy or something else, one sees the deeds of worthy men who were there in past times as if they were present. And it is the same for speech. For when one hears a story being read, one perceives the happenings as if one saw them in the present. And since one renders into the present what is in the past by these two things, that is painting and speech, it well seems that it is by these two things that one comes to the memory.[47]

Then the writer addresses his lady directly as "bele tres douce amie" and contends that if he cannot be present in her company, he would like to stay always in her memory if possible. For this reason he is sending "these two things in one." In the illustration immediately below, the writer is portrayed handing to the lady a rolled up manuscript of his bestiary.[48] The text then continues:

> For I am sending in this writing, painting and speech, to say that, when I am not present, these writings, by their painting and their speech, will make me present in your memory.
> And I will show you how this writing holds painting and speech. For it well seems that there is speech, because all writings are made to show speech and to be read; and when one reads them, they go back to the nature of speech. Then again, there is painting and it seems that writings do not exist unless they are painted. And also this writing is of such meaning that it requires painting. For it is the nature of beasts and birds that they are more recognizable painted than described.[49]

This somewhat confused statement of the function of words and images is not only underscored by the writer's reiteration of "on voit, on veist," but is explained visually in illustrations of Memory as a woman at the portals of the House of Memory.[50] As depicted in an early fourteenth-century manuscript, Lady Memory stands at the entrance of a castle, between two doors. On one door is a large ear; on the other an eye. Clearly the images that one "sees" in the memory are to be achieved by impressions that first enter through these doors of sight and hearing.

We cannot determine whether individual bestiarists such as Philippe de Thaon and Guillaume le Clerc[51] shared Richard's concept of the relationship and function of word and picture. However, we can admit the possibility that in the bestiary and in certain kinds of didactic literature, the manner in which the moral precepts were presented was designed to enable the reader to retain them by fixing a series of images in the mind that could be recalled at will. Indeed, the bestiary may have owed its popularity in part to the facility with which it might be remembered. For here were the *imagines agentes,* each one in its place and with its accustomed rubric that externalized the rhetorician's chambers of memory. Whether they almost fill their frames from side to side or allow for backdrops that can be plain or patterned, brilliantly colored or glittering with gold leaf, they vibrate with movement. Infused with animation, giving an impression of gesture, at times flamboyant and even violent, they hint at subtle significance, dazzle us with their strangeness, and compel us to search out the allegory. The arresting quality of the figures and their pertinence to the accompanying text suggest that the bestiary was to reach the *oculum imaginationis* through the eye and the ear, and that words and images were to combine to fix doctrinal mysteries and moral precepts in the memory.

## Notes

1. *Mediaeval Latin and French Bestiaries,* rev. ed. (Chapel Hill: University of North Carolina Press, 1962), p. 44.
2. Ed. F. J. Carmody (Berkeley: University of California Press, 1948), I.xv.1; cf. Cicero, *De oratore,* trans. E. W. Sutton and H. Rackham, Loeb Library (London: Heinemann, 1942), I.5.18; Isidore, *Patrologia latina,* 83, col. 564: "Rerum omnium Thesaurus memoria est."
3. See Frances A. Yates, *The Art of Memory* (London: Routledge and Kegan Paul, 1966), pp. 96–99; Beryl Smalley, *English Friars and Antiquity in the Early Fourteenth Century* (Oxford: Blackwell, 1960), pp. 114–115.
4. For an exponent of a system very similar to that of the artificial memory in this century, see A. R. Luria, *The Mind of a Mnemonist,* trans. Lynn Solotaroff (New York: Basic Books, 1968), and his description of S who possessed a fantastic memory: "When S read through a long series of words, each word would elicit a graphic image. And since the series was fairly long, he had to find some way of distributing these images of his (and this habit persisted throughout his life), he would 'distribute' them along some roadway or street he visualized in his mind. . . . Frequently he would take a mental walk along that street . . . and slowly make his way down, distributing his images at houses, gates, and store windows. . . . This technique of converting a series of words into a series of graphic images explains why S could so readily reproduce a series from start to finish or in reverse order; how he could rapidly name the word that preceded or followed one I'd select from the series. To do this, he would simply begin his walk, either from the beginning or from the end of the street, find the image of the object I had named, and 'take a look at' whatever happened to be situated on either side of it." S's visual patterns of memory differed from the more commonplace type of figurative memory by virtue of the fact that his images were exceptionally vivid and stable; he was also able to "turn away" from them, as it were, and "return" to them whenever it was necessary (pp. 31–33). In noting that S's images represented "a fusion of graphic ideas and synesthetic reactions," Luria quotes S: "When I hear the word *red* I see a man in a red shirt coming toward me: as for *blue,* this means an image of someone waving a small blue flag from a window." See also A. N. Leontiev, *The Development of Memory* (Moscow: Academy of Communist Education, 1931) and *Problems of Mental Development* (Moscow: Academy of Pedagogical Sciences, 1959); A. A. Smirnov, *The Psychology of Recall* (Moscow: Academy of Pedagogical Sciences, 1948). Recently psychologists have begun to give serious attention to the principles and techniques of artificial memory, and it has been revitalized by such writers as Gordon H. Bower, in "Analysis of a Mnemonic Device: Modern Psychology Uncovers the Powerful Components of an Ancient System for Improving Memory," *American Scientist,* 58

(1970), 496–510. An interesting account of the later application of the system in the nineteenth century and a detailed examination of its use by Samuel Clemens, is given by Thomas M. Walsh and Thomas D. Zlatic, "Mark Twain and the Art of Memory," *American Literature*, 53 (1981), 214–231. References in *Notes & Queries*, ser. I, v, 227, 305–355; II, vii, 257, 304, 442, 476, 485, are to various mnemonic systems rather than the classical art of memory. The exception is a note by T. J. Buckley, ser. II, vii (1959), 366, who quotes the *Penny Cyclopaedia*, xv.90, on the system in classical rhetoric.

5. See Yates, *The Art of Memory;* also Harry Caplan, "Memoria: Treasure-House of Eloquence," *Of Eloquence: Studies of Ancient and Medieval Rhetoric*, ed. Anne King and Helen North (Ithaca, New York, and London: Cornell University Press, 1970), pp. 196–246; Walter J. Ong, *Ramus, Method, and the Decay of Dialogue* (1958; rpt. New York: Octagon Books, 1974), and "Memory as an Art," *Rhetoric, Romance and Technology* (Ithaca, New York, and London: Cornell University Press, 1971), pp. 104–112; John R. Reed, "Memory," *Victorian Conventions* (Athens: Ohio University Press, 1975), pp. 401–439; Raymond B. Waddington, "Shakespeare's Sonnet 15 and the Art of Memory," *The Rhetoric of Renaissance Poetry*, ed. Thomas O. Sloan and Raymond B. Waddington (Berkeley: University of California Press, 1979), pp. 96–122. The major early texts are *Rhetorica ad Herennium*, trans. Harry Caplan, Loeb Library (London: Heinemann, 1954); Cicero, cited above, and Quintilian, *Institutio oratoria*, trans. H. E. Butler, Loeb Library (London: Heinemann, 1921–1922).

6. There were, of course, many possibilities for *loci:* the signs of the zodiac and the 360 decans are reputed to have been used by Metrodorus of Scepsis, and heaven and hell by Boncompagno da Signa and others in the thirteenth century.

7. See Paolo Rossi, *Clavis universalis* (Milan and Naples: Riccardo Ricciardi, 1960), p. 282.

8. For text, see Beryl Rowland, "Bishop Bradwardine, the Artificial Memory, and the *House of Fame*," in *Chaucer at Albany*, ed. Russell Hope Robbins (New York: Burt Franklin, 1975), p. 59, ll. 160–164.

9. Yates, *The Art of Memory*, pp. 60–79.

10. See *The Parisiana Poetria of John of Garland*, ed. trans. Traugott Lawler (New Haven and London: Yale University Press, 1974), p. 237. See also B. Rowland, "The Medievalizing of the 'Ars Memorativa,'" in *Bamberger Beiträge zur Englischen Sprachwissenschaft*, ed. Wolf Dietrich Bald and Horst Weinstock, 15 (1984), 197–203.

11. Raymond D. Di Lorenzo, "The Collection Form and the Art of Memory in the *Libellus super ludo shachorum* of Jacobus de Cessolis," *MS*, 35 (1973), 205–221; see also H. J. R. Murray, *A History of Chess* (Oxford: Clarendon Press, 1962), ch. V, "The Chess Moralities."

12. Yates, *The Art of Memory*, p. 57.

13. *Patrologia latina*, 77, col. 128.

14. G. R. Owst, *Preaching in Medieval England* (New York: Russell and Russell, 1965), p. 351.

15. *Mirk's Festial: A Collection of Homilies by Johannes Mirkus* (John Mirk), ed. T. Erbe, *EETSES*, 96 (1905), 186. See also G. R. Owst, *Literature and Pulpit in Medieval England* (Oxford: Blackwell, 1961), pp. 137–146 on images.

16. *Morale Scolarium of John of Garland (Johannes de Garlandia)*, ed. Louis John Paetow (Berkeley: University of California Press, 1927), pp. 174, 243: "Templi sculpturas morum dic esse figuras, / Vivas picturas in te gere non perituras." See also *De mysteriis ecclesie*, ed. F. G. Otto (Gissae: 1847), ll. 60–61, where there is a modification in the second line of the quotation to include "animarum."

17. See Owst, *Preaching*, p. 294. For memory and images, see also Douglas Gray, *Themes and Images in the Medieval English Religious Lyric* (London: Routledge and Kegan Paul, 1972), pp. 40–42.

18. XI.ii. 20–21.

19. Milan edition, 1808; Paolo Rossi, *Clavis universalis*, pp. 272–275. See also Yates, *The Art of Memory*, pp. 86–91.

20. Yates, *The Art of Memory*, p. 109. Vienna, OeNB Cod. 5395.

21. Adolf Katzenellenbogen, *Allegories of the Virtues and Vices in Medieval Art* (New York: Norton, 1964), p. 55.

22. Ibid., pp. 55–56.

23. R. A. Pack, "An *Ars memorativa* from the Late Middle Ages," *AHDLMA*, 46 (1979), 243. For illustration see Yates, *The Art of Memory*, plate 4b.

24. See Rosemond Tuve, *Allegorical Imagery* (Princeton: Princeton University Press, 1966), p. 20. Reproduced from Oxford, Bodleian, MS Douce 5, fol. 234, published Lyons, 1511.

25. Oxford, Bodleian, MS Bodley 602, fol. 10; MS Bodley 764, fol. 74$^v$; Brussels, Bibl. Roy. MS 10074, fol. 146$^v$; London, Brit. Lib. MS Add. 24686, fol. 13. See also Florence McCulloch, pp. 168–169; Beryl Rowland, *Animals with Human Faces: A Guide to Animal Symbolism* (Knoxville: University of Tennessee Press, 1973), pp. 139–140; *Birds with Human Souls: A Guide to Bird Symbolism* (Knoxville: University of Tennessee Press, 1978), p. 154.

26. Montague Rhodes James, *The Bestiary* (Oxford: Roxburghe Club, 1928), p. 1.

27. McCulloch, p. 71.

28. See Xenia Muratova, "The Decorated Manuscripts of the Bestiary of Philippe de Thaon," *Third International Beast Epic, Fable and Fabliau Colloquium*, ed. J. Goossens and T. Sodmann (Köln: Böhlau, 1981), pp. 217–246; "Problèmes de l'origine et des sources des cycles d'illustrations des manuscrits des bestiaires," *Epopée animale fable fabliau*, ed. G. Bianciotto and M. Salvat (Paris: Publications de l'Université de Rouen, 1984), pp. 383–408; *I Manuscritti miniati del bestiario medievale*, in *Settimae di studio centro italiano di studi sull'alto medioevo*, XXXI (Spoleto: Panetto and Petrelli, 1985), pp. 1319–1372; "Bestiaries: An Aspect of Medieval Patronage," *Art and Patronage in the English Romanesque*, ed. Sarah Macready and F. H. Thompson, Society of Antiquaries of London, Occasional Paper (new series) VIII (London: Thames and Hudson, 1986), pp. 118–144. I wish to express my appreciation of Dr. Muratova's extremely detailed and comprehensive studies.

29. V. A. Kolve, *Chaucer and the Imagery of Narrative: The First Five Canterbury Tales* (Stanford: Stanford University Press, 1984), p. 177. This learned and remarkably stimulating work was published after I had begun this paper. In his first chapter, Kolve deals comprehensively with medieval faculty psychology and the widespread knowledge of the three-cell theory of the brain. He con-

siders Richard de Fournival's preface an important illustration of the medieval concept of image-making in the memory process, but does not regard it as having specific reference to the artificial memory.

30. McCulloch, pp. 94–95; for illustration, see Rowland, *Animals,* p. 34 (MS Bodley 764, fol. 22ᵛ).

31. McCulloch, pp. 148–150; Rowland, *Animals,* p. 132 (MS Bodley 764, fol. 7ᵛ); T. H. White, *The Bestiary* (New York: Putnam, Capricorn Edition, 1960), pp. 14–17.

32. McCulloch, p. 95; Rowland, *Animals,* p. 36 (MS Bodley 764, fol. 14); White, pp. 28–29.

33. McCulloch, pp. 155–156; Rowland, *Birds,* pp. 130–132 (Oxford, Bodleian MS Ashmole 1511, fol. 46ᵛ); White, pp. 132–133.

34. MS Bodley 764, fol. 41ᵛ. Alternatively, this calf may be bellowing. See *English Rural Life in the Middle Ages,* Bodleian Picture Book no. 14 (Oxford: Oxford University Press, 1965), p. 6.

35. McCulloch, pp. 193–196 and plates I–X.

36. White, pp. 54–55.

37. "The Illustrated Medieval Aviary and the Lay-Brotherhood," *Gesta,* 21 (1982), 70–71.

38. Ibid., pp. 63–74.

39. Ibid., p. 63.

40. Ibid., p. 71.

41. *Li Bestiaires d'amours di Maistre Richart de Fornival,* ed. Cesare Segre, Documenti de Filologia, no. 2 (Milan: R. Ricciardi, 1957), p. clvi.

42. See Gabriel Bianciotto, "Sur le *Bestiaire d'amour* de Richart de Fournival," *Epopée animale, fable, fabliau,* ed. G. Bianciotto and Michel Salvat (Paris: Publications de l'Université de Rouen, 1984), pp. 107–119.

43. Oxford, Bodleian MS Douce 308, fol. 91ᵛ.

44. Ibid., fol. 97.

45. Ibid., fol. 94.

46. Ibid., fol. 86dᵛ. The illustration is reproduced in Kolve, p. 10.

47. "Et pour chu Diex, ki tant aime l'omme qu'il le velt porveoir de quant ke mestiers lui est, a donne a homme une vertu de force d'ame ki a non memoire. Ceste memoire si a .ij. portes, veir et oir, et a cascune de ces .ij. portes si a un cemin par ou on i puet aler. che sont painture et parole. Painture sert a l'oel et parole a l'oreille. Et comment on puist repairier a le maison de memoire et par painture et par parole, si est apparant par chu ke memoire, ki est la garde des tresors ke sens d'omme conquiert par bonte d'engien, fair chu ki est trespasse ausi comme present. Et a che meisme vient on per painture et par parole. Car quant on voit painte une estoire, ou de Troies ou d'autre, on voit les fais des preudommes ki cha en ariere furent, ausi com s'il fussent present. Et tout ensi est il de parole. Can quant on ot .i. romans lire, on entent les aventures, ausi com on les veist en present. Et puis c'on fait present de chu ki est trespasse par ces .ij. coses, c'est par painture et par parole, dont pert il bien ke par ces .ij. coses poet on a memoire venir."

48. Oxford, Bodleian MS Douce 308, fol. 91ᵛ.

49. "Car je vous envoie en cest escrit et painture et parole, pour che ke, quant je ne serai presens, ke cis escris par sa painture et par sa parole me rende a vostre memoire comme present. Et je vous monsterai comment cis escris a painture et parolle. Car il est bien apert k'il a parole, par che ke toute escripture si est faite pour parole monstrer et pour che ke on le lise; et quant on le list, si revient elle a nature de parole. Et d'autre part, k'il ait painture si est en apert par chu ke lettre n'est mie, s'on ne le paint. Et meesmement cis escris est de tel sentence k'il painture desire. Car il ise de nature de bestes et d'oisaus ke miex sont connissables paintes ke dites."

50. Paris, Bibl. Nat. MS fr. 1951, fol. 1; see Kolve, p. 26.

51. For detailed considerations of these two writers, see Xenia Muratova, "The Decorated Manuscripts of the Bestiary of Philippe de Thaon (The MS 3466 from the Royal Library in Copenhagen and the MS 249 in the Merton College Library, Oxford) and the Problem of the Illustrations of the Medieval Poetical Bestiary," cited above, and "Les Miniatures du manuscrit fr. 14969 de la Bibliothèque Nationale de Paris (Le Bestiaire de Guillaume le Clerc) et la tradition iconographique franciscaine," *MRom*, 28: 3–4 (1978), 141–148.

# Willene B. Clark

## 2. The Aviary-Bestiary at the Houghton Library, Harvard

When I first became interested in the manuscript that is the subject of this study, it was privately owned and unavailable for consultation.[1] I wrote to Florence McCulloch in the hope that she had information about it, and she very generously loaned me a set of prints of the illustrations, making possible a study of the iconography and style. Recently, when the manuscript was presented to the Houghton Library, Harvard University, I was able to study it firsthand and to confirm and build upon the observations which Professor McCulloch had conveyed to me in conversation and in her seminal book on bestiaries.[2]

The Harvard manuscript is one of the smallest of bestiaries and makes no pretense at elegance, yet it occupies an important place among extant thirteenth-century books.[3] Its fame derives not from the main part of the manuscript, but from a separate, two-quire booklet of bird and animal pictures added at the beginning, images designed to serve as models for illustrating the texts which follow. The first of these texts is the Aviary (*De columba deargentata, Libellus ad Rainerum conversum . . . , De tribus columbis*, fols. 15–58), a work of Christian allegory much like the bestiaries but with birds as subjects, written about mid-twelfth century by Hugh of Fouilloy, prior of St.-Laurent-d'Heilly, a small Augustinian house near Amiens.[4] Following the Aviary is a bestiary in the version erroneously attributed to St. John Chrysostom and known as the Dicta Chrysostomi, or DC; it was compiled as early as the eleventh century (fols. 60–87).[5] Both texts in the Harvard manuscript were intended to have illustrations for each of the creatures, but, except for several incomplete diagrams in the Aviary, they have only spaces for pictures. The DC version is seldom illustrated, and this set of miniatures intended for it, plus a text with spaces for illustrations, add further significance to the Harvard manuscript. On the basis of style, both the illustrations in the opening booklet and the script in the texts can be related to Parisian work of the 1230s or 1240s.[6]

Because the Harvard Aviary-Bestiary has not been studied since the 1940s, a number of issues need to be reexamined and updated, among them the nature of the two treatises, the relationships between the model book and the texts, certain physical features of the model book, and the place of production. Moreover, the Harvard manuscript has a twin in the Dubrowsky Collection of the Leningrad Gos. Publ. Bibl. Saltykova-Shchedrina, MS lat. Q.v.III.1, which has not been mentioned previously in literature on the Aviary and bestiary. This manuscript shares contents, iconography, and painting style with Harvard, but integrates the pictures into the text of both Aviary and bestiary.[7] A comparison of these two manuscripts with each other, and with manuscripts related to them textually and iconographically, reveals new information about Aviary and bestiary production, and demonstrates the fluid relationships which can exist between one beast-moral manuscript and another.

Little is known of the early history of the Harvard Aviary-Bestiary. Its first recorded owner is Johannes Spergaz I [*Iuris*] B [*baccalarius*], whose fifteenth-century *ex libris* appears at the head of the text. Later inscriptions in the manuscript include the signatures of William Cheslyn (eighteenth century), who signed the recto and verso of the second flyleaf at the front, and who might be a reader or borrower; and of John Jorrom (eighteenth century), an owner who wrote a verse anathema on the first end flyleaf, and who may have lived in Leicestershire.[8] In the seventeenth or eighteenth century a John Ballammy signed his name near the fold on the final flyleaf, perhaps at the time of a rebinding of the manuscript. Although the name Spergaz may be German or Flemish, and Cheslyn and Jorrom appear to be English, the places of residence are unknown for former owners. There is no trace of the manuscript throughout the nineteenth century; it reappeared about 1939 or 1940 when sent on consignment by Marks and Co. of London to Dawson's Book Shop, Los Angeles.[9] In 1941 it was purchased by H. P. Kraus, New York,[10] and in 1946 Kraus sold it to Philip Hofer of Cambridge, Massachusetts, who presented it to the Houghton Library in 1983 in honor of Roger S. Wieck.

## The Text

The Harvard Aviary text is complete, while most bird chapters of the DC bestiary have been omitted in deference to the Aviary, and both texts have received textual and pictorial interpolations. There are seven textual additions to the Aviary. The first two are chapters from a Second Family Latin bestiary, the *Noctua* (Owl) and the Crow, originally in the order Pelican, *Nycticorax* (Owl), *Noctua,* Raven, Crow, but now misbound.[11] There is an extension of the Eagle chapter, from an unknown source,[12] and at the end of the Aviary are five more added chapters, for the Coot, Ibis, Dove (2), and Peridexion Tree, all from a B-Is bestiary.[13] All but the *Noctua* and the Dove have model-book illustrations (Fig. 2.2, top, the Peridexion Tree, inscribed *de columbis et s[er]pente*). These interpolations are typical of the changes which medieval compilers or copyists made in beast-moral texts, and which occur frequently enough in bestiaries to have occasioned a number of distinct versions.[14] On the other hand, such changes are unusual in the Aviary, which retains a remarkable integrity, both textual and pictorial, throughout its tradition.[15]

DC bestiaries vary more than most other versions in their choice of chapters, but the Harvard and Dubrowsky copies are alone in their inclusion of four chapters (Asp, Wolf, Dog, Firestones) from a bestiary version which McCulloch calls "H."[16] Two other chapters (Diamond, Conch) derive from the B-version *Physiologus,* source of the DC bestiary.[17] All bestiary interpolations in Harvard are illustrated in the model book, along with the other bestiary pictures. These textual additions in both Aviary and bestiary, from four different bestiary versions (B *Physiologus,* B-Is, H, and Second Family) and an unknown source, are typical of the complexities of beast-moral literature.

## The Model Book

For their part, the illustrations raise issues which are every bit as complicated. Ives and Lehmann-Haupt were the first to show that the two opening quires of the Harvard manuscript constitute a model book.[18] The miniatures are fully painted and placed one after another in rectangular frames, from one to six to a page (Figs. 2.1, 2.2). Most model books or pattern sheets contain only line drawings; the painted designs of the Harvard manuscript form one of only two sets of fully colored model-book designs before the fourteenth century.[19] They are the only complete set of model pictures for any text, here two texts. Altogether there are seventy different subjects illustrated: the usual thirty for the Aviary, plus four more for added chapters, and thirty-six for the bestiary, including its added chapters (see appendix to this article).[20] Only the painted portions of the

Aviary diagrams (e.g., Fig. 2.3) are included in the model book, while the Harvard text section contains only the geometries and texts of the diagrams. The model-book character of the opening quires is confirmed by the fact that many of the designs are punched for copying, the largest surviving collection of medieval miniatures so treated. The punched miniatures will be discussed later.

While the spaces left for illustrations in the text conform to frame shapes in the model book, they are often too small to have accepted the model-book designs directly.[21] A question therefore arises as to the original relationship between the two sections of the Harvard manuscript. The model-book folios are slightly larger than the text folios, and the parchment quality of the model book is different from that of the text.[22] The original stitching-hole patterns are markedly different for the model book and for the text. The inscriptions on the paintings and the script of the text are also different. The earliest foliation is in the text section, which originally began with fol. 1 (see n. 3). Faintly inked Roman numerals, probably from the fifteenth century, beside the miniatures correspond with the thirteenth-century text foliation, indicating where each design would have been placed (visible in Figs. 2.1, 2.4). It should be recalled that the binding is also from the fifteenth century, which may indicate the period when the two portions of the manuscript were brought together. It may have been Spergaz, the fifteenth-century owner, who put in the Roman numerals so that a reader could find the corresponding chapters in the text.[23]

While a model book for the DC bestiary might have been very useful, considering the likelihood that the new text would be copied from an unillustrated manuscript, it would be superfluous for most Aviary copies, for the Aviary was specifically intended for illustrations, and most Aviary models would have had pictures. The few added Aviary miniatures in the Harvard model book would hardly justify the time it took to paint all the rest. The justification for the model book is probably that it was made by a group of professional manuscript painters, as the evidence below suggests, for their own use.

The separation of the model book and text section is also curious, but may be explained by the following hypothesis. The text, which has been corrected by a second scribe, may also have been intended as an exemplar in the shop. As soon as the scribe had written the first quire, he could have handed it over to a painter working from the booklet of pictures, and the two could then have worked almost simultaneously, one quire apart at all times. Such a procedure would mean that the new book could be completed far more quickly than one first written in its entirety and then illustrated, all from a single illustrated model. The time saved would be a decided advantage for a commercial enterprise.[24] If the work was indeed carried out in this manner, it may have required more of a "team" effort on the part of painter and scribe than current thinking about professional production in Paris of the 1240s would suppose.[25] Such a theory of team production would explain how the picture section, though separate, could have remained with the text so that the two could eventually be bound together.[26]

## The Miniatures

In the Aviary tradition the miniatures in most illustrated copies tend to follow a standard program of designs, which includes allegorical pictures of two trees (where birds nest), three diagrams, and twenty-three "portraits" of birds. The Harvard and Dubrowsky manuscripts carry this program, with a few pictorial variants.[27] Among these variants the Blackbird miniature is the most interesting, appearing only in these two Aviaries. It shows a bird in a tree, and below a nimbed man leaving his clothes to one side (Fig. 2.4). The scene illustrates a tale from St. Gregory's *Dialogues* which is recounted in the Aviary, chapter 48: the bird is the Devil in disguise, and the man is St. Benedict about to subdue temptation by rolling naked in nettles, seen here as trees.[28]

The Harvard bestiary's miniatures represent one of only eleven instances of illustrations among the thirty-two known DC bestiaries.[29] Most DC illustrations derive from the *Physiologus* tradition, with sufficient regional variations in details to preclude strong relationships between copies.[30] The Harvard manuscript's *Physiologus* miniatures include, among others, the Lion erasing its spoor and breathing life into its cub (Fig. 2.2), the Panther leading the animals (Fig. 2.2), and the Fox feigning death.[31] There are several designs that have been individualized by the artist or his model, of which the Beaver is an example. In bestiaries the Beaver discourages the hunter by biting off its testicles, which are sought for their medicinal property. Here the animal is also shown standing on its hind legs to display the results.[32]

There are two painters at work in the Harvard model book, identifiable in the miniatures with human figures.[33] The first, who is the more talented of the two, painted the Cedar, Blackbird, and Caladrius illustrations of the

Aviary, and the Siren, the first Beaver miniature, and probably the Centaur and the Wolf designs (both damaged) in the bestiary. His figures have well-drawn faces with pointed nose, almond eyes, and glancing pupils, and a mouth with straight upper lip (Fig. 2.4).[34] His colleague is responsible for the Lion, the Unicorn, the second Beaver design, and the Basilisk, and is known by coarser faces with staring eyes and small mouths turned down at the corners (Fig. 2.5). The drapery of both artists tends to be flat and arranged in a few large folds, although in some instances there are shaded troughs and loose waist-line folds to give volume to the cloth (Fig. 2.2). It has not been possible to differentiate the artists' hands among the bird and animal pictures, but it is likely that each painter decorated the entire leaf side on which he painted scenes with human figures. Many Aviary birds are placed in a round frame surrounded by red and blue rectangular borders, sometimes with modest white filigree in the interstices (Figs. 2.1, 2.4).

## Place of Production

The figure painting provides the means for associating the style of the Harvard model book with Parisian artists whom Robert Branner called the Dominican Group, painters who decorated the well-known Bible begun after 1236 for the convent of St. Jacques in Paris (Paris, Bibl. Nat. MS lat. 16719–16722), and who were active probably one or two decades before 1250. Like the Harvard text, the Dominican Bible was corrected by still another hand, and this manuscript too is considered an exemplar.[35] Painter 1 of the model book is close in style to Branner's third master in the Bible (Figs. 2.4, 2.6), and Painter 2 to his fourth master.[36] The filigree in the Aviary frames is identical with that in another product of the Dominican Group, a Missal, Paris, Bibl. Nat. MS 8884, painted by Branner's fourth master.[37] On the other hand, the Harvard model book is wanting in the precision used in making the Bible and other liturgical books produced by the Dominican Group's painters, and it lacks the Bible's luxurious burnished gold. Like most Parisian books of the period, the model book's colors are dominated by rose and blue, but in contrast with the Dominican Group's finished books, the model book's colors are weak and dull, the rose somewhat brownish, and the blue toned down by gray. As the Dubrowsky manuscript attests, it was not the subject matter that ruled out the use of high quality pigments; it was almost certainly the utilitarian nature of the model book that was responsible. Other colors in the miniatures are brown, beige, various grays, and green. In the text section there are red and blue two- and three-line initials with good, though not distinctive, pen-scroll decoration comparable to Parisian work of the 1230s and 1240s, but not identical with pen-scroll in other Dominican Group books. The Dominican Group painters were professional artists, and almost certainly made the model book for their own use, and in concert with one of a number of scribes and calligraphers probably worked in the manner suggested above.

## The Harvard and Dubrowsky Manuscripts

A Dominican Group painter, who relates closely to Painter 2 of the Harvard manuscript, is responsible for the decoration of the Dubrowsky Aviary-Bestiary, but the script, calligraphy, and frame types do not relate to Harvard's (Fig. 2.7). Nevertheless, because of similarities between the two books, it is tempting to suppose that Dubrowsky was made from the two parts of the Harvard manuscript. Although substantially larger than Harvard and with smaller miniatures, Dubrowsky is identical with it in contents, and, with minor variations, also in the design of its miniatures, which now fill the spaces left for them in the text.[38] Dubrowsky includes all textual additions of Harvard and illustrates those which are illustrated in the model book, but with the added Aviary chapters in the correct order. Despite these similarities, it is more reasonable to suppose that the Dubrowsky and Harvard manuscripts were based on the same model, for while Dubrowsky includes miniatures for two bestiary chapters, the Whale and the Dragon, which are missing from Harvard,[39] it lacks the *capitulum* texts usually found in Aviary miniature borders and present in Harvard. Although the Harvard and Dubrowsky Aviaries share most variants, Harvard has a variant in some instances when Dubrowsky maintains the more common reading.[40] Thus, neither manuscript is able to claim more completeness than the other; they depend on a common and more authentic model (or models) for both Aviary and bestiary.

It goes without saying that there are differences, beyond just those of measurement, between the model-book pictures and those in the finished manuscript. Most obviously, Dubrowsky has the complete diagrams, whereas the model book has only the center bird images. In contrast to Harvard, the Dubrowsky manuscript was decorated with great care, even elegance, although this painter's figures are less accomplished than those of his Harvard colleagues. Like the Harvard artists he used no gold, but his colors are richer and brighter than theirs.[41] His figures often differ from Harvard's in body position (compare the Unicorn miniatures of Figs. 2.1 and 2.8). In addition to the two miniatures omitted in Harvard, there are differences between the two manuscripts in some of the designs. For the Peridexion Tree miniature no space is left in either manuscript's text, but whereas in Dubrowsky the design occurs frameless in the lower margin, it is a framed, integral part of the Harvard model book.[42] For the bestiary's Dog chapter Dubrowsky depicts several species of dogs, two of which the Harvard artist misrepresents as lions. The Cedar miniature of the Aviary is essentially the same in both manuscripts, but where in Harvard the tree has no leaves of any kind, in Dubrowsky it has leaves resembling quilting. The "quilted" tree, according to evidence elsewhere, was probably in the original Aviary, reinforcing the supposition of greater authenticity in the model which the two manuscripts must have shared. Judging by the non-figural ornament in the Dubrowsky manuscript, this artist was trained in a tradition apart from the Dominican Group. The frames of his miniatures are irregular in shape and without floral filigree, and the patterns he gave the grounds are entirely different from those in Harvard.

The Harvard and Dubrowsky manuscripts are related in several rather convoluted ways to seven other more or less contemporary Aviary-Bestiary manuscripts. Only one of these, however, has a DC bestiary; five have an H bestiary and one a B-Is.[43] In the manuscripts with H bestiary the Aviary is followed by chapters for the Coot and Ibis, as in the Harvard manuscript. All seven Aviaries have similar text variants, which, not surprisingly, relate to those of the Harvard Aviary and its Dubrowsky twin.[44] Each of the three bestiary versions in the group has its own iconographic program, but six of the total of nine manuscripts share distinctive miniatures for the Sawfish, with a small boat facing a winged sea-serpent (Fig. 2.5), and for the Whale, with two men on the creature's back, and a small dish-shaped boat below, its sail looped around an unstepped mast (missing in Harvard).[45] An Aviary frame type similar to that of Harvard is also typical of the group.

To judge by style, the whole group is Parisian: four manuscripts, including Harvard and Dubrowsky, were painted by artists who are known to have worked in Paris, and three others by artists whose work has a strong Parisian look.[46] If all manuscripts were indeed made in Paris, then the H-version bestiary is likely to be Parisian, too, for it is known only in these manuscripts. The group's three different bestiary versions, the interpolations from four bestiary versions in the Harvard and Dubrowsky manuscripts, and the bestiary miniatures shared by manuscripts in the group, would have necessitated a great deal of cumbersome borrowing of manuscripts, unless scribes and artists had access to a center where an Aviary and at least four bestiary models were located. At such a center scribes would be able to copy from any of the texts and painters to choose popular common images to insert in the pictorial programs of their chosen models. In fact, there is evidence that the abbey of St. Victor in Paris owned bestiaries in at least two of the group's versions, and an illustrated Aviary.[47] As an important Parisian educational and ecclesiastical institution with an extensive library and active scriptorium, St. Victor is a likely place for the center of Aviary and bestiary production which is suggested by these manuscripts.

The bestiaries of Harvard and Dubrowsky have a special relationship with the other DC bestiary of the group, in British Library MS Sloane 278. Although the Aviary text variants of Sloane are not always congruent with those of Harvard and Dubrowsky, the three manuscripts share so many bestiary variants that they could have had the same DC text model.[48] The bestiary illustrations of Sloane, however, relate more to other manuscripts of the group than to Harvard, presenting another typical bestiary conundrum. The Sloane style is probably Flemish, attributable perhaps to a northerner working in Paris.

## Other Evidence of Production Methods

Much information on medieval copying methods is found in the Harvard Aviary-Bestiary, which gives every indication of frequent use by copyists.[49] The method most in evidence is the rare punch-transfer technique, which is found most often in Aviary and bestiary manuscripts.[50] In this method the outlines of a design were punched with a sharp instrument, probably through to a sheet of parchment beneath, which became the actual means of transfer when it was pounced with dark powder to transfer the design through the holes.[51] In the Harvard manuscript, twenty-six miniatures for the Aviary and fifteen for the bestiary are punched. As with punched miniatures elsewhere, the punching occurs usually in the main elements of a design. Here it is the bird or animal that is punched, and occasionally the round borders of the Aviary pictures.[52] Thus a painter could transfer the essentials required by the tradition, but place them in his own decorative context; or he could use the element punched in a new design. The reason for the relatively high incidence of punching in Aviaries and bestiaries may be that the birds and animals are decorative forms and well suited to design contexts of all sorts.

The punch transfer method's potential for causing damage is made obvious in the condition of many of the Harvard model-book pictures. Although the punches were made with a very small, sharp instrument, in some instances they were made so carelessly as to be clearly visible. Sometimes the instrument punched through two leaves, as witnessed in several miniatures by holes which cannot be assigned to the miniature on the reverse side (Fig. 2.8).[53] Further damage was done in other ways. The parchment is discolored and the miniatures are often severely rubbed, which could have been produced by repeated copyings by one or more tracing methods.[54] Prominent holes appear in the center of all the round Aviary pictures, both punched and not, which have disturbed the paint. They were made undoubtedly by an overly large compass point, perhaps in a tracing procedure where the copyist drew the new round border by using the center of the model's miniature seen through the tracing material (Figs. 2.4, 2.8). All such abuse indicates that the model book had little intrinsic value for the copyists, for whom it was only a means toward an end, and therefore not worthy of careful handling.

In its pristine state the little booklet of miniatures would have looked tidy and appealing, despite its somewhat perfunctory execution, for the painting is professional and in a fashionable style of the time. Even in its present condition, the Harvard Aviary-Bestiary, both model book and text, remains a precious document for the evidence it contains relating not only to beast-moral compilation but also to production methods and Parisian bestiary production. Moreover, with the Dubrowsky manuscript, it is an important addition to the corpus of books decorated by the Dominican Group painters and to the small number of illustrated DC bestiaries. The Harvard Aviary-Bestiary as a whole is a compelling medieval manuscript which will undoubtedly continue to receive scholarly attention.

## Appendix
### ILLUSTRATIONS IN THE HARVARD AVIARY-BESTIARY
*(An asterisk indicates that the design is punched for copying and which specific parts of the design.)*

Aviary: (Pt. 1) *Prologue miniature (Dove and Hawk under arches, fol. 1), *Dove diagram (fol. 1ᵛ), Three Doves (*Noah, David, *Christ; fol. 2), *Hawk for Hawk diagram (fol. 2), Turtledove diagram (with *Palm not bird at center, fol. 2ᵛ), *Turtledove miniature (not authentic, fol. 3), Cedar inhabited by king (?Christ, fol. 3); (Pt. 2) *Pelican reviving chicks (fol. 3ᵛ), *Nycticorax (fol. 3ᵛ), *Raven pecks corpse's eye (fol. 4), *Crow (not authentic, fol. 4), *Cock (fol. 4ᵛ), *Ostrich with horseshoe in beak (fol. 4ᵛ), *Vulture (fol. 5), *Crane (fol. 5), *Kite (fol. 5ᵛ), *two flying Swallows (fol. 5ᵛ), *Stork with snake in beak (fol. 6), Blackbird (St. Benedict about to roll in nettles, miniature not authentic, fol. 6), *Owl (*Bubo,* fol. 6ᵛ), Jay atop tree (fol. 6ᵛ), *Goose with goslings (fol. 7), *Heron on shore (fol. 7), Caladrius prophesying life and death (fol. 7ᵛ), *two miniatures of Phoenix on pyre (fols. 7ᵛ, 8), *Partridge (fol. 8), *four Quail in grass (fol. 8), *Hoopoe (fol. 8), Swan (fol. 8ᵛ), *Peacock (fol. 8ᵛ), *Eagle (fol. 8ᵛ); not authentic: Ibis (fol. 8ᵛ), *Coot (fol. 9), Peridexion Tree (dragon, tree with doves, fol. 9).

Bestiary: Lion followed by hunter (fol. 9), Lioness breathes on cub (fol. 9), Panther leads animals (fol. 9), hunter stabs Unicorn with head in virgin's lap (fol. 9), Siren below boat with sailors (fol. 9ᵛ), *Centaur with bow (fol. 9ᵛ), *Hydrus enters Crocodile's mouth and exits side (fol. 9ᵛ), *Wild Ass (fol. 9ᵛ), Hyena atop corpse (fol. 9ᵛ), Ape mother carries two young (fol. 9ᵛ), *Elephant, stream, mandrake on hill; Elephant mother and young in lake (fol. 10), *Asp with tail in ear (fol. 10), Wolf at sheepfold bites leg, shepherd sleeps (fol. 10), Dogs and lions [an error] at city gate (fol. 10ᵛ), four Firestones on hill (fol. 10ᵛ), three Diamants in matrix (fol. 10ᵛ), Conch on shore (fol. 10ᵛ), *Antelope by river (fol. 11), *Sun Lizard (Lacerta) traverses tower (fol. 11), men in boat face winged *Sawfish (Serra, fol. 11ᵛ), Vipers copulate by mouth, birth from side (fol. 11ᵛ), *two Stags at water (fol. 12), Goat and traveler (fol. 12), *Fox feigns death (fol. 12ᵛ), *Ostrich looks at sun (Assida, fol. 12ᵛ), *hunter, dogs, Beaver castrates self/*hunter, dogs, Beaver displays loss (fols. 13, 13ᵛ), irregular rows of Ants (fol. 13ᵛ), Hedgehogs roll on grapes (fol. 14), Salamander (a dragon, fol. 14), *Weasles walk/*copulate by mouth (fol. 14ᵛ), Basilisk, man dying, man dead (fol. 14ᵛ).

*I would like to thank Dr. Rodney G. Dennis of the Houghton Library, Harvard University, and Dr. Tamara Pavlovna Voronova of the Gos. Publ. Bibl. M. E. Saltykova-Shchedrina, Leningrad, for their kindness in providing me full access to the two manuscripts discussed in this study. My Marlboro College col-*

*league Professor Dana Howell was my guide through the essays in Russian, and Professor Helen Zakin very kindly read the paper and provided helpful suggestions for its improvement. A version of this paper was read at the New England Medieval Conference, November 1987, and in Leningrad, March 1988.*

## Notes

1. The only extended study to date is Samuel A. Ives and Hellmut Lehmann-Haupt, *An English 13th Century Bestiary* (New York: H. P. Kraus, 1942). Their findings are summarized in R. W. Scheller, *A Survey of Medieval Model Books* (Haarlem: de Erven F. Bohn, 1963), no. 13, pp. 101–103; and in *Harvard College Library, Illuminated & Calligraphic Manuscripts* (Exhib. cat., Cambridge: Harvard College, 1955), no. 22; and reviewed by Dorothy Miner, *Art Bulletin*, 25 (1943), 88–89.

2. Florence McCulloch, *Mediaeval Latin and French Bestiaries*, rev. ed. (Chapel Hill: University of North Carolina Press, 1962), p. 31, n. 33 and p. 42.

3. Cambridge, Harvard University, Houghton Library MS Typ 101: 160 × 110/115 (110 × 80) mm, outer vertical edges cropped, [2+] 14 + 73 [+2], modern foliation [2+] 89, thirteenth-century foliation [2+] 14 + lxxii [+2], 1 column, 24 lines of *textualis*, dark brown ink, ruled by hard point, 2 double-vertical and 2 triple-horizontal bounding lines, modern signatures, slightly discolored parchment, somewhat heavier in the first two quires; fifteenth-century brown leather covers with paste-downs from a fifteenth-century sacred text. Fols. 32/36–33/37 and 64–66 reversed in later binding. Several names (see below) and a number of later and uninformative scribblings and drawings on the flyleaves; on the second flyleaf a drawing (eighteenth/nineteenth century?) of a Beaver chewing a stick, a subject with a source in natural history illustration, not the bestiary. Chapters added to Aviary and bestiary (discussed below), and textual extensions, from as yet unidentified sources, in chapters on the Crow and the Eagle.

4. The Aviary text is printed by J. P. Migne, *Patrologia latina*, 177: 13–56; I have completed a critical edition and English translation of the text, and a study of the illustrated Aviary manuscripts, which are forthcoming. For the Aviary, see also W. B. Clark, "The Illustrated Medieval Aviary and the Lay-Brotherhood," *Gesta*, 21 (1982), 63–74, with bibliography, and for Hugh of Fouilloy, H. Peltier, "Hugues de Fouilloy, Chanoine regulier, prieur de Saint-Laurent-au-Bois," *Revue du Moyen Age Latin*, 2 (1946), 25–44. The Aviary is composed of sixty chapters in two parts, the first built around diagrams of several birds and trees, the second a series of essays on individual birds. In his *Patrologia latina* edition of the Aviary, Migne conflated several chapters of Pt. 1, resulting in a text of fifty-six chapters.

5. The DC bestiary text is in Friedrich Wilhelm, "Der ältere und der jüngere *Physiologus*," *Denkmäler deutscher Prosa des 11. und 12. Jhs.*, II (1916; new ed. Munich: Max Hueber, 1960), pp. 17–44; see the historical discussion by Nikolaus Henkel, *Studien zum Physiologus im Mittelalter* (Tübingen: Max Niemeyer, 1976), pp. 29–34, and McCulloch, *Mediaeval Bestiaries*, pp. 41–44.

The number of chapters in DC bestiary copies varies, with the average about 27; McCulloch, p. 42.

6. In Ives and Lehmann-Haupt, p. 23, n. 1, the manuscript is said to be English and of the second third of the thirteenth century.

7. I. P. Mokretsova and V. L. Romanova, *Frantsuzskaia knizhnaia miniatiura XIII veka v sovietskikh sobraniiakh 1270 – 1300* (*Les manuscrits enluminés français du XIIIe siècle dans les collections soviétiques 1270 – 1300*) (Moscow: Iskousstvo, 1984), no. X and pp. 29 – 30, partial color facsimile, plus black-and-white reproductions of all other miniatures. They note, p. 29, the close relationship between the Leningrad and Harvard manuscripts. Also, Alexandre de Laborde, *Les principaux manuscrits à peintures conservés dans l'ancienne Bibliothèque Impériale de Saint-Pétersbourg*, 2 vols. (Paris: SFRMP, 1938), no. 24; N. Garelin, "Dve rukopisnikh bestiaria Ross. Publitchnoi Biblioteki," *Sbornik Publitschnoi Biblioteki*, 2 (1924), 267 – 269; Xenia Muratova, *The Medieval Bestiary* (Moscow: Iskusstvo, 1984), reproductions pp. 141, 142, 144, 153 – 156, 163 – 166, 170, 171, 175, 177.

8. Only the name of Cheslyn has been noted so far in the literature on the manuscript. Jorrom's anathema reads: "If anyone this Book doth steal, Hee shall be sent to Lester gaol." A fourth name, that of John Ballammy, is written in a late eighteenth- or nineteenth-century hand near the spine on the verso of the second end flyleaf and might represent a reader.

9. It was advertised for sale in Dawson's Book Shop catalog for April 1940, Item 95, pp. 22 – 23. I am grateful to Glen Dawson for sending me a copy of the catalog.

10. Hans Kraus's purchase of the book from Dawson's is confirmed by Roland Folter of H. P. Kraus in a letter to me dated 11 February 1985.

11. The chapters are presently in the order Pelican, *Noctua*, Raven, *Nycticorax*, and Crow, the result of a reversal of ff. 32 and 33 (see above, n. 3). The April 1940 catalog of Dawson's Book Shop, p. 22, states that the Harvard Aviary-Bestiary is unbound, but that its binding is present. It was rebound after April 1940, but it cannot be determined when the four leaves were reversed (see above, n. 3). I have used the Latin for *Nycticorax* and *Noctua* to distinguish the two forms of owl from one another, and from the *Bubo*, which occurs later in the Aviary; modern science is uncertain as to which owl each term refers. The Second Family bestiary is discussed by McCulloch, *Mediaeval Bestiaries*, pp. 34 – 38.

12. *Item quomodo si cui martyr blandiatur et capitulo Ysaias ultimo glosa Deus tamquam misericors . . . ut aiunt qui de animalium scribere naturis.*

13. The first interpolated Dove chapter is erroneously ascribed to Hugh of Fouilloy (*Hugo prior*) in the rubric. The texts for these chapters are printed in Max Friedrich Mann, "Der Bestiaire Divin des Guillaume le Clerc," *Französiche Studien*, 6 : 2 (1888), 47 – 48, 55 – 56, 64 – 67. See also McCulloch, pp. 28 – 30.

14. The versions are discussed most fully by McCulloch, *Mediaeval Bestiaries*, chs. 2 and 3.

15. Two translations of the Aviary can be said to constitute separate versions, but each exists in only one manuscript. One is a fragment in Portuguese (Buenos Aires, Coll. Prof. Serafin da Silva Neto); see J. Mota, et al., *Livro das Aves* (Rio

de Janeiro: Instituto Nac. do Livro, 1965); the other a French verse paraphrase (Paris, Bibl. Nat. MS fr. 24428, ff. 49–52; for the latter, McCulloch, *Mediaeval Bestiaries,* pp. 57, 76). A small group of Aviary manuscripts has truncated texts and reordered chapters, but depends nevertheless on the main branch.

16. The H version is erroneously attributed in the *Patrologia latina,* 177: 55–84, to Hugh of St. Victor. McCulloch, *Mediaeval Bestiaries,* p. 42, n. 58, is incorrect in identifying a single leaf in Paris, Arsenal Lib. MS lat. 394, which also contains a DC bestiary, as being from an Aviary.

17. The B-version *Physiologus* is identified as the DC source by Francesco Sbordone, "La tradizione manoscritta del *Physiologus* latino," *Athenaeum: Studi periodici di letteratura,* NS 27 (1949), 253; see also Henkel, *Studien,* pp. 30–31. Sbordone lists the varying contents of the several DC bestiary families which he discusses.

18. *An English Bestiary,* pp. 24–25, where the miniatures are described as being in a single quire. The two quires are irregular, the first composed of five bifolios, the second of two.

19. The other is actually a bifolio of pattern sheets made in Germany about 1200 (Vatican MS lat. 1976, first two folios); D. J. A. Ross, "A Late Twelfth-Century Artist's Pattern Sheet," *Journal of the Warburg and Courtauld Institutes,* 25 (1962), 119–128.

20. The standard Aviary program is described in Clark, "The Illustrated Medieval Aviary," pp. 69–70, where the Hawk is erroneously called the Falcon. Three chapters in the Harvard Aviary text, *Noctua,* the two added Dove chapters, and the Peridexion Tree have no space for a picture; only the Peridexion Tree is found in the model book. In the bestiary text there are spaces but no pictures for the Whale and the Dragon; there is only one space for the two Elephant pictures, which are frequently combined. Several subjects, such as the Beaver, are divided into two framed pictures.

21. Spaces in the Aviary text, apart from the Pt. 1 diagrams, are oval in shape, and would have accommodated the round inner frames of the Aviary pictures. They average 10 to 12 lines or 36 to 40 mm in height. Aviary model-book pictures average about 55 mm in height. In the bestiary, spaces are usually square like the model-book pictures, fairly regular in size, and average about 11 lines, or 49 cm, in height; corresponding model-book pictures are often larger, more varying in size, and measure from about 60 to 36 mm in height.

22. Ives and Lehmann-Haupt, p. 24, noted the difference in parchment quality.

23. James Douglas Farquhar, "The Manuscript as a Book," in *Pen to Press: Illustrated Manuscripts and Printed Books in the First Century of Printing,* Exhib. Cat. (Baltimore: University of Maryland, Johns Hopkins University, 1977), p. 83, in describing later medieval manuscripts, notes that occasionally the miniatures were numbered, but either for account purpose or to refer to numbered sketches to be used as models.

24. Compare the pecia system for copying university texts in thirteenth-century Paris, in which the text was loaned in small booklet units to a number of scribes at once, so that the entire text would not be tied up by one scribe over a long period of time. See Jean Destrez, *La pecia dans les manuscrits universitaires du XIIIe et du XIVe siècle* (Paris, 1935), and Graham Pollard, "The *pecia* System

in the Medieval Universities," in *Medieval Scribes, Manuscripts and Libraries: Essays Presented to N. R. Ker* (London: Scolar Press, 1978), pp. 145–161.

25. Branner, p. 10, discusses the "dissociation of the different steps in book-making"; see also J. J. G. Alexander, "Scribes as Artists: The Arabesque Initial in Twelfth-Century English Manuscripts," in *Medieval Scribes, Manuscripts and Libraries,* p. 90. Conversely, Karen Gould, "Terms for Book Production in a Fifteenth-Century Latin-English Nominale (Harvard Law School Library MS. 43)," *The Papers of the Bibliographical Society of America,* 79 (1985), 75–99, points out, p. 92, that even in the fifteenth century specialization was not rigid and that artisans had to cooperate in given circumstances.

26. Interestingly enough, another Aviary-Bestiary, Paris, Bibl. Nat. MS lat. 2495B, to which the Harvard manuscript relates in both text variants and iconography, is bound with an illustrated but incomplete copy of its bestiary, which reproduces the main manuscript almost exactly. Here, however, it is a question of a complete model and a copy, not a pictorial model book and copy.

27. The visual variants of Harvard and Dubrowsky include: the Palm instead of a bird in the Turtledove diagram, and anecdotal scenes for the Raven, Jay, Black-bird, Goose, Caladrius, Phoenix, Partridge. As is customary in an Aviary, the Pelican is shown anecdotally, reviving its young.

28. Aviary, ch. 48 of my edition, in Clark, *The Medieval Book of Birds,* forthcoming; also in Migne, *Patrologia latina,* 177 : 44. St. Grégoire, *Dialogues,* ed. Adalbert de Vogüe, *Sources chrétiennes* (Paris: Ed. du Cerf, 1978–81), II, p. 36, l. 1, to p. 38, l. 19.

29. Henkel, *Studien,* p. 29, n. 43, lists 29 copies, to which can be added Munich, Staatsbibl. clm 16189 and Brussels, Bibl. Roy. MS 18421–29, both fully illustrated, and the Dubrowsky manuscript.

30. Even fewer illustrated *Physiologus* manuscripts survive. The earliest illustrated Latin version is the famous ninth-century Bern, Bürgerbibliothek MS 318, published in facsimile by C. von Steiger and O. Homburger (Basel: Alkuin-Verlag, 1964). The earliest surviving illustrated Greek version is Milan, Bibl. Ambrosiana MS E.16.Sup., of c. 1100; M. L. Gengaro, "A proposito delle inedite illustrazioni del Phisiologus greco della Biblioteca Ambrosiana," *Arte Lombarda,* 3 (1958), 19–27, and Xenia Muratova, "L'arte Longobarda et il 'Physiologus,'" in *Atti del 60 Congresso internaz. di studi sull'alto medioevo,* Milan, 1978 (Spoleto: Cent. Ital. di Studi Sull'Alto Medioevo, 1980), pp. 547–558.

31. For the popular bestiary images, see McCulloch, *Mediaeval Bestiaries,* plates I–X, and Beryl Rowland, *Animals with Human Faces* (Knoxville: University of Tennessee Press, 1973). See appendix of this article for Harvard bestiary designs.

32. Fol. 13ᵛ; reproduced in Ives and Lehmann-Haupt, fig. 7. Curiously enough, the Beaver displaying also occurs in the later thirteenth-century English Second Family bestiary, London, British Library MS Harley 4751, another example of the many anomalous relationships between bestiaries.

33. Lehmann-Haupt's view, in *An English Bestiary,* p. 22, that the paintings of the Aviary are superior to those of the bestiary cannot be supported.

34. Ives and Lehmann-Haupt, fig. 3, for the Caladrius.

35. For the Dominican Group, Branner, *Manuscript Painting in Paris,* pp. 59–60,

65, 207–208, who gives sources, p. 208, for the Dominican Bible's role as exemplar. Scheller, *A Survey of Medieval Model Books,* was correct in his observation, p. 103, that the Harvard manuscript was "used in a well-organized centre of book production."

36. Branner, fig. 95 (third master), fig. 97 (fourth master).

37. Branner, fig. 104.

38. Leningrad, Gos. Publ. Bibl. Saltykova-Shchedrina MS lat. Q.v.III,I: 229 × 161 (176 × 103) mm, [5+] 54 [+5], 1 column, 31 lines of *textualis,* dark brown ink, ruled by leadpoint, double-horizontal and single-vertical bounding lines. Fols. 6 and 7 reversed; a number of leaves glued in on stubs in more recent times; seventeenth-century white vellum covers. (?)Coll. Chancellor Pierre Seguier (d. 1672), no. 1202 (seventeenth century), then through his daughter Marie to his grandson Henri-Charles de Cambout (1664–1732), Duke of Coislin and Bishop of Metz, who left his library to St.-Germain-des-Prés, Paris, as no. 1131; Coll. Pierre Dubrowsky (1754–1816), a Russian diplomat and bibliophile; Leningrad, Imperial Library, 1805. For Seguier and Coislin, see Alfred Franklin, *Les anciennes bibliothèques de Paris* (Paris: Imprim. Imp., 1867), I, pp. 117–120; for Dubrowsky, Michel François, "Pierre Dubrowski et les manuscrits de Saint-Germain-des-Prés à Leningrad," in *Mémorial du XIVe centenaire de l'abbaye de S. Germain-des-Prés* (Paris: Librairie philosophique J. Vrin, 1959), pp. 333–341. Among designs which vary from the Harvard manuscript: no curtains over a bed in the Caladrius miniature; Goose with one gosling instead of two; includes the hunter in the Antelope scene; includes the Beaver castrating itself; has all dogs in Dog miniature instead of Harvard's dogs and (erroneously) lions.

39. Reproduced by Mokretsova and Romanova, p. 159.

40. Based on my edition; see above, n. 28. Complete data for the DC bestiary text is not available for comparison.

41. The colors are dominated by a dark gray-blue and rose, and include also a medium blue, gray-green, gray, beige, and a bright red.

42. Reproduced by Mokretsova and Romanova, p. 168.

43. London Brit. Lib. MS Sloane 278, with a DC bestiary; Oxford Bodleian Lib. MS Bodley 602, with a B-Is bestiary (McCulloch, pp. 28–30); and with H bestiary Paris, Bibl. Nat. MSS lat. 2495A and 2495B, Chalon-sur-Saône Bibl. Mun. MS 14 from the abbey of La Ferté, Cambridge Sidney Sussex College MS 100, and Valenciennes Bibl. Mun. MS 101 from the abbey of St. Amand. Two other bestiaries are related to the group: the first, Paris, Bibl. Nat. lat. 11207, of the Second Family, is related through its painters, who also worked in the Chalon-sur-Saône and Valenciennes manuscripts; the second, with an H bestiary similar to those of the group, is Paris, Bibl. Nat. MS lat. 14429, with an Aviary that does not, however, relate to these either textually or pictorially, despite the manuscript's obvious Parisian production.

44. Based on my forthcoming edition; see above, n. 28.

45. Both designs appear in lat. 2495B and Chalon-sur-Saône 14, the Whale in Sidney Sussex 100, and the Sawfish in Sloane 278. For Leningrad's designs, Mokretsova and Romanova, pp. 159, 172, where in the Whale the artist has,

quite mysteriously, enlarged the boat and put it, without sail, beneath the Whale's belly.

46. The Sidney Sussex, Chalon-sur-Saône, and Valenciennes manuscripts were made by artists defined as Parisian by Robert Branner, *Manuscript Painting in Paris During the Reign of Saint Louis* (Berkeley, Los Angeles, London: University of California Press, 1977), the first by a painter of his Bari Atelier, the latter two painted by his Amiens Atelier; Branner does not list these manuscripts. On the basis of style, the two Bibliothèque Nationale manuscripts are probably Parisian. The ninth manuscript of the group, Bodley 602, is English, and related only by its Aviary variants.

47. Victorine editions (Paris 1526, Rouen 1617) of the works of Hugh of St. Victor include material from the Aviary and the H and Second Family versions of the bestiary, all attributed to Hugh. The Rouen edition states that the texts were drawn from manuscripts in the St. Victor library: *ex manuscriptis eiusdem operibus quae in Biblioteca Victorina servantur*. The late thirteenth-century Paris lat. 14429, with its independent Aviary and an H bestiary, was at St. Victor at an early date, and to a degree conforms to the Aviary variants in the printed editions, although not enough to suppose a direct relationship. The Second Family bestiary mentioned in n. 43 has no known early provenance.

48. Like Harvard and Leningrad, but also like the H bestiary, the Sloane Bestiary omits the birds in favor of the Aviary. Using the DC text in Sbordone, "La tradizione" as basis, the Sloane and Harvard/Leningrad variants include: 266,2 *Filius primitivus meus: Fm. primogenitus;* 266,10 *eo: Domino;* 267,6 *satis hoc animal: animal satis;* 267,14 *om et + Cocodrillus.* Sbordone, p. 256, placed Sloane 278 alone in his text group f, to which the Harvard and Leningrad DC texts should also be assigned.

49. There has been a tendency for scholars to assume, because some medieval painters' model books have been preserved, that their use was widespread. The rarity of surviving model books, however, and their varying characters and contexts, urge caution in any general assumptions. Scheller, *A Survey of Medieval Model Books,* lists only 31, and he notes, p. 6, that the Harvard manuscript is the only model book (strictly speaking) known from the period between 1230 and 1350! For recent skepticism about model-book use by stained-glass painters, Michael Cothren, "The Choir Windows of Agnières (Somme) and a Regional Style of Gothic Glass Painting," *Journal of Glass Studies,* 28 (1986), p. 52, n. 23. Pattern sheets may have been more in use in the late Middle Ages; see, for example, E. Melanie Gifford, "Pattern and Style in a Flemish Book of Hours: Walters Ms. 239," *Journal of the Walters Art Gallery,* 45 (1987), 89–102.

50. Florence McCulloch, *Mediaeval Bestiaries,* p. 75, n. 17, was the first to draw attention to punched miniatures in bestiaries (London, Brit. Lib. MS Add. 11283 and Brussels, Bibl. Roy. MS 8340) other than the Harvard manuscript.

51. The technique of punching for copy transfer is discussed by Lehmann-Haupt, pp. 35–41; Scheller, *A Survey,* pp. 101, 103; Dorothy Miner, "More about Medieval Pouncing," in *Homage to a Bookman: Essays on Manuscripts, Books, and Printing for H. P. Kraus* (Berlin: Mann, 1967), pp. 87–107; and James Douglas Farquhar, *Creation and Imitation* (Fort Lauderdale: Nova/NYIT University Press, 1976), p. 65.

52. Miner, "More About Medieval Pouncing," p. 91 and passim, discusses the se-
    lectivity of the punching and shows, in an example where model and copy are
    both known, that the copyist had chosen certain elements of the design to il-
    lustrate a different text. One possible new use for bird and animal pictures was
    in heraldry.

53. This confusion is especially evident in the Heron and Phoenix miniatures
    which are back to back in the Aviary, and in which the punches are unreadable
    as forms. In the bestiary, one of the Stags was punched through the two fol-
    lowing leaves. A reader or owner, probably long after the thirteenth century,
    "connected the dots" of the punches at the back of the Dove diagram (fol. 1ᵛ),
    thereby placing a second dove incongruously between the two birds of the
    Aviary's Prologue miniature (Fig. 2.2).

54. Medieval tracing methods are discussed by Farquhar, *Creation*, pp. 65–69.

FIGURE 2.1. Harvard Aviary: the Owl (*bubo*), the Jay, the Goose, the Heron, fols. 6ᵛ–7. (Photo: courtesy Florence McCulloch; by permission of the Houghton Library, Harvard University)

FIGURE 2.2. Harvard Aviary and Bestiary: the Ibis, the Peridexion Tree, the Lion and Lioness, the Panther, the Unicorn, fol. 9. (Photo: courtesy Florence McCulloch; by permission of the Houghton Library, Harvard University)

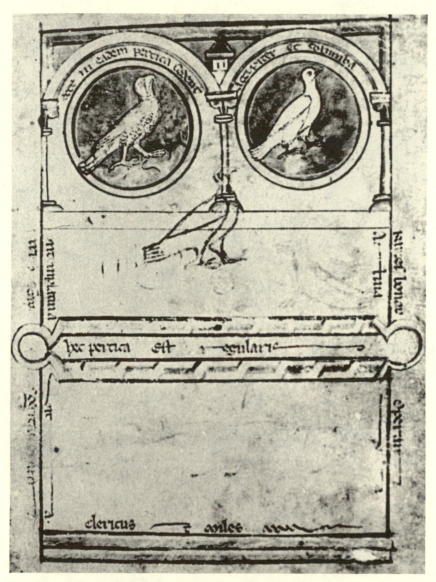

FIGURE 2.3. Harvard Aviary: Prologue miniature, fol. 1 (see n. 52). (Photo: courtesy Florence McCulloch; by permission of the Houghton Library, Harvard University)

FIGURE 2.4. Harvard Aviary: the Blackbird with St. Benedict, fol. 6. (Photo: by permission of the Houghton Library, Harvard University)

FIGURE 2.5. Harvard Bestiary: the Sawfish, fol. 11ʳ. (Photo: courtesy Florence McCulloch; by permission of the Houghton Library, Harvard University)

FIGURE 2.6. The Dominican Bible (Paris, Bibl. Nat. MS 16720, fol. 181ᵛ, II Esdras). (Photo: Paris, Bibl. Nat.)

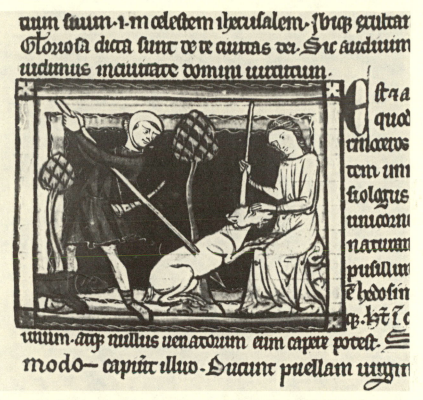

FIGURE 2.7. Dubrowsky Aviary-Bestiary (Leningrad, Gos. Publ. Biblioteka M. E. Saltykova-Shchedrina MS lat. Q.v.III.1, fol. 38ᵛ): the Unicorn. (Photo: Gos. Publ. Bibl. M. E. Saltykova-Shchedrina)

FIGURE 2.8. Harvard Aviary: the Ostrich (with the Vulture showing from reverse side) and punches, fol. 4ᵛ. (Photo: by permission of the Houghton Library, Harvard University)

# Xenia Muratova

## 3. Workshop Methods in English Late Twelfth-Century Illumination and the Production of Luxury Bestiaries

The striking similarities between the Ashmole and Aberdeen Bestiaries were first noticed by M. R. James, who defined them as "sister manuscripts." He dated them to the late twelfth century and classified them in his Second Family of bestiaries, a classification adopted by Florence Mc-Culloch.[1] In James's opinion, "the fine bestiaries belong rather to the North of England than to the South."[2] He saw in the Aberdeen Bestiary "a replica of Ashmole 1511."[3] T. S. R. Boase and M. Rickert noted the relationship between the two manuscripts, which are described by F. Klingender as "the Aberdeen-Ashmole group."[4] J. Einhorn sees in one of the Aberdeen Bestiary images a variant of the corresponding illumination in Ashmole 1511.[5] Boase viewed each manuscript as the work of a different artist, while Nigel Morgan sees in the illuminations of the Ashmole Bestiary "later work in the same manner, probably by the same artist" who worked in the Aberdeen manuscript, which he considers to be "the earliest luxury copy of the Second Family of bestiaries."[6] Morgan defines the Ashmolean manuscript as a "companion book" to the one at Aberdeen.[7]

Elsewhere I have used the term *manuscrits frères* to refer to the two bestiaries[8] and concluded that the cycles of illustrations of the two manuscripts are unquestionably the work of different artists belonging to the same artistic milieu.[9] Although the Aberdeen artist is more attached to the solid, Romanesque order of proportions and forms, whereas the elegant language of the Ashmole artists reveals Gothic tendencies, the Aberdeen Bestiary could hardly have been created any earlier than the Ashmole Bestiary. The former contains several compositions that are overcharged and clumsy in comparison with the same scenes in the Ashmole Bestiary. The Aberdeen artist manifests a certain difficulty in combining figures and organizing pictorial space in comparison with the ease of composition in

Ashmole. The Aberdeen scenes often exceed the limits of the written space. The intense colors and a particularly rich ornamental decoration of clothing in the Aberdeen Bestiary seem to hide the helplessness of a pupil who does not understand articulation of the human figure and who is not capable of varying gestures and movements with the same mastery as the Ashmole artist.[10] For these reasons, I believe the Aberdeen Bestiary to be a free copy of a more refined manuscript.

While no one doubted the closeness of the two manuscripts, the exact nature of their relationship remains undefined. A detailed comparison of decoration, paleography, and codicology confirms this close relationship of the two bestiaries on the one hand, and their individual characteristics on the other, but does not provide definitive evidence of the details of the relationship.[11] Despite individual interpretations in the two manuscripts, one could also suggest the possibility of a common model.

On the basis of style alone, it is very difficult or even impossible to determine which manuscript is earlier. The Romanesque qualities of the Aberdeen Bestiary in comparison with the Gothic tendencies of Ashmole could suggest that Aberdeen is the earlier in execution. The ornament in both is typical of the last quarter of the twelfth century: leafy filigree of Ashmole, painted initials on colored grounds, and vinescrolls with inhabiting white beasts in Aberdeen. The Ashmole minor initials may be related to Romanesque initial decoration of the north of England, especially in Durham.[12] The Aberdeen minor initials, accompanied sometimes by rich pen flourishes rigidly disposed in the margins, reveal tendencies that will develop in the decorated letter of the first half of the thirteenth century, in particular in manuscripts originating most likely in London and Oxford.[13]

There are, however, indications other than the style which point to the Aberdeen and Ashmole Bestiaries as the products not only of the same artistic milieu, but of the same workshop. The two books are fruits of the same conception, executed differently. They testify to, by concealed evidence, specific relations among the artists of an important atelier specializing in the production of luxury manuscripts for individual patrons.

In the lateral margins of fol. 93$^v$ of the Aberdeen Bestiary, which contains the end of Isidore of Seville's essay on the Ages of Man and the miniature for the Firestones,[14] there are fairly clearly discernible leadpoint sketches of the principal elements of the miniature, with its two scenes in two registers (Fig. 3.3). These sketches are situated slightly higher on the page than the painted miniature. One can make out even the horizontal lines dividing the registers and the bordering lines. The upper drawing represents two human figures flanking a tree and with stones in their hands. The hand of the right figure is repeated twice: raised to the level of the head, and in a slightly lower position. There are slight traces of plants sketched at either side. The drawing below shows two figures embracing above a small mountain surrounded with tongues of flame. The remains of a short and carefully erased inscription is not readable.

Such faint leadpoint line drawings are characteristic of preparatory sketches found occasionally in twelfth- and thirteenth-century manuscripts, and their authenticity cannot be doubted.[15] These are not, however, preliminary drawings to be covered by paint, but are the much rarer case of a draft suggestion to the painter of the manuscript by another artist, perhaps the headmaster of the shop.[16] Comparison of the drawings with the Firestones miniature produces an important conclusion. The sketch is sufficiently clear to discern the positions and dimensions of the figures in both scenes, and to see that these do not conform to the figures in the Aberdeen miniature. The figures of the sketch are finer, their postures freer, their gestures more graceful, and their more delicate heads on very thin necks are smaller. The stones which they hold in their hands in the upper zone have an elongated shape, in contrast to the rounded stones of the miniature. In the lower scene of the miniature the figure on the right places his arm on the shoulder of his companion, while the sketch shows the reverse. The flames are lower in the sketch than in the miniature.

The Aberdeen painter appears to have followed the indications of the sketch, but interpreted them in his own way, modifying the type and the attitudes of the figures. On the other hand, the marginal Firestones sketch in Aberdeen corresponds exactly to the miniature of the Firestones in the Ashmole Bestiary: the postures, gestures, and proportions of the figures and the form of the stones and the flames coincide exactly (Figs. 3.3 and 3.4). The dimensions of the figures and the height of the registers are also exactly like those in the Ashmole miniature.[17] This correspondence of the sketch to the miniature of Ashmole bears witness to the Aberdeen artist's use of Ashmole itself, and not a common model. The changes in the gesture of the hand in the upper zone show that the draughtsman did not use any mechanical method of transfer. The drawings permit a conclusion that the Aberdeen and Ashmole Bestiaries were almost contemporary works: the Aberdeen manuscript could have been made either simultaneously with Ashmole, or slightly later, while the Ashmole Bestiary was still in the shop.[18]

An examination of margins of the Aberdeen manuscript shows two more, but hardly discernible, traces of erased drawings on fols. 44$^v$ and

68$^v$. On fol. 44$^v$, near the miniature for the Vulture, one can see traces of a circle and of the heads of two affronted birds within. The diameter of the circle (6.3 cm) coincides exactly with that of the Vulture miniature in Ashmole, but not of Aberdeen (with a diameter of 6.8 cm).

The discovery in the Aberdeen Bestiary of the marginal sketches corresponding to the designs of the Ashmole Bestiary lead to the conclusion that the two manuscripts were produced in the same workshop and that the cycle of illuminations of Aberdeen is based directly on that of Ashmole. The traces of marginal sketches in Aberdeen are not numerous enough to afford a clear view of the character of the relationships among the artists participating in the execution of the two manuscripts, but they provide new and important indications concerning the methods of work in English workshops during the period of transition from Romanesque to Gothic.

The refinement in draftsmanship, and the graceful character and proportions of the figures suggest that these sketches were done by one of the artists of the Ashmole Bestiary. The Aberdeen Bestiary artist who drew the disproportionate figures with large shoulders and short necks, and who gave the woman only one breast, could not produce these graceful, finely proportioned figures; the Adam Naming the Animals miniatures of the two manuscripts demonstrates the differences in quality (Figs. 3.1 and 3.2). The author of the sketch was perhaps the headmaster of the workshop, or at least a principal artist. He was a master of linear stylization who possessed a fine sense of proportion and rhythm, and whose virtuosity has left the imprint of an elegant standard on the whole cycle of the illuminations in the Ashmole Bestiary.

The marginal sketches provide only the essentials of the composition, the details being left to the imagination and talent of the artist executing the design in paint. The fact that the copy was made from sketches rather than from the model manuscript itself permitted the artist still more freedom to modify the details of his composition. Hence the variations and modifications in details of the compositions in the Aberdeen Bestiary in comparison with Ashmole. The headmaster presented to the artist executing the Aberdeen Bestiary a precise pictorial motif corresponding in its dimensions to the compositions in the model manuscript, but this motif was not to be copied literally.

Thus, the connection between the Aberdeen and Ashmole Bestiaries touches in a way upon the problem of freedom or dependence of the medieval artist, a topic much discussed in modern art history.[19] But it not only corroborates the general statement that the freedom of the medieval artist consisted in the interpretation of the model, it also provides another concrete example of the basic working method of the medieval artist in interpreting a prototype. In this instance it is not a matter of reinterpretation of an early prototype, but the modification of a contemporary model at a particular stage of the creative process.

The comparison of these two manuscripts demonstrates the fundamental attitude of the Romanesque and Early Gothic artist who neither strives for nor is satisfied with an exact copy. Each new manuscript was, in a sense, a new and unique creation, presenting an individual interpretation of the model according to the artist's personality and susceptibility to the artistic tendencies of his period.

An important aspect of practice was the extensive use of model books and collections of patterns in a shop.[20] It is probable that the shop master in some specific cases provided drawings to be interpreted by a particular artist, for instance in the case of apprentices. For the trained artists, however, it must have sufficed for the master to point out which models to use. It is clear that the workshop which produced the two bestiaries possessed a storehouse of exempla and patterns, including various motifs of animals. The use and assemblage of motifs from such a storehouse is particularly evident in the large miniatures of the Creation of Animals and of Adam Naming the Animals (Figs. 3.1 and 3.2). The iconography of both scenes has several points in common with analogous representations in Sicilian and south Italian mosaics, as well as in the mosaics of San Marco, Venice.[21] These miniatures represent in both manuscripts a collection of various motifs of animal figures used also in the miniatures of the bestiary proper: the Lion, the Stag, the Dogs, the Cats, the Horse, the Elephant, the Goat, the Bull, the Peacock, the Ram, and the Boar. The Squirrel and Hare are not mentioned in this version of the bestiary, but are present in traditional scenes of the Creation. The Squirrel and Hare are already encountered in the same scenes in earlier bestiaries such as MS lat. Q.v.V.1. of the Leningrad Public Library (fols. 2ᵛ and 5), the first known bestiary accompanied by scenes of the Creation. The presence of hares, which appear to be unknown in England before the thirteenth century, in the creation of animals of both manuscripts also relates these representations to models from south Italy or Venice.[22]

Although the Aberdeen artist's rendering of figures does not express the figure's movements or gestures, or the configuration of drapery, as finely as the Ashmole painter does, the treatment of animal forms and their placement in the frames is skillful in both manuscripts. In the animals of the Aberdeen Bestiary there is no trace of the awkwardness which strikes the eye in the representations of the Creator. To the Aberdeen painter's virtuosity of outline in animal designs, equal to that of his Ashmole counterpart, is added a particular taste for rich and refined ornamental elaboration of silhouettes and forms. The difference between representation of human and animal figures may be due to the use of different models, and to a different approach to the models, that is, to possible half-mechanical methods of transfer—stencils, mirror, or geometrical devices—for the representation of animals. The outlines of the majority of animals are very similar in both manuscripts, which seems again to suggest mechanical transfer, but detailed comparison of the dimensions of comparable animals in the two books shows that they almost never coincide.[23]

The reversal of direction of some of the animals in various scenes of both manuscripts (the cats in the Creation scene; a small dog in Aberdeen's Adam Naming the Animals, Fig. 3.1; the Wolf in Aberdeen) might also result from the use of half-mechanical methods of transfer of images. One of the methods of mechanical or half-mechanical transfer was pouncing.[24] The Ashmole manuscript shows no evidence of the pricking of miniatures for this transfer method, but there are many pricked designs in Aberdeen. The verso of the leaves with pricked images has often been dirtied by the charcoal dust used for pouncing. Some miniatures have suffered because of the pricking of a miniature on the reverse side, as in the first Dog scene (fol. 18).[25] Of course, it is difficult to date these prickings. The ancient evidence, on the reverse side of the pricked leaves, of their practical use allow the supposition, however, that the prickings could not have been made much later than the execution of the manuscript. Possibly the manuscript remained in the paintshop for some time and was used as a model, or served as model in another shop. The existence of these early prickings and the evidence of their use suggest perhaps that the Aberdeen and Ashmole Bestiaries were not a unique pair, but two manuscripts which managed to survive from a much larger series. The developed use of the half-mechanical methods of transfer bear witness to a workshop that was large and well organized, similar to those which were developed in the thirteenth century.[26] The extensive use of exempla, the repetition of animal patterns in various compositions, as well as the repetition and variation of the same attitudes in several figures, indicate a standardization of production in the shop, but also a tradition of fine workmanship which permitted a uniqueness to each manuscript.

Elsewhere I have suggested the participation of three artists in the execution of the Ashmole Bestiary.[27] In the Aberdeen Bestiary the situation is unclear. It is not simply a matter of the differentiation of artists' hands in Aberdeen, but of determining participation in different phases of execution.[28] I am inclined to think that two artists took part in the Aberdeen Bestiary's decoration, one a master who did the marginal sketches for a number of miniatures and who chose the exempla and patterns for the rest of the designs. He may have executed some of the preliminary drawings for the second artist to paint. The second artist, possibly an apprentice, may have executed the major part of the preliminary drawings and the painting. The decoration of the Aberdeen Bestiary could be the "chef d'oeuvre" of his apprenticeship, executed in accordance with the indications of the headmaster. There is a certain contradiction between somewhat rough and awkward human forms and a particular richness and refinement of the ornamental work, including the rosettes and arabesques. The second artist did not participate in any way in the decoration of the Ashmole Bestiary.

The high level to which the art of interpretation of models was carried is especially striking in the production of English workshops of the end of the twelfth and beginning of the thirteenth century. This art guaranteed a richness, individuality, and variety of styles, and a uniqueness for each manuscript. With all the lively circulation of models and a particular independence in the re-elaboration of those models, this production is distinguished by a high artistic standard. There were many highly placed and wealthy patrons to support a surprisingly large production of luxury manuscripts—a characteristic feature of English society and culture in the transitional period from the Romanesque to the Gothic.[29] The marginal drawings of the Aberdeen Bestiary and the peculiarity of their relationship to both manuscripts reveal important unknown aspects of the practices in the English workshops producing illuminated manuscripts around 1200.

*I could hardly find a better topic to honor the memory of Florence McCulloch than two manuscripts which mark the apogee of production of English illuminated bestiaries: Bodleian Library MS Ashmole 1511 and Aberdeen University Library MS 24. Although I never met Dr. McCulloch, her work on the bestiaries has been an important source and starting point of my own work.*

## Notes

1. M. R. James, *The Bestiary* (Oxford: Roxburghe Club, 1928), pp. 14ff., 55–59; "The Bestiary in the University Library," *Aberdeen University Library Bulletin,*

36 (1928), 529–531; and *A Catalogue of the Medieval Manuscripts in the University Library Aberdeen* (Cambridge: Cambridge University Press, 1932), pp. 18ff. Florence McCulloch, *Mediaeval Latin and French Bestiaries* (Chapel Hill: University of North Carolina Press, rev. ed., 1962), p. 36.

2. James, *The Bestiary,* p. 59.

3. Ibid., p. 55.

4. T. S. R. Boase, *English Art 1100–1216* (Oxford: Clarendon Press, 1953), p. 295. Margaret Rickert, *Painting in Britain: The Middle Ages* (Harmondsworth: Penguin, 1954), p. 100. Rickert notes a trio of manuscripts, adding Bodleian Douce 151 to the Ashmole and Aberdeen Bestiaries. Francis Klingender, *Animals in Art and Thought* (London: Routledge and Kegan Paul, 1971), pp. 388, 392.

5. Jürgen W. Einhorn, *Spiritalis unicornis* (Munich: Wilhelm Fink, 1976), p. 277.

6. Boase, *English Art,* p. 295; Nigel Morgan, *Early Gothic Manuscripts,* I (Oxford and London: Oxford University Press and Harvey Miller, 1982), p. 64.

7. Morgan, p. 65.

8. Xenia Muratova, "Les manuscrits 'frères': un aspect particulier de la production des Bestiaires enluminés en Angleterre à la fin du XIIe et au début du XIIIe siècle," in *Actes du Colloque: Artistes, artisans et production artistique au Moyen Age,* Rennes: CNRS, Université de Rennes, 1983, vol. 3. "Etude du manuscrit," pp. 47ff. I use the term *manuscrits frères* to describe illuminated bestiary manuscripts in which the iconographic schemes are essentially the same and executed in a similar manner; the term paraphrases James's "sister manuscripts" and Adolph Goldschmidt's *Schwester-Handschriften,* introduction to Alexandra Konstantinowa, *Ein englisches Bestiar des zwölften Jahrhunderts in der Staatsbibliothek zu Leningrad* (Berlin: Deutscher Kunst Verlag, 1929).

9. Muratova, "Etude du manuscrit," pp. 47ff.

10. This is particularly true of the Creator figure. In the scenes of the Creation of birds, of animals, and of Eve (fols. 2, 2$^v$ and 3) and in the scene of Adam naming the animals (fol. 5), the Aberdeen artist gave to this figure the same harsh gesture, whereas the artist of the Ashmole Bestiary subtly varied gestures, poses, and gracious turns. Thus, the different images of the Creator furnished by the Ashmole and Aberdeen artists are the result not only of different artistic conceptions and personal languages but also of different levels of skill. The comparison of the dimensions and of the proportions of the figures in both manuscripts also shows a particular refinement of proportions of the human figure in the Ashmole Bestiary (e.g., in the scene of the Separation of Light from Darkness, fol. 4, the height of the figure of the Creator, 9.3 cm; of his head, 1 cm; of his feet, 1 cm) contrary to the more solid and heavy figures in the Aberdeen Bestiary (e.g., in the same scene, fol. 1, the height of the figure of the Creator, 11.2 cm; of his head, 1.6 cm; of his feet, 1.5 cm). Thus, in the scene of the Ashmole Bestiary the head constitutes 9.3% of the height of the figure. In the same scene in the Aberdeen manuscript the head constitutes the seventh part of the figure.

11. A comparison of the codicology, style, iconography, technical processes, and miniatures in the two manuscripts appears in my study "Etude du manuscrit," *Bestiarium* (Paris: Club du livre, 1984), 13–55.

12. The small filigree initials in the Bible of Hugh of Puiset (Durham Cath. Lib. MS A.II) compare well with those of Ashmole. The chiaroscuro initials of Ashmole (fols. 85, 92) find parallels in some initials in the Copenhagen Psalter (Royal Lib. MS Thott 143,20), e.g., fol. 30.

13. The Aberdeen Bestiary is a fairly early case of the decoration of margins with pen flourishes. They take the form of long "rods" ornamented with small blue and red cluster patterns. Far richer and more varied decoration of this type is found in manuscripts of 1230–1250 ascribed to London and Oxford, e.g., Oxford, New College MS 322 and Stockholm, Nat. Mus. MS B 2010 (Morgan, *Early Gothic*, I, pp. 113–114, 121–123).

14. These are the first known instances of the Firestones miniature divided into two compartments, although the two consecutive events (man and woman beckoning to one another with gestures; they are surrounded by flames) appear together, united in one scene, in Bodleian MS Laud. Misc. 247 (fol. 141$^v$) of the 1120s. For the same scene on the door of the church of Alne, see Muratova, "Les cycles des bestiaires dans le décor sculpté des églises du XIIe siècle dans le Yorkshire, et leur relation avec les manuscrits des bestiaires enluminés," in *Atti del V Colloquio della Societa Internazionale per lo studio dell'epica animale, della favola e del fabliau* (Turin-St. Vincent, 1983; Alexandria, 1987). In the Leningrad Bestiary, Gos. Public Lib. MS Q.v.V.I., fol. 34$^v$, and New York, Pierpont Morgan Lib. MS 81, fol. 33$^v$, the man and woman are shown embracing on the summit of a hill surrounded by flames; for the Leningrad and Ashmole versions, Muratova, *The Medieval Bestiary* (Moscow: Iskusstvo, 1984), p. 115. The relating of the Firestones to Adam and Eve at the Fall occurs as early as the tenth-century *Physiologus* in Brussels (Bibl. Roy. MS 10066-77, fol. 141$^v$). The miniatures of the Ashmole and Aberdeen Bestiaries have traits in common with the Fall depicted in the mosaics of the Cappella Palatina in Palermo; on iconography related to the models of the Sicilian mosaics, Muratova, "Etude du manuscrit," pp. 36ff., and "I manoscritti miniati del bestiario medioevale: origine, formazione e sviluppo dei cicli di illustrazioni. I bestiari miniati in Inghilterra nei secoli XII–XIV," in *L'uomo di fronte al mondo animale nell'alto medioevo. Trentunesima Settimana di studio*, V. 31 (Spoleto: Panetto and Petrelli, 1985), II, pp. 1335, 1347, and "The Manuscripts of Bestiaries: An Aspect of Medieval Patronage," in *Art and Patronage in the English Romanesque*, ed. S. Macready and F. H. Thompson (London: Society of Antiquaries, 1986), pp. 133ff. The Firestones text in Ashmole 1511 is that of the B-version *Physiologus*.

15. For instance, the preparatory drawings in Cambridge, Trinity College MS O.I.64, Bede's *Life of St. Cuthbert*, of c. 1200; Morgan, *Early Gothic*, I, no. 12, pp. 59–60. The Apocrypha drawings in the Winchester Bible are less sketchy, with a certain precision of outline; C. M. Kauffmann, *Romanesque Manuscripts 1066–1190* (London: Harvey Miller, 1975), pp. 108–112, and *English Romanesque Art 1066–1200* (Exhib. cat., London, 1984), no. 64b, 65, pp. 121–122. On preparatory drawings in medieval manuscripts, Henry Martin, "Les esquisses des miniatures," *Revue archéologique*, II (1904), pp. 17ff.

16. In late twelfth- and early thirteenth-century manuscripts it is more common to find traces of written instructions to the artist, one of the more interesting ex-

amples being in the Rochester Bestiary, Brit. Lib. MS Roy. 12.F.XIII, with numerous marginal directions in French to the painter; see fols. 29$^v$, 30$^v$, 35–36$^v$, 42$^v$–43$^v$, and especially fols. 52$^v$, 53$^v$, 54$^v$, 56, 57, where only spaces for miniatures occur.

17. Dimensions of the Aberdeen miniature: 11.5 × 12.4 cm with frame, 10.5 × 11.5 cm without frame. The dividing line between registers is at a height of about 2.5 cm, and the height of each scene 5.6 cm. The height of each marginal drawing in the Aberdeen manuscript is 5 cm. The Ashmole scenes also measure 5 cm in height. The heads of the Aberdeen figures measure 1 cm in height, in Ashmole 0.7 cm, and in the sketch 0.7 cm.

18. Morgan, *Early Gothic*, I, pp. 63 and 65, suggests c. 1210 as a date for the Ashmole Bestiary and c. 1200 for Aberdeen. In my commentary on the Ashmole Bestiary, "Etude du manuscrit," pp. 49ff., I propose c. 1205–1215 for this manuscript's production. After a new comparison with related manuscripts, such as the St. Louis Psalter in Leiden (Univ. Lib. MS 76 A), I am inclined now to think that both the Ashmole and the Aberdeen Bestiaries should be dated to about 1200.

19. Emile Mâle, *L'art religieux en France au XIIe siècle* (Paris: Armand Colin, 1922), pp. 107, 117–118, 151; E. de Bruyne, *Etude d'esthétique médiévale*, 3 vols. (Bruges: De Tempel, 1946), II, and in the Spanish edition, II, pp. 419ff.; Erwin Panofsky, *Gothic Architecture and Scholasticism* (New York: Meridian, 1957), pp. 23, 27–28; Paul Frankl, *The Gothic: Literary Sources and Their Interpretation* (Princeton: Princeton University Press, 1960), p. 836; R. Assunto, *La critica d'arte nel pensiero medioevale* (Milan: Il Saggiatore, 1961), pp. 118ff.; Xenia Muratova, *Artists of the French Gothic: Problems of the Theory and Practice* (Moscow: University of Moscow, 1988).

20. On medieval model books, Hans Hahnloser, *Villard de Honnecourt* (Vienna, 1935; Graz, 1972); S. A. Ives and H. Lehmann-Haupt, *An English 13th Century Bestiary* (New York: H. P. Kraus, 1942); R. W. Scheller, *A Survey of Medieval Model Books* (Haarlem: De Erven F. Bohn, 1963); Dorothy Miner, "More about Medieval Pouncing," in *Homage to a Bookman: Essays on Manuscripts, Books, and Printing for Hans P. Kraus* (Berlin: Mann, 1967), pp. 87–101; Helmut Lehmann-Haupt, *The Göttingen Model Book* (Columbia: University of Missouri Press, 1972), pp. 11–13.

21. See above, n. 14.

22. See the contribution of R. Delort during the discussion of Muratova, "I manoscitti miniati." Hares are present in the miniatures of MS 132 in the Montecassino Library, fol. 171, dated 1023; in the Creation of the animals on the Salerno ivories; and in the Creation of the animals in the mosaics of San Marco, Venice.

23. See above, n. 11. Examples of comparative measurements of animal length in the two bestiaries are: the horse in the Tiger miniature, 4.1 cm in Aberdeen, 4.4 cm in Ashmole; the Pard, 5.2 cm in Aberdeen, 5 cm in Ashmole; the Hyena, 6.5 cm in Aberdeen, 5.3 cm in Ashmole; the Bonnacon, 4.9 cm in Aberdeen, 5.6 cm in Ashmole.

24. On this technique, Ives and Lehmann-Haupt, *An English Bestiary;* Dorothy

Miner, review of Ives and Lehmann-Haupt in *Art Bulletin,* 25 (1943), 88–89, and "More about Medieval Pouncing"; Scheller, *A Survey,* pp. 101–103.

25. Other Aberdeen Bestiary miniatures with prickings are: Adam and Eve in the Creation of Eve, fol. 3; man in Hyena miniature, fol. 11$^v$; the Apes, fol. 12$^v$; archer in Magpie scene, fol. 37; Hoopoe, fol. 36$^v$; Viper, fol. 66$^v$; Amphisbaena, fol. 68$^v$. None corresponds in dimensions with the Ashmole miniature, or with miniatures in two other bestiaries with a similar program, Cambridge Univ. Lib. MS Ii.IV.26 and Oxford, St. John's College MS 61 (for example, the human figure in the Hyena miniature is 6.5 cm in length in Ashmole and 7.2 cm in Aberdeen, where the legs of this figure are in a different position). It is important to remember, however, that the half-mechanical transfer methods, stencils, pouncing, mirror, and so forth, provide the artist with only an approximate outline of the figures and facilitated his work, but there was always room for reinterpretation of the outline drawing.

26. Miner, "More about Medieval Pouncing," p. 103.

27. Muratova, "Etude du manuscrit," pp. 46ff.

28. Compare Henry Martin, *Les peintres de manuscrits et la miniature en France* (Paris: H. Laurens, 1909), pp. 23ff.

29. See *Art and Patronage in the English Romanesque* (see above, n. 14).

FIGURE 3.1. Aberdeen Bestiary: Adam Naming the Animals (Aberdeen Univ. Lib. MS 24, fol. 5). (Photo: W. B. Clark)

FIGURE 3.2. Ashmole Bestiary: Adam Naming the Animals (Oxford, Bodleian Lib. MS Ashmole 1511, fol. 9). (Photo: Conway Library, Courtauld Institute of Art)

FIGURE 3.3. Aberdeen Bestiary: the Firestones (Aberdeen Univ. Lib. MS 24, fol. 93ᵛ). (Photo: Conway Library, Courtauld Institute of Art)

FIGURE 3.4. Ashmole Bestiary: the Firestones (Oxford, Bodleian Lib. MS Ashmole 1511, fol. 103ᵛ). (Photo: Conway Library, Courtauld Institute of Art)

# Guy R. Mermier

## 4. The Phoenix: Its Nature and Its Place in the Tradition of the Physiologus

The moment we open the vast and fascinating book of medieval history, we are immediately immersed in the symbolic world which forms the basis of the primitive mind for whom St. Augustine formulated a dynamic in the phrase "per visibilia et invisibilia." We know that man, awakened from his cosmic sleep, sought almost instinctively, through his relationship with the stars, the rocks, the plants, and the animals around him, to understand and organize the chaos of his world. Nature was thus at the beginning of humanity; it was the "magister docens" for man, source of his life, of his fear, and consequently of his religion. All the herbals, aviaries, lapidaries, and bestiaries thus owe their origin and their use to the Augustinian concept that the symbol gives man the means to understand himself and to prevail. Rare indeed are the Church Fathers who in their teaching have not turned to nature, and to the animals in particular. The fact is, if man is often complex and obscure, the animal offers constant and unequivocal qualities which serve as a mirror for man. The bestiaries offer thus a "socialized" fauna and a concrete language which far surpasses that of the naturalists, for whom a lion is a lion.

The present study of the phoenix will offer only a brief inroad into one aspect of animal symbolism. As superficial as that may be, it will, however, provide an opportunity to organize somewhat and to clarify the principal nuances which form the myth of the phoenix in the antique and medieval tradition of the *Physiologus,* and to view the implications of those nuances for the French bestiaries of the high Middle Ages.[1]

First a brief word on the *Physiologus.* The name comes from the Greek *Physiologos,* which means "the naturalist," and it remains a question as to whether it refers to a book of ancient wisdom or the name of an author. Even today doubt persists, but one thing remains certain: all versions of the text are alike in appealing to the authority of this anonymous naturalist with the formula "Physiologus says." The work, of which the original was Greek, seems to have been written at Alexandria in the early years of Christianity, about the second century of our era.[2] The *Physiologus* was known and used at a very early date by the Church Fathers: St. John Chrysostomos, Clement of Alexandria, St. Epiphany, St. Basil the Great, St. Ambrose, and St. Jerome. St. Justin Martyr was the first Christian author of the School of Alexandria to have consulted the work and Origen the first to have cited it and commented upon it.[3] There is also a question as to whether the original *Physiologus* included allegories. The prevailing theory today is that the interpretations, of a symbolic, didactic, and religious character, were added by one or several Christian authors.[4] In any case, for purposes of this study, it is the allegorized or moralized *Physiologus* which is of interest.[5] The influence of this work on the Middle Ages was incalculable, being second only to the Bible in the number of versions in which it appeared.[6]

At first glance, the history of the phoenix appears all too familiar, so often has the bird been represented in paintings, sculpted in stone or wood, and engraved on coins. It appears with equal frequency in fables, and even more popularly, in publicity for firemen and fire-insurance companies. A more serious effort to find its deep mythic reality will encounter enormous complexities and stunning contradictions.

According to the accounts of encyclopedias and dictionaries, the phoenix is a mythological bird associated especially with the cult of the sun in ancient Egypt, and which, having died, is reborn of its own ashes.[7] To this is occasionally added that it was a unique bird of great beauty, with a melodious song and shining or scarlet plumage.[8] The matter appears quite simple until the article by McDonald or the works of van den Broek and Hubaux-Leroy are brought to bear.[9] These studies bring to light the multiplicity of variants in the tradition of the phoenix.

To begin, we shall present in a schematic fashion the phoenix in the antique tradition, exclusive of the *Physiologus,* and thereafter the *Physiologus* traditions, both Eastern and Western.

## I. THE PHOENIX IN SOURCES OTHER THAN THE *PHYSIOLOGUS*

Below is a classification of the principal elements of the myth of the phoenix: the name by which the bird is called, its gender, its food, its appearances, the length of its life, the places it frequents, its death, and its resurrection.

### A. NAME

The phoenix is known as (1) a purple bird or *avis regia;* [10] (2) phoenician; [11] (3) benu (purple heron); [12] (4) palm tree.[13]

## B. Gender

The bird is referred to variously as *singularis, unicus avis,*[14] *asexual;*[15] male and female;[16] male;[17] female;[18] and androgynous or hermaphroditic.[19]

## C. Food[20]

(1) The winged worm born from the ashes of the burnt phoenix feeds on water and "dry fodder" at the seashore; (2) the phoenix neither eats nor drinks; (3) according to Ovid, the phoenix touches neither seeds nor plants, but feeds only on drops of incense and the juice of amomum; (4) according to Claudian (*Phoenix*) the phoenix does not eat fatty things or quench its thirst at fountains. It feeds only on the pure rays of the sun and the mists raised by the wind.

## D. Appearances[21]

1. According to Tacitus (*Annales* vi, 28), the phoenix appeared for the first time in Egypt in the reign of Sesoris, about 1300 B.C., then under Amasis (529–526 B.C.) and under Ptolemy III Evergetes, who died in 221. According to Larcher, Tacitus was mistaken in placing the arrival of the phoenix in Egypt two years too early.[22] In fact, Pliny, Solinus, and Dio Cassius pushed back by two years the date proposed by Tacitus.[23]

2. The appearance of the phoenix is linked also to important political events, to the founding of cities or temples, as well as to important moments in the Bible.[24]

## E. Lifespan

Larcher writes of Tacitus, "He does not doubt the existence of the phoenix. . . . This learned historian reports almost every story told in his day about this bird; but he adds prudently that the details about it are uncertain and mixed with fables. 'There are variations,' he says, 'in its lifespan; most people say it lives five centuries; some say fourteen hundred and sixty-one years.'"[25] We shall soon see, in the analysis which follows, that even Tacitus was far from guessing the incredible number of variations that the lifespan of the phoenix was to inspire. One of the constants of the phoenix myth is that after a certain lifespan it died and was then reborn.[26] The span can be 500 years,[27] more than 500 years,[28] 540 years,[29] 650 or 654 years,[30] 1,000 years,[31] 1,461 years,[32] 7,006 years,[33] 93,312 and 97,000 years,[34] 972 human generations.[35]

## F. Life and death of the phoenix

1. Geographic associations: India;[36] Egypt and Heliopolis;[37] Paradise, Elysium;[38] Arabia, Ethiopia, Assyria, Phoenicia;[39] the Temple of the Sun near Panchaia;[40] Lycaonia;[41] Syria;[42] Lebanon.[43]

2. Preparations for death: aware of the approach of death, the phoenix prepares a pyre made of various materials (Fig. 4.1).[44]

3. Composition of the pyre:[45] aromatic substances and spices; fennel and amber (electrum); cinnamon and myrrh.[46]

4. The death of the phoenix: the fundamental myth of the phoenix is that in dying it renews its life. The nest-pyre is generally at Heliopolis. The bird immolates itself, and from its ashes is born the new phoenix. In addition to this tradition there is another, equally vivid, according to which the phoenix dies and decomposes on its nest. From its remains, that is, from the fluid issuing from the decomposition of the body, a worm is reborn that is quickly metamorphosed into a phoenix bird.[47] Often the myth of the worm is amplified in a curious way: wings grow from the worm which, after three days, becomes the new phoenix. According to Pliny and Manilius, the worm emerges from the marrow of the corpse's bones. For Clement of Rome and Cyril of Jerusalem the worm issues from the decomposed flesh of the corpse. Ambrose and Lactantius also mention the role of fluid in the metamorphosis of the phoenix. Most often the pyre is ignited by heat from the rays of the sun.[48] Certain versions expand this myth and report that in order to set itself ablaze, the bird beats its body with its wings. In certain cases, for the pseudo-Jerome for instance, the bird beats its wings at sunrise and the heat enflames the amber placed among the aromatic substances on an altar.[49] There is another, less violent, version of the death of the phoenix: according to Lactantius, the bird, having covered its nest with aromatic substances, stretches itself over the nest and dies there.[50]

## G. Resurrection of the phoenix

The traditional resurrection of the phoenix is made from the ashes of the pyre on which it was consumed. In certain versions the resurrection takes place in a ball of myrrh. Horapollo reports an original version according to which the phoenix, feeling its death draw near, opens its side, and from fluid issuing from the wound is born the new bird which flies toward Heliopolis where the old bird dies at dawn.[51] The young bird then returns to its homeland while the Egyptian priests bury the old dead bird. We have already encountered the worm phase, and that of the worm which acquired wings before becoming the new phoenix. Among the phenomena which accompany the resurrection are rain and dew.[52]

## II. The phoenix in the oldest, mostly non-Latin *Physiologus* versions

The phoenix-like characteristics in these versions can be summarized as follows:

### A. Name
In all cases the bird is called "phoenix."

### B. Gender
The *Physiologus* assumes that the bird is above sexuality.[53]

### C. Physical representation of the phoenix
The representations are usually vague, with the sources referring only to a "bird." It is compared, however, to a peacock,[54] and given an aureole made of the rays of the sun. The extraordinary beauty of the bird is also noted, a beauty enhanced by precious stones studding its plumage: sapphires, emeralds, and so forth.[55] The Vienna *Physiologus* attributes to the phoenix a physical trait usually given to the crocodile by the *Physiologus*, that it cannot move its upper jaw.[56] The same manuscript adds that its plumage is parti-colored, that it is tall in stature and as big as a small island. Its head is adorned with rays and it has 365 rounded plumes. It further adds that its feet are made of a single piece of skin and webbed like those of ducks and geese.

### D. Food
The subject is rarely addressed. According to the Vienna *Physiologus* the winged worm lived near the sea, feeding on water and dry matter. According to the Greek *Physiologus*, the phoenix fed upon the Holy Spirit.[57]

### E. Appearances
The phoenix usually makes its appearance to die and be reborn. According to the Greek *Physiologus* the phoenix goes to Heliopolis to burn itself up "in the new month, Nisan or Adar, that is, Phamenoth or Pharmouti."[58]

### F. Life and death

1. Geographic associations: India, Egypt, Heliopolis;[59] Lebanon;[60] Paradise.[61]

2. Preparation for death: the ancient versions are in general agreement on the fact that the bird prepares its own pyre and lights it.[62]

3. Composition of the pyre: usually the nest-pyre is made of vine branches or of twigs soaked in aromatic essences which the phoenix lights in one way or another.[63]

4. Death of the phoenix: either it is consumed on a pyre[64] or it decomposes.[65]

5. It has a lifespan of either a complete era[66] or 500 years.[67] The latter is the more common form of the legend.

### G. Resurrection of the phoenix

Nearly all versions say that (1) the priest of Heliopolis examines the ashes of the altar where the bird was burnt, and finds there a worm; (2) the second day the worm is transformed into a young bird; (3) the third day the bird becomes an adult in the image of its predecessor.[68]

### H. Symbolism

The innovation of the *Physiologus,* in comparison with antique and pagan traditions, is to present the phoenix as a symbol of Christ and the Resurrection.[69]

## III. The phoenix in the Latin *Physiologus*

We shall not repeat the basic work of Florence McCulloch, to whom we warmly dedicate these pages.[70] We shall conclude this present study with the Latin versions that are closest to those of the French bestiaries: the Latin *Physiologus,* versions Y and B; a prototype of the version which McCulloch called B-Is; an excerpt from the *Etymologiae* of Isidore of Seville.[71]

### A. Latin *Physiologus*, Y version

According to chapter IX of this version, the bird is of Indian origin. At the end of "quingentos annos" it enters "in ligna Libani" and "implet alas suas aromata."[72] Then it gives a sign to the priest of Heliopolis who prepares the pyre upon which the bird will immolate itself. On the second day an "avicullam pusillam" issues from the ashes, a small bird that becomes an adult, "aquilam magnam," on the third day.[73] The new bird greets the priest and "vadit in antiquum locum suum." In the last paragraph of text the phoenix symbolizes Christ, "Phoenix personam accipit Salvatoris."

## B. Latin *Physiologus*, B version

The author of this version emphasizes immediately that the bird is a symbol and image of Christ, "Est aliud volatile quod dicitur phoenix; huius figuram gerit dominus noster Jesus Christus." According to this version, the phoenix is of Indian origin and after "expletis quingentis annis vitae suae" it goes to the forest of Lebanon, there to fill its wings with various aromatic substances. The bird goes to Heliopolis where it finds the priest who has prepared its nest-pyre. The bird arrives and burns itself up. The priest then comes and, examining the ashes, finds "ibi vermiculum modicum suavissimo odore fragrantem."[74] The next day the bird has taken shape and the day after that (the third day) it is a new adult phoenix. And the version concludes, "Ergo sicut iam supra diximus, personam accipit salvatoris nostri."

## C. The *Physiologus* of the B-Is type (British Library MS Royal 2.C.XII)[75]

The text begins with a rapprochement between the phoenix and Christ, "Est aliud volatile quod dicitur phoenix. Huius figuram gerit Dominus noster Iesus Christus." The bird is from India, "Indie partibus," and after "expletis quingentis annis vitae suae" it goes to Lebanon and "replet utrasque alas diversis aromatibus." It then goes to Heliopolis, meets the priest there and is consumed. As in the Latin version B a worm is born from the ashes and soon takes the form of a small bird. The third day "veniens sacerdos invenit eam iam in statu suo integram atque factam avem fenicem." The bird greets the priest and "evolat et pergit ad locum suum pristinum." The text ends with the association of the bird with Christ, "Ergo sicut iam supra diximus personam accipit Salvatoris Nostri."

## D. Excerpt from the *Etymologiae* of Isidore of Seville (XII, XIV, XVII, XIX)

In this case the bird is of Arabic origin and after having lived "quingentis et ultra annis," it gathers aromatic materials and puts itself upon a pyre which it lights by exposure to the rays of the sun. Finally, it is reborn of its own ashes.[76]

## IV. The phoenix in the French *Physiologus* tradition: The bestiaries of Philippe de Thaon, Gervaise, Guillaume le Clerc of Normandy, and Pierre de Beauvais[77]

### A. The bestiary of Philippe de Thaon, lines 2217–2246[78]

In the first part (lines 2217–2246) the text follows the Latin version B interpolated with passages from Isidore,[79] but without the worm phase of the phoenix. Philippe, like Isidore, states that the phoenix is of Arabian origin. To burn itself up, the phoenix utilizes a pyre, but the priest does not intervene. Philippe and, later, Pierre de Beauvais are the only French writers to detail the physical appearance of the phoenix. According to Philippe, the bird "cume cisne est truvez," an error that McCulloch explains by saying that Philippe confused "olorem" with "colorem."[80] He adds in his description that the bird is "purprins" (line 2224). In a second part, Philippe follows closely the Latin version B. After it is burnt, the phoenix becomes a worm which the priest of Heliopolis discovers and, on the third day the worm becomes an adult phoenix which is the symbol of Christ.[81]

### B. The bestiary of Gervaise[82]

Gervaise also maintains the Christ symbolism, and like Guillaume le Clerc, he stresses the uniqueness of the bird. Like Guillaume and Pierre de Beauvais, as we shall see, Gervaise gives India as the native land of the phoenix. He does not mention the physical appearance of the bird, but stipulates that it is a bird "mult . . . bien chantanz," a trait that does not occur in Isidore or in the three other Latin versions reviewed above. The phoenix lives 500 years and, feeling itself grow old, it seeks "un arbre"[83] where it can gather the spices and aromatic materials which make up its pyre. Gervaise adds to these last some precious stones.[84] The phoenix itself lights its pyre and from the ashes is born a worm which is transformed on the third day into an adult phoenix. The article ends with the Christ symbolism.

### C. The bestiary of Guillaume le Clerc of Normandy[85]

Guillaume follows the tradition of the Latin type B-Is (e.g., Royal 2.C.XII) closely. The phoenix lives in India; it is "sanz per" and when it has reached 500 years of age it collects spices.[86] The bird goes away to die in the city of Leopole.[87] It makes a sign to the priest to prepare a pyre and, having been burnt, it is reborn first in the form of a worm which becomes a bird on the third day. Guillaume's chapter ends with the Evangelical symbolism of the phoenix as a figure of Christ.

### D. The bestiary of Pierre de Beauvais

#### 1. Long version [88]

Pierre retains the Christ symbolism of the phoenix. The bird originates in India and is a beautiful bird, "a grant merveille," and wears "sor son cief une creste comme paon." Its chest, "pis," and its neck "li resplendist de rouge color et reluist comme fin or." Finally, "vers la coe est autresi blou comme li purs ciels quant il est clers." [89] When it feels the time of its death approach the phoenix flies toward a mountain called Lebanon.[90] There, at the top of a tree, the bird builds its nest-pyre. Without the aid of the priest the phoenix lights the pyre and is consumed, to be reborn in the form of a new phoenix at the end of three days. There is no mention of a worm phase. In conclusion Pierre returns to the comparison of the phoenix with Christ.

#### 2. Short version [91]

This is unquestionably a reduction of the long version.[92] The text begins with the comparison of the phoenix with Christ and repeats the features of the long version in simply suppressing all description of the physical characteristics of the bird. The text also ends with the Christ symbolism.

## Conclusion

If the ensemble of French bestiaries is compared with the tradition which preceded them, it appears that the French versions of the phoenix derive only in small measure from the tradition, and in particular from the Latin B-Is branch, however, with additions, originating in interpolations from texts foreign to the *Physiologus* tradition. This says that the variants often depend on small points of detail, and the changes that can be observed derive above all from the ancient authors' view of *inventio*.

If the various French versions of the bestiary are compared, it is clear that, except for the Philippe de Thaon version, the bestiaries of Gervaise, Guillaume, and Pierre are very alike. Of the four French bestiaries it is certainly that of Philippe which is the most diverse and the best written. After

Philippe, it is Guillaume who shows the most talent in his narration. Guillaume does not hesitate to say "I" and to introduce metaphors that are not lacking in poetic content. Nevertheless Guillaume is best known for the importance he gives to theological symbolism (a third of his text). The two versions of Pierre totally lack poetic content. Pierre not only writes in prose, but he is clearly uninterested in the lessons that he teaches. There are other variations among these texts, but they are usually of a semantic type, as in the case of Lebanon, which is a sort of wood, a forest, or a mountain.

Nevertheless, it must be admitted that, despite all that has been done to the present, many questions remain to be resolved, not the least being that of the sources of the interpolations. Thus, the *Physiologus* is far from having given up all its secrets, for the phoenix as well as for the other elements of which it is composed. It is hoped, however, that the present study will at least have made clear the complexity of the tradition of the phoenix, and that it will further the distinguished work of the scholar whose memory we honor with affection in this volume.[93]

*Notes*

1. This study will consider only the didactic-theological tradition of the *Physiologus* (the moralized *Physiologus*), leaving aside the non-moralized bestiaries, and in particular the bestiaries of love, secular works interesting in themselves but of little use to the present purpose. Moreover, nothing will be said of the developments of the sixteenth century, including the work of Thomas Browne, whose skepticism in regard to the legend of the phoenix is nevertheless fascinating. On the *Physiologus*, its nature and tradition, see the following general studies: Max Goldstaub, "Der *Physiologus* und seine Weiterbildung besonders in der lateinischen und in der byzantinischen Literatur," *Philologus*, Supplementband 8, Heft 3 (1899–1901), 339–404; Nikolaus Henkel, *Studien zum Physiologus im Mittelalter* (Tübingen: Max Niemeyer Verlag, 1976); Friedrich Lauchert, *Geschichte des Physiologus* (Strasbourg: Karl J. Trübner, 1889); Max Friedrich Mann, "Der Bestiaire Divin des Guillaume le Clerc," *Französische Studien*, 6:2 (1888); Ben E. Perry, "Physiologus," in Pauly-Wissova, *Real Encyclopädie der Classischen Altertumswissenschaft*, 20, pt. 1 (Stuttgart: J. B. Metzlersche, 1941), cols. 1074–1129; *Physiologus*, trans. Michael J. Curley (Austin and London: University of Texas Press, 1979); Francesco Sbordone, *Ricerche sulle fonti e sulla composizione del Physiologus greco* (Naples: Arti grafiche G. Torella, 1936); Max Wellmann, "Der *Physiologus*, eine religionsgeschichtlich-naturwissenschaftliche Untersuchung," *Philologus*, Supplementband 22, Heft 1 (1930), 1–116.

2. Florence McCulloch, *Mediaeval Latin and French Bestiaries* (Chapel Hill: University of North Carolina Press, 1962); Curley, pp. ix–xliii.

3. Lauchert, pp. 65–79; Max Wellmann, "Der *Physiologus*, eine religionsgeschicht- lich-naturwissenschaftliche Untersuchung," pp. 5–10; Sister Mary Francis McDonald, "Phoenix Redivivus," *The Phoenix*, 14 (1960), 187–206.

4. McCulloch, p. 19; Lynn Thorndike, *History of Magic and Experimental Science* (New York: Macmillan, 1929), I, p. 500.

5. See above, n. 1.

6. See Samuel A. Ives and Hellmut Lehmann-Haupt, *An English 13th Century Bestiary* (New York: H. P. Kraus, 1942), p. 6: "With the exception of the Bible itself, there is probably no other work which has won such unqualified popu- larity and been translated into as many languages as the *Physiologus*. Thus by the fifth century we find it translated from Greek into Ethiopic, Armenian, Syrian, and Latin, and later into Arabic and Georgian, while in the later Middle Ages it spread to Western Europe and is found in Anglo-Saxon, Old High German, Middle High German, Icelandic, English, French, Provençal, North Italian and Spanish."

7. On the Egyptian tradition, see H. Bonnet, *Reallexikon der ägyptischen Reli- gionsgeschichte* (Berlin: Walter de Gruyter, 1952); Roelof van den Broek, *The Myth of the Phoenix According to Classical and Early Christian Traditions* (Lei- den: E. J. Brill, 1972); McDonald, pp. 195–197.

8. See in J. P. Clébert, *Bestiaire fabuleux*, pp. 298–302, the article "Phénix"; see also Willy Ley, *Dawn of Zoology* (Englewood Cliffs, NJ: Prentice Hall, 1968), p. 63 and n. 2, and p. 260.

9. Jean Hubaux and Maxime Leroy, *Le Mythe du Phénix dans les littératures grecque et latine* (Liège, Paris: Droz, 1939); van den Broek; Anne Clark, *Beast and Bawdy* (New York: Taplinger, 1975), pp. 25–37; McDonald, pp. 188–195 (on the tradition of the phoenix in Hebrew); Curley, introduction, pp. ix–xxxiii.

10. The phoenix was called "avis regia" because it represented the bonds of unity between the king and his successor. On the word "purple," it is known that Herodotus and Isidore of Seville associated the Greek word "foinis" with the word signifying the color purple (see van den Broek, pp. 61–62). On He- rodotus and the phoenix, McDonald, p. 187. Original sources include: Isidore, *Etymologiae*, XII,7,22, ed. J. André (Paris: Soc. d'Edition "Les Belles Let- tres," 1986); Hrabanus Maurus, *De universo*, 8,6 (Migne, *Patrologia latina* 3, 246A); Pseudo-Hugh of St. Victor (Hugo de Folieto), *De bestiis et aliis rebus*, I, 49 (*Patrologia latina*, 177, 48c); Honorius of Autun, *Speculum lati- norum*, IV (ed. G. Goetz, Leipzig, 1889) 75: II, V: 199, 27; see also van den Broek, p. 51, n. 4.

11. See H. G. Liddell and R. Scott, *A Greek-English Lexicon* (Oxford: Claren- don Press, 1953); Ovid, *Metamorphoses*, XV, 393. The Greek word "foinis" has sometimes been associated with the word meaning "Phoenician." This asso- ciation is not surprising if one considers that in antiquity the poets scarcely ever made a distinction between Syria, Assyria, and Phoenicia. However, it seems more probable that this association is due merely to simple etymological relationships.

12. The benu (benou) is a legendary sacred bird venerated by the Egyptians of Heliopolis and identified with the phoenix. See Clébert, *Bestiaire fabuleux*,

"Phénix"; Albert Stanburrough Cook, *Old English Elene, Phoenix and Physiologus* (New Haven: Yale University Press, 1919), p. xliiii. Egyptologists have thought that the Greek word "foinis" was the result of the pronunciation of the name of the Egyptian bird "benu" (pronounced "bwa" or "bwane"). This view allows us at least to see how Herodotus and Hecataeus of Meletus were able to recognize the Greek phoenix in the benu of Heliopolis (see van den Broek, p. 21, n. 5).

13. Placidus Lactantius (*De ave phoenice*) notes the flight of the phoenix to Syria and its death on or in a palm tree (see Cook, pp. xxxiii–xxxviii). It is not impossible that the association of the words "phoenix" and "palm tree" was due to the homonym of the two words in the Bible translations of the classical period. See Isidore, *Etymologiae*, XVII,7,1; Hubaux-Leroy, pp. 100–125.

14. Isidore, *Etymologiae*, XII, 7,22; van den Broek, ch. 10; P. H. Larcher, "Mémoire sur le Phénix, ou recherches sur les périods astronomiques des Egyptiens," *Mémoires des Inscriptions et Belles Lettres*, Classe d'histoire et de littérature ancienne I (Paris: Imprimerie Royale, 1815), 166–307. According to Pomponius Mela, the phoenix is never conceived by the coupling of a male and a female, nor brought forth as other animals (Larcher, p. 175).

15. Van den Broek, pp. 360, 421.

16. Maximus Confessor, *Epistolae*, XIII (PG 91, 519A); van den Broek, pp. 359–360, 365–366, 388–389.

17. Van den Broek, p. 360.

18. Laevius, *Pterygion phoenicis* (fragment in Charisius, *Ars grammatica*, IV, 6, 268–272, 360, 396; Macrobius, *Saturnalia*, III, 8: 366; *Carmen in laudem solis*, 31, 33, 35; Dracontius, *Romulea*, X, 10.

19. Achilles Tatius, *Laucippe et Clitophon*, III, 25, 7; van den Broek, pp. 364–365; Clark, p. 41 (objection of Thomas Browne).

20. Van den Broek, pp. 335–356; on item C,2, van den Broek, p. 356, n. 5; Larcher, pp. 10, 101.

21. Van den Broek, p. 107, n. 3; Tacitus, *Annales*, VI, 28; van den Broek, pp. 108, 113ff.

22. Larcher, p. 193.

23. Van den Broek, pp. 113–114.

24. Thus, the birth of Christ occurred in the year 5,500 after the creation of the world, that is to say, at the time of the eleventh appearance of the phoenix. It appeared also at the sacrifice of Abel and at the departure of the Children of Israel from Egypt under the leadership of Moses. See van den Broek, pp. 125, 127 n. 2, 128; the Coptic *Sermon on Mary*, ll. 33–35 (trans. and ed. in van den Broek, pp. 44–47).

25. Tacitus, *Annales*, VI, 28; Larcher, p. 192. This period of 1,461 years was known as the Sothic period (van den Broek, pp. 26–32).

26. Lucian, *Hermotimus*, 53; Libanius, *Orationes*, XVII, 10; van den Broek, p. 67, nn. 1, 2, pp. 67–112 and ch. 5.

27. This number is given by Tacitus, Herodotus, Ovid, Pomponius Mela, Pliny, and Seneca, among others (Larcher, p. 196). Certain editors of Horapollo have corrected 500 to 7,000, and even to 1,461! (Larcher, p. 196). Some editions of

Aurelius Victor and many manuscripts give the phoenix only 50 years of life (Larcher, pp. 194–195); Tacitus, *Annales,* VI, 28; Herodotus, *Historiae,* II, 73, 1; Ovid, *Metamorphoses,* XV, 395 (for others see van den Broek, p. 68, n. 6).

28. Isidore, *Etymologiae,* XII,7, 22; Hrabanus Maurus, *De universo,* VIII, 6 (*Patrologia latina,* 3, 246B); Honorius of Autun, *Speculum Ecclesiae; de paschali die* (*Patrologia latina,* 172, 936A); Pseudo-Hugh of St. Victor (Hugh of Fouilloy), *De bestiis et aliis rebus,* I, 49 (*Patrologia latina,* 177, 48C); Reinerus, *De ineptis cuisdam idiotae libellus,* in *Monumenta Germaniae Historica, Scriptores,* 20, 597.

29. According to Manilius, one of the sources for Isidore of Seville and Pliny, this number is also noted by Solinus. Pliny, *Historia naturalis,* X, 4; Solinus, *Collectanea rerum memorabilium,* 33,12; Theodoric, *De mirabilibus mundi,* 767–768. The oldest editions of Pliny read "660 years," but as van den Broek, p. 69, notes, "This can hardly have been the original reading."

30. According to Syncellus, *Chronographia,* 334c (*Die Fragmente der griechischen Historiker,* ed. F. Jacoby, Leiden, 1961, p. 463); and Suidas, *Lexicon,* art. "foinis," 69, 165.

31. Van den Broek, pp. 69–70; Larcher, p. 191. The Greek Nonnus (*Dionysiaca*), Martial (*Epigrammata,* V, 7, 2), Pliny (*Historia naturalis,* XXIX, 29), Lactantius (*De ave phoenice,* 59), and Claudian (*Phoenix,* 27) give 1,000 years of life to the phoenix. See also Ausonius, *Epistolae,* XX, 9; Gregory of Tours, *De cursu stellarum ratio,* 12; Nonnus, *Dionysiaca,* XL, 395; John of Gaza, *Descriptio tabulae mundi,* II, 209; *Appendix Physiologi,* 25 (Sbordone, ed.). A certain number of rabbis give the bird the same number of years, but, according to them, this lifespan was accorded the bird together with the capacity for self-reproduction in compensation for not having succumbed, like all other animals, to the enticements of the female, and for abstaining from eating forbidden fruit (Larcher, p. 191).

32. Tacitus, *Annales,* VI, 28. Van den Broek, writes, p. 70, "Although Tacitus does not say so, this figure of 1,461 years must be related to the Egyptian Sothic period"; see also van den Broek, pp. 20–32.

33. Chaeremon, *Hieroglyphica,* frg. 3 in Tzetes, *Chiliades,* V, 395–398 (see Jacoby, ed., *Die Fragmente der griechischen Historiker,* III, C, I, Leiden, 1958, p. 147); van den Broek, p. 72; Larcher, pp. 187–188.

34. It was Plutarch who gave the phoenix a lifespan of 97,000 years. Larcher, p. 190, corrects this: "Selon la traduction d'Ausone, elle est de 93,312 ans."

35. Hesiod, frg. 304 (Merkelbach-West), see van den Broek, pp. 72, 80 n. 2, 76–112.

36. Lucian, *De morte peregrini,* 27; *Navigium,* 44; Philostratus, *Vita Apollonii Tyanaei,* III, 49; Sidonius, *Carmina,* II, 407, and others (see van den Broek, p. 305, n. 3); Hubaux-Leroy, review by Nilsson, *Gnomon,* 17 (1941), p. 214; van den Broek, p. 306, n. 2; Larcher, p. 173.

37. Celsus in Origen, *Contra Celsum,* IV, 98; Aelian, *De natura animalium,* VI, 58; Philostratus, *Vita Apollonii Tyranaei,* III, 49 (who says that the phoenix lives in India, builds its nest near the sources of the Nile, and goes to Egypt to die). The Greek *Physiologus* has Egypt as the cremation place of the phoenix. See also Lactantius, *De ave phoenice.* Hecataeus of Miletus (Herodotus, *Historiae,*

II, 71, 73) recognized the classical phoenix in the benu of Heliopolis (see van den Broek, p. 403, n. 3); Tzetzes, *Chiliades,* V, 393, has the phoenix living in Egypt but dying in Ethiopia (see Nilsson's review of Hubaux-Leroy, 214); Diodorus Siculus, *Biblioteca hist.,* XVII, 50, 4; van den Broek, pp. 305–307; McDonald, pp. 195–197; A. S. Cook, pp. xlv–li.

38. According to the *Physiologus of Pseudo Basil,* 21 (Sbordone), the phoenix brings its perfume from Paradise (see also the Coptic *Sermon on Mary,* 22–23; van den Broek, p. 45). Ovid was the first to locate the phoenix in Elysium (*Amores,* II, 6, 49–54). See also Lactantius, *De ave phoenica;* van den Broek, p. 326, writes, "The view that the phoenix lives in Paradise is also found in the rabbinical traditions"; Cook, pp. lii–lx.

39. For Arabia, see: Manilius, in Pliny, *Historia naturalis,* X, 3 (see van den Broek, p. 305, nn. 1, 2) 4; Tacitus, *Annales,* VI, 28; Pomponius Mela, *De chorographia,* III, 84; Herodotus, *Historiae,* II, 73. For Ethiopia, see: Achilles Tatius, *Leucippe et Clitophon,* III, 25, 4; Tzetes, *Chiliades,* V, 393 (see above, n. 37). For Assyria see: Ovid, *Metamorphoses,* XV, 393 (however, see van den Broek, p. 52); Lactantius Placidus, *Narrationes fabularum Ovidianorum,* XV, 37; also van den Broek, p. 307. For Phoenicia see: Assyria (van den Broek, pp. 52, 53 n. 1); also van den Broek, pp. 149, 175, 305–307; Larcher, pp. 172–173.

40. Pliny, *Historia naturalis,* X, 4 (reporting from Manilius). See K. Ziegler, *Panchaia,* in Pauly-Wissowa-Kroll, et al., *Real-Encyclopaedia der classicien Altertumswissenschaft,* 18, 3 (1949), 493–495; van den Broek, pp. 149–150, 156, 189–190.

41. Ambrose, *De excessu fratris,* II, 59 (see van den Broek, p. 306, n. 5); van den Broek, p. 190.

42. Lactantius, *De ave phoenice,* 61–64, 65–70; McDonald, pp. 201–202; van den Broek, pp. 51–57.

43. Greek *Physiologus* (Sbordone) 17 (see also Byzantine *Physiologus* [Sbordone] 10), Coptic *Sermon on Mary,* 22–23 (van den Broek, p. 45). On the substitution of Lebanon for India, see van den Broek, p. 309.

44. Claudian, *Phoenix,* 17–20, 30–42, 83–88, 200, 236 (van den Broek, p. 163). According to Claudian the young phoenix bore the remains of the old phoenix to Heliopolis where they were burnt.

45. According to Lactantius (*De ave phoenice,* 79–82, 83–88) the pyre was made of aromatic materials and essences (van den Broek, pp. 163–164, 168–169, 171, and n. 4; see also van den Broek, pp. 51–53).

46. Manilius in Pliny, *Historia naturalis,* X, 4; also Pliny, *Historia naturalis,* XII, 85 (see van den Broek, p. 168, n. 2); Ovid, *Metamorphoses,* XV, 398–400 (see van den Broek, p. 164, n. 2); Artemidorus, *Onirocritica,* IV, 47; Hubaux-Leroy, pp. 65–97; van den Broek, pp. 164–174, 179, 307–309.

47. See the objection of Thomas Browne in Clark, p. 42.

48. McDonald, pp. 200–203.

49. Van den Broek, p. 206, n. 7; p. 179, n. 5; *Appendix Physiologi* (Sbordone), 2.

50. Lactantius, *De ave phoenice,* 91–94; *Physiologus of Ansileubus* (fragmenta in Glossario inserta), 12 (Pitra, *Spicilegium Solesmensis,* III, 419). According to Lactantius, 95–98, the burning takes place after the death of the bird (see van den Broek, p. 211, n. 1).

51. Van den Broek, p. 159; Guy R. Mermier, *Le Bestiaire de Pierre de Beauvais, version courte* (Paris: A. G. Nizet, 1977), p. 63; see also van den Broek, p. 211, n. 3.

52. Van den Broek, pp. 212–213. See the Persian translation of Kazwini's *Cosmography* in R. J. F. Henrichsen, *De phoenicis fabula apud Graecos, Romanos et populos orientales commentatio,* II (Hauniae, 1827), 21 (see van den Broek, p. 214, nn. 2, 5); Byzantine *Physiologus* (Sbordone), 10; Epiphanius, *Ancoratus,* 84, 6; Coptic *Sermon on Mary,* 17, 26 (van den Broek, pp. 45–47); Arabic *Physiologus* (Land, *Anecdota Syriaca,* IV, 155) 6; *Physiologus of Vienna* (Sbordone), pp. 24–26; Albertus Magnus, *De animalibus,* XXIII, 110.

53. Van den Broek, pp. 388–389.

54. For example, in the bestiary British Library MS Harley 3244 the phoenix is represented with the head of a peacock.

55. Aelian, *De natura animalium,* XVII, 23 (van den Broek, p. 256, n. 6).

56. *The Physiologus of Vienna* [OeNB MS 1010] (Sbordone), pp. 6–7. See Herodotus, *Historiae,* II, 68; Aristotle, *Historia animalium,* I, ii (492b, 23).

57. Van den Broek, pp. 338, 356; Lauchert, *Geschichte des Physiologus,* F. Sbordone, *Physiologus* (Milan: In aedibus societatis Dante Alghieri-Albrighti, Segati, etc., 1936); E. Peters, *Die griechische Physiologus und seine orientalischen Uebersetzungen* (Berlin: S. Calvary, 1898).

58. Van den Broek, pp. 130–131 and nn. 2, 4; Lauchert, pp. 229–279; Curley, pp. 73–74.

59. In the Arabic *Physiologus* the phoenix goes from India to Lebanon to gather aromatic materials and returns to India to burn itself up (Lauchert, pp. 87–88). According to the *Physiologus of Vienna,* the phoenix builds its nest-pyre "in the neighborhood of Heliopolis, in the region of Gade's, outside our world, near the sea."

60. Lauchert, p. 80, n. 1, pp. 80–81; Charles Cahier, *Nouveaux mélanges d'archéologie, d'histoire et de littérature,* I (Paris: Firmin Didot, 1874), p. 123.

61. According to the *Physiologus of Pseudo Basil* (Sbordone).

62. As in the *Physiologus of Vienna,* the Greek *Physiologus,* the Armenian *Physiologus,* and the descendants of the Greek *Physiologus* in Latin and other languages.

63. In the Greek *Physiologus* and the Armenian and Ethiopian versions of the *Physiologus* the pyre is made of vine twigs, while in the *Vienna Physiologus* the pyre is of wood imbued with aromatic essences.

64. Van den Broek, p. 206, n. 7.

65. See the *Physiologus of Vienna,* where the decomposed body becomes a sort of fluid; van den Broek, pp. 186–187 and p. 189, n. 2.

66. According to the *Physiologus of Vienna.*

67. See Charles Cahier, *Nouveaux mélanges . . .* I, pp. 106–138, for the Armenian *Physiologus.*

68. Ovid, *Metamorphoses,* XV, 400–402; van den Broek, pp. 186–187; McCulloch, pp. 158–160. Other examples in Cahier, p. 123, and Curley, p. 13.

69. Cahier, p. 123; McDonald, pp. 197–204, on the use of the phoenix by the Church Fathers.

70. McCulloch, *Mediaeval Latin and French Bestiaries.*

71. *Physiologus latinus; éditions préliminaires, versio B,* ed. F. J. Carmody (Paris: Li-

brairie E. Droz, 1939); *Physiologus latinus, versio Y,* ed. F. J. Carmody, University of California Publications in Classical Philology XII, 1941, 95–134; on the B-Is version and the *Etymologiae* excerpt, McCulloch, pp. 21–44.

72. McCulloch, p. 158, n. 134.

73. McCulloch, p. 158, n. 135.

74. It might be noted that the great difference between the Y and B versions is in the inclusion by B of the worm episode.

75. Apart from insignificant details, MS Royal 2.C.XII is very close to B and is closely enough associated with Y to permit the designation of a "family tie" between them.

76. One notes suddenly that the worm phase is absent, that for the lifespan of the phoenix Isidore indicates more than 500 years, and that to burn itself the bird faces the sun and beats its wings. Moreover, Isidore does not mention the priest, omits the bird's greeting to the priest, all details of the resurrection, and the motif of the three days. In sum, the Isidore excerpt clearly represents a tradition both different and simplified from that of the Greek *Physiologus* and the three Latin texts, Y, B, and the B-Is of Royal 2.C.XII.

77. See McCulloch, pp. 159–160.

78. *Le Bestiaire de Philippe de Thaün,* ed. Emmanuel Walberg (Lund: H. Möller, 1900). See McCulloch, pp. 47–54.

79. McCulloch, p. 28.

80. McCulloch, p. 159.

81. Philippe presents some notable variants, despite his similarities with the Latin version B. For the lifespan of the phoenix, Philippe follows Isidore and offers an original lesson with regard to the manner in which the bird is smeared with balm before going to burn itself at Heliopolis. When it has become the new phoenix, it goes *el gault,* but Philippe does not mention the forest of Lebanon. He adds to B and B-Is the symbolism of the wings representing the two Testaments.

82. "Le Bestiaire de Gervaise," ed. Paul Meyer, *Romania,* 1 (1872), 420–443.

83. Here the tree represents the forest of Lebanon or the mountain Lebanon. Pierre de Beauvais speaks of "vergeles des liban," underscoring the confusion which exists concerning the name Lebanon.

84. McCulloch, pp. 41–44. This allusion to stones is found only in Guillaume le Clerc.

85. Max Friedrich Mann, "Der Bestiaire Divin de Guillaume le Clerc," *Französische Studien,* pp. 37–73 (see above, n. 1). See McCulloch, pp. 28–30.

86. Guillaume does not mention Lebanon. He is content to say only "de la desertine s'en vole."

87. But it is Heliopolis which is in question.

88. Charles Cahier, *Mélanges d'archéologie et d'histoire de littérature,* II (Paris: Firmin Didot, 1851), pp. 85–232; III (1853), pp. 203–288; IV (1856), pp. 57–87. As a sequel to my edition of the short version of Pierre de Beauvais, *Bestiary,* I am preparing a new critical edition of the long version. I shall in fact return in detail to the short version, using the very helpful comments of my colleagues and reviewers. My work has been considerably delayed by the fact that the

fourth manuscript of the long version, formerly in the Phillips collection and then the property of a private British individual, Philip Robinson, has totally disappeared after the sale of Robinson's manuscripts at Sotheby. About twenty years have elapsed since my search and eventual discovery of the manuscript that is now lost again. Thus, I feel entitled to go ahead with an edition of the long version based on only three manuscripts. Should the lost manuscript reappear, I would of course publish subsequent findings.

89. McCulloch, pp. 158–162. These details are absent from Pierre's short version, and also from the other bestiaries.

90. McCulloch, pp. 159–160.

91. See Guy Mermier, *Le Bestiaire de Pierre de Beauvais, version courte.*

92. Guy Mermier, "De Pierre de Beauvais et particulièrement de son bestiaire: vers une solution des problèmes," *Romanische Forschungen,* 78:2/3 (1966), 338–371.

93. I would like to express my thanks to the editors of this volume for their patient, careful editing and helpful suggestions. The following are several useful titles for the study of the phoenix in the tradition considered in this article: John Bugge, "Virgin Phoenix," *Medieval Studies,* 37 (1976), 332–350; R. T. Clark-Rundle, "The Legend of the Phoenix," *University of Birmingham Historical Journal,* 2:1 (1949), 2:2 (1950), 105–140; Nikolaus Henkel, *Studien zum Physiologus im Mittelalter* (Tübingen: Max Niemeyer, 1976); M. Laurent, "Le phénix, les serpents et les aromates dans une miniature du XIIe siècle," *L'Antiquité Classique,* 4 (1935), 375–401; Frank Lothar, *Die Physiologus-Literatur des englischen Mittelalters und die Tradition,* diss., Tübingen, 1971, on the phoenix, pp. 136–150; and Francesco Sbordone, "La fenice nel culto di Helios," *Revista Indo-Grego-Italica,* 19 (1935), 1–46.

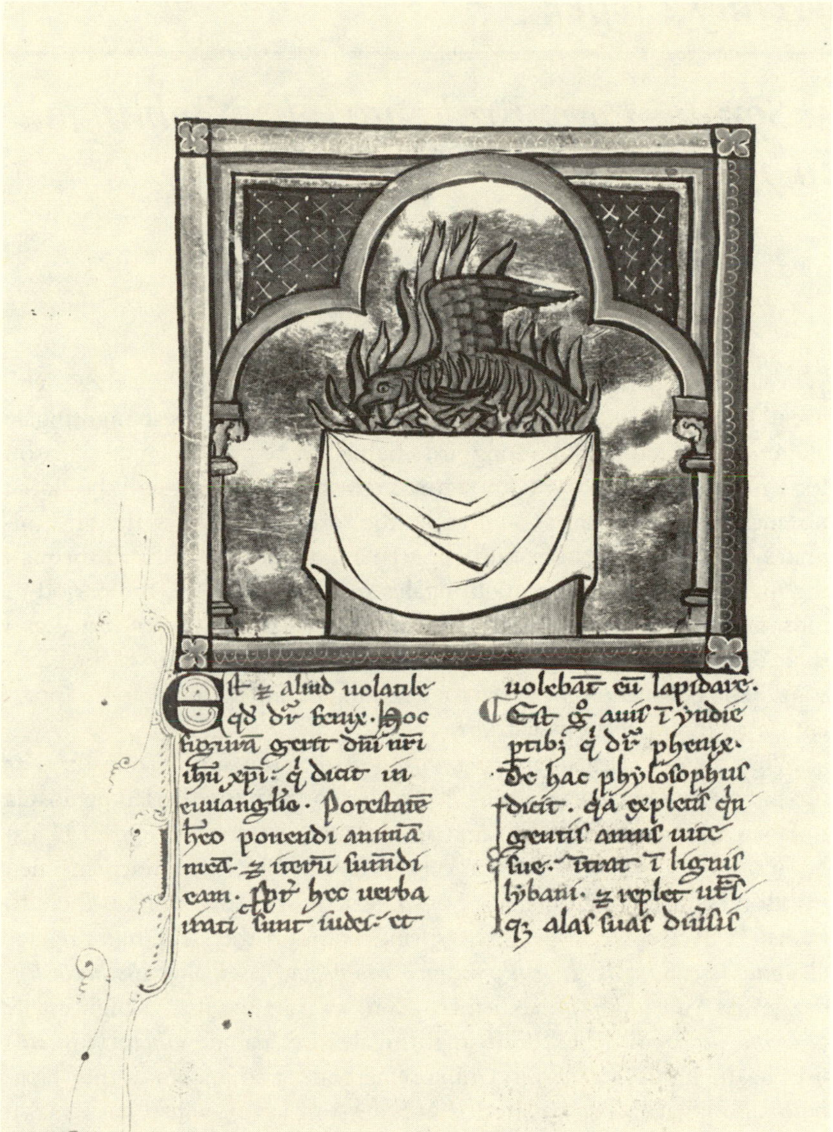

FIGURE 4.1. The immolation of the phoenix (Malibu, California, J. Paul Getty Museum MS Ludwig XV, 3, fol. 74ᵛ). (Photo: J. Paul Getty Museum)

*Wendy Pfeffer*

# 5. *Spring, Love, Birdsong: The Nightingale in Two Cultures*

Why connect spring, love, birdsong, and the nightingale? For those who live in North America, unfamiliar with the song of a European nightingale and unacquainted with the songbird's habits, there may be, in fact, reason for wonder. For those who know the nightingale better, there should be no question. Europeans should know the songbird well, for the bird migrates annually to Western Europe, arriving at the end of April through the middle of May. There, nightingales mate in mid-May; the period of most notable vocalizing extends from mid-April to the end of June,[1] and there is no way to indicate in print the variety and musicality of the bird's song.[2] The connections between the nightingale and spring become apparent, as do its connections with love.

What is particularly interesting with regard to this spring songster is its ubiquity. A bird called "nightingale" is known from the Iberian peninsula to Japan, though it is not the same bird in every country. As Arthur Hatto has written, "The truth is that at certain levels of literary refinement men insist on having a 'nightingale,' even if, strictly speaking, none is there to be had."[3] Western Europe is the spring home of the "true nightingale" (*Daulias luscinia*, alias *Luscinia megarhynca megarhynca*, alias *Erithacus luscinia*, alias *Sylvia luscinia*); Northern Europe hears the thrush-nightingale (*Luscinia luscinia*). The "Pekin nightingale" or "robin" (*Liothrik luteus*) lives in the Himalayas and in China, where it is also known as the "Japanese nightingale." Yet that bird is unknown in Japan, which has its own nightingale, the *uguisu* (*Cettia cantans*, alias *Homochlamys cantans*). And in Persia there is a nightingale which is probably the *bulbul* of Perso-Arabian poetry (*Daulias itafizi*).[4] Even the Indian subcontinent claims a nightingale, although the bird in question is a cuckoo, with quite a different song. Despite the differences in species and geography, all authors recognize the nightingale for its song, and all associate the bird with spring.

The nightingale is the most frequently cited bird in the medieval literature of Western Europe. In the *Carmina burana,* for example, there are
twenty-one poems which contain references to the nightingale.[5] Of these
Latin poems, eleven treat the nightingale in some detail, frequently identifying the bird as *philomena* and thereby associating the songbird with
Ovid's myth of Procne and Philomela (*Metamorphoses,* VI, 416–669). The
nightingale is a mournful singer of love for the poets of these Latin lyrics,
an augur of spring and an inspiration for the poets as well. As an example
of the nightingale in these lyrics, let us consider one poem, "Revirescit et
florescit," Poem 173. Here the happiness of the bird is contrasted with the
feelings of the poet who sees death as the outcome of his emotion:

> Philomena
> per amena
> silve quando volitat
> exultando
> et cantando
> statim tui glorior.
> miserere
> quia vere
> in hac pena dulcissima morior! (ll. 10–18)

(When *philomena* flies through the pleasant woods, exulting and singing, at
that moment I boast of you. Have mercy, because truly I die in this most
sweet pain.)

The bird represents the natural world in spring, which the poet has chosen
not to describe. Rather, he reserves verbs normally applied to the natural
world to himself:

> Revirescit
> et florescit
> cor meum a gaudio.
> ab hac peto
> corde leto,
> quam numquam deserui
> tota mente,
> ut repente
> donet michi gratiam, si merui. (ll. 1–9)

(My heart grows green again and flowers from joy. Of her whom I never
entirely forgot, with a happy heart I ask, that immediately she grant me
favor, if I merit it.)

Compressed into eighteen lines are the ideas of spring, of the poet's long-ing, and of his eventual unhappiness, all three tied to the image of the nightingale, for the bird is a part of spring and is perceived as expressing emotions similar to those of the poet. For these reasons, the nightingale becomes a receptive audience for this lyricist.

In European vernacular poetry the nightingale has similar functions, and there is a whole vocabulary directly related to the songbird.[6] For the Occitan troubadours, the nightingale is perceived as a parallel to the poet, inciting the troubadour to sing or reminding the poet of his unhappiness in love and his inability to compose. It is important to note an additional element associated with the nightingale in troubadour lyrics: the bird fre-quently serves as a messenger in Occitan poetry. Consider, for example, Bernard de Ventadour's Poem 43, "Can la verz folha s'espan."[7] Here the time is spring and the nightingale signals that the time has come for love:

> Can la verz folha s'espan
> e par flors blanch' el ramel,
> per lo douz chan des auzel
> se vai mos cors alegran.
> Lancan ve.ls arbres florir
> et au.l rossinhol chantar,
> adonc deu.s ben alegrar
> qui bon' amor sap chauzir. (ll. 1–8)

(When the green leaves open and white flowers appear on the branch, my heart is happy because of the sweet song of the bird. When he sees the trees flower and hears the nightingale sing, then he who knows how to sing a good love ought to be happy.)

Curiously, although the nightingale is the most frequently cited bird in medieval European poetry, it is a latecomer to the bestiary tradition. The nightingale is not included in early Latin bestiaries and is first noted in the bestiary of Pierre de Beauvais.[8] Those authors who did include the nightingale in their works of natural history depended ultimately on St. Ambrose for the description of the bird. Ambrose spoke of the noctur-nal activity of the female nightingale, guarding her eggs and staying awake at night by singing.[9] Isidore of Seville, obsessed as he was with etymology, wrongly associated *luscinia* with *lucinia*, the lightbearer—for Isidore, the nightingale was the bird that heralded the dawn (a role more often associ-ated with the lark).[10] These ideas were repeated by medieval authors, in texts like the twelfth-century *De bestiis et aliis rebus*[11] or the fourteenth-century French *Poème moralisé sur les propriétés des choses*.[12] It would appear, and the paucity of citations should make clear, that the nightingale was only marginally associated with the medieval bestiary tradition.

What role does the nightingale have in Asian literature? In Persian literature, the nightingale is "defined" in Farid Ud-din Attar's *Mantiq ut-Tair* (*The Conference of the Birds*).[13] Although the work itself is a Sufi philosophical treatise, a number of the birds involved in the poem's debate are described, and the characteristics attributed to these birds remained fixed to them in Persian literature. The author's invocation of the nightingale is as follows:

> Salutations, O Nightingale of the Garden of Love! Utter your plaintive notes caused by the wounds and pains of love. Lament sweetly from the heart, like David. Open your melodious throat and sing of spiritual things. By your songs show men the true Way. Make the iron of your heart as soft as wax, and you will be like David, fervent in the love of God.[14]

Here we have the nightingale identifiable by its sad song, associated beyond a doubt with love. But the nightingale is no mere singer of love; he is knowledgeable in all of love's secrets, and he himself is devoted to the Rose, the sole object of his attentions:

> If I am parted from my dear Rose I am desolate, I cease my singing and tell my secrets to none. My secrets are not known to everyone; only to the Rose they are known with certainty. So deep in love am I with the Rose that I do not even think of my own existence; but only of the Rose and the coral of her petals. . . . The Rose which blooms today is full of longing, and for me smiles joyously. When she shows her face under the veil I know that it is for me. How then can the nightingale remain a single night deprived of the love of this enchantress?[15]

Within the context of the *Mantiq ut-Tair,* the nightingale is so firmly attached to the Rose that it cannot be persuaded to seek the Simurgh, a symbol of God. Another aspect of the nightingale's attachment to the Rose is its suicidal behavior for the sake of love, a trait best known to English readers through Oscar Wilde's story "The Nightingale and the Rose." In Wilde's story, the nightingale gives its life and song for love, singing all night and pressing its breast against a thorn so that the bird's song constructs the rose and its heart's blood stains the flower red.[16] Ironically, the nightingale does its heroic deed for a student in love, although the student "could not understand what the nightingale was saying to him, for he only knew the things that are written down in books."[17]

Again in this story the songbird is portrayed as the voice of Love. The bird describes love as "wiser than philosophy . . . mightier than power,"[18] and the song of the nightingale in its last night of singing tells of love—first of the birth of love, then of passion, and last of love perfected by death. Wilde's message is that the nightingale itself is the perfect lover.

Does the nightingale play a specific role in Arabic lyric? In the *muwash-shah,* for example, where the theme of love is manifest, "the imagery used to depict the state of the lover and his beloved seems to stem from . . . Arabic love poetry (*ghazal*)."[19] Stock metaphors are used,[20] and "imagery involving birds is quite common."[21] However, as Linda Compton has noted with regard to imagery drawn from nature, "Nature [appears] . . . as a carefully cultivated and planned garden or meadow. It is beautiful but controlled."[22] And although Henri Pérès has stated that the love of nature seen in Andalusian poetry is a result of the peasant origin of most of the poets,[23] at the same time he demonstrates that the cadre of preference for these same poets was "l'Espagne, les villes et les lieux de plaisance."[24]

Still, there are birds to be found in this body of poetry. For example, a small sparrow is used to evoke feelings of tenderness:[25]

> I love a gazelle. Loving him is bewitching me.
> > What a killer he is!
> His glances have made my heart like a frightened bird.
> And the heart did not stop being bewildered about love
> > as long as he made it sick.

Although Arabic poets may wish for the freedom of a bird in order to fly unnoticed to their beloved,[26] bird imagery is often related to a lack of freedom or to psychological captivity.[27]

> And the good bird alighted at my house at sunset.
> Around the net of cunning he picks up kernels of hearts.
> As soon as he descended he flew away, so here is a song
> > of the sad one:
> > "If only you could have seen what kind of a bird
> > > alighted at my house and stopped beside me!
> > When he saw the trap, he balanced his wings
> > > and departed.

Here the melancholy tone of the poem is carried through to the end, for the bird takes the lover's heart, leaving the lover behind.[28]

If there is an image taken from nature that keeps its "assigned role," it is the wind. "The wind as messenger is a familiar Arabic motif."[29] As Compton has noted, "Traditionally, the wind is a messenger, and is asked to carry messages to the loved ones far away or . . . the wind may be called upon to help the lover see his beloved when they are threatened by a *raqib* [spy]." Furthermore, the wind often stirs the mind of the poet.[30]

We have noted certain poetic themes associated with the nightingale in Western and Eastern cultures in the Middle Ages. In Europe, the nightingale may represent spring, the poet, the poet's love, or his song. The bird may serve as a strongly sexual metaphor as well. In Arabic literature these same roles are shared by the songbird with the wind. Despite the decades of debate over possible Arabic influences on medieval European literature, with regard to courtly love, in particular, it seems clear that with reference to the figure of the nightingale there was no influence whatsoever. I concur wholeheartedly with Samuel Stern, who wrote, "Arabic poetry could not have exercised a decisive influence on troubadour poetry."[31] As Peter Dronke remarked in his introduction to *Medieval Latin and the Rise of European Love-Lyric,* "Researches . . . should be concerned with the variety of sophisticated and learned *development* of *courtois* themes, not with seeking specific origins for the themes themselves."[32] Dronke argues that courtly love can exist in many languages and cultures not necessarily in communication with one another. We know that there was a long tradition of vernacular love song in medieval Europe, and I have argued elsewhere that folk songs are the probable source of most nightingale imagery in medieval vernaculars.[33] The true nightingale's song is remarkable only during its mating season in the spring. Although the bird does winter in North Africa, its song is not at all distinctive during the winter. I believe the same is true for the song of other birds known as nightingales. It is unlikely, therefore, that Arab authors would use the nightingale and its song as a multifaceted image in their lyrics, and far more appropriate that the meanings associated with the nightingale in Western Europe were more often associated with the wind in Arabic writings. That there are similarities in imagery cannot be denied, but as Dronke and Stern, among others, have noted, these must be explained as parallel developments.[34] And why not? After all, love is universal.

*This contribution was originally presented at the Annual Meeting of the Modern Language Association of America, Los Angeles, California, 28 December 1982, in a session organized by the International Courtly Literature Society.*

*Notes*

1. H. F. Witherby, et al., *The Handbook of British Birds* (London: H. F. and G. Witherby Ltd., 1938), pp. xii and 189–190.

2. Herman Heinzel, Richard Fitter, and John Parslow, *The Birds of Britain and Europe with North Africa and the Middle East* (London: Collins, 1972), p. 254

3. Arthur Hatto, ed., *Eos: An Enquiry into the Theme of Lovers' Meetings and Partings at Dawn in Poetry* (The Hague: Mouton, 1965), p. 793.

4. Ibid., p. 793.

5. *Carmina burana: die Liebeslieder,* ed. Alfons Hilka and Otto Schumann (Heidelberg: Carl Winter, 1941).

6. Elisabeth Schulze-Busacker, *Le vocabulaire de la nature dans la poésie des troubadours: Etude descriptive,* diss., Paris-Sorbonne, 1974, p. 1052: "La classe de oiseaux des champs . . . contient 20 verbes pour l'action du rossignol . . . des 9 vocables désignant leurs traits caractéristiques, il y en a 7 qui se rapportent au rossignol. L'indication d'une partie du corps (*cors*, 'coeur') et le terme collectif *parelha* concernent également le rossignol qui est l'oiseau le plus cité dans la poésie troubadouresque."

7. Bernard de Ventadour, *Chansons d'amour,* ed. Moshé Lazar (Paris: Klincksieck, 1966).

8. J. M. Telfer, "The Evolution of a Medieval Theme," *Durham University Journal* 45 (n.s. vol. 14), no. 1 (December 1952), 31.

9. St. Ambrose, *Hexaemeron,* Liber V, xxiv.85, in J. Migne, *Patrologia latina* (Paris, 1882), vol. 14, col. 254.

10. Isidore of Seville, *Etymologiarum sive originum libri XX,* ed. W. M. Lindsay (Oxford: Clarendon, 1911), book XII, vii.37. On the lark, see William Shakespeare, *Romeo and Juliet,* act 3, scene 5, and Wendy Pfeffer, *The Change of Philomel: The Nightingale in Medieval Literature* (Bern and New York: Peter Lang, 1985), p. 44.

11. *De bestiis et aliis rebus,* in J. Migne, *Patrologia latina* (Paris, 1879), vol. 177.

12. *Poème moralisé sur les propriétés des choses,* ed. Gaston Raynaud, *Romania,* 14 (1885), 442–484.

13. Farid Ud-din Attar, *The Conference of the Birds (Mantiq ut-Tair): A Philosophical Religious Poem in Prose,* tr. C. S. Nott (London: Routledge and Kegan Paul, 1961).

14. Ibid., p. 9.

15. Ibid., pp. 14–15.

16. Oscar Wilde, *The Works of Oscar Wilde* (six volumes in one) (Roslyn, New York: Black's Readers Service, 1927), pp. 520–524.

17. Ibid., p. 522.

18. Ibid.

19. Linda Fish Compton, *Andalusian Lyrical Poetry and Old Spanish Love Songs: The Muwashshah and Its Kharja* (New York: New York University Press, 1976), p. 60.

20. Ibid., p. 48.

21. Ibid., p. 65.

22. Ibid., p. 74.

23. Henri Pérès, *La Poésie andalouse en arabe classique au XI<sup>e</sup> siècle: ses aspects généraux et sa valeur documentaire,* Publications de l'Institut d'études orientales, Faculté des lettres d'Alger (Paris: Adrien-Maisonneuve, 1937), p. 473.

24. Ibid., p. 115.

25. Compton, p. 65.

26. Ibid., p. 75.

27. Compton, p. 101; Pérès, p. 242.

28. Compton, p. 101.

29. Ibid.

30. Ibid., pp. 74–75.

31. Samuel Miklos Stern, "Literary Connections between the Islamic World and Western Europe in the Early Middle Ages: Did They Exist?" in *Hispano-Arabic Strophic Poetry: Studies by Samuel Miklos Stern,* ed. L. P. Harvey (Oxford: Clarendon, 1974), p. 217.

32. Peter Dronke, *Medieval Latin and the Rise of European Love-Lyric,* 2nd ed. (Oxford: Clarendon, 1968), p. xvii, Dronke's emphasis.

33. Pfeffer, *The Change of Philomel.*

34. Stern, p. 216; Dronke, passim.

# Jeanette Beer

## 6. Duel of Bestiaries

The traditions of the bestiary underwent unexpected transformation in Richard de Fournival's *Le Bestiaire d'amour*.[1] A genre that had been devoted to Christian moralizing now became affiliated with the profane literature of love. The process involved more than a mere transposition of metaphors. The juxtaposition of the two known traditions was a provocation to both, for *Le Bestiaire d'amour* transcended all conventions by its ambivalence.

Ambivalence is not, of course, infrequent in the corpus of French courtly literature. Generally, however, the interplay between superficial message and underlying meaning emerges, meticulously explained perhaps by some critic's leavening study on "courtly irony," "courtly malice," or "aesthetic distance." For some reason the disharmony between convention and real content in *Le Bestiaire d'amour* has frequently been ignored, and the work continues to elicit a bewildering range of critical verdicts. In the nineteenth century it was either ignored or damned with faint praise by the old classics of criticism (Lanson, Tuffrau, and company). In this century it is all too often admired—or detested—on inappropriate grounds: its conventional courtliness.[2] Yet *Le Bestiaire d'amour* was as antipathetic to courtly idealism as was, later, Jean de Meun's portion of *Le Roman de la rose*. Moreover, Richard's contemporaries were well aware of the provocation that had been dealt to popular vogues, and some of them reacted accordingly. One demonstration of contemporary protest to Richard's Aristotelian bestiary was the anonymous *Response* (itself a bestiary) which was appended to several late manuscripts of *Le Bestiaire d'amour*.[3] Together the two works constitute an early "querelle de la rose" which was just as personal and impassioned as its celebrated descendant.

Superficially *Le Bestiaire d'amour* abounds in conventionalities. Repetitive love declarations are courteously addressed to "ma bele, tredouce amie," containing all the accepted topoi from contemporary love literature: enduring devotion, inferiority to the beloved, danger from "faux

amants," and the importance of discretion. Even the "clerc" versus "chevalier" debate finds expression in the clerical Richard's warnings to his lady
against his unworthy rivals, the "vultures," "vipers," and "hydras" of love.
As for the time-honored bestiary traditions, Richard explicitly asserts the
authority of the ancients in his prologue. *Le Bestiaire d'amour* was not
intended as a zoological treatise that would correct scientific error.

Conventions need not be used to conventional purpose, however, and
*Le Bestiaire d'amour* undermines the very conventions it exploits. Dominating the whole is Richard's initial declaration that the desire for wisdom is a
characteristically human property: "Toutes gens desirent par nature a savoir." The *sententia* was Aristotle's. It had served to introduce his *Meta-
physics,* establishing the premise that rationality was a characteristically
human property, which distinguished man from the other animal species.
What must necessarily be concluded then from Richard's subsequent use
of the "lower" animal species as exempla for the human love condition?

The use of animal symbolism for human love was not, of course, a novelty in itself. Several lyric poets had occasionally employed such imagery,
and Richard was familiar enough with their work to cite from it.[4] Their
metaphors were, however, sporadic, and the device was only one of many
means by which the *canso* achieved its lyric ends. *Le Bestiaire d'amour* was
sustained metaphor, the complete transference of a given set of Chris-
tianized symbols to the alien context of profane love (Fig. 6.1). Its very title
was therefore a philosophic statement, which forced reevaluation of two
given literatures. Richard's premise was formulated thus: "Par la nature
d'une beste (set) on le nature d'une autre" (*Bestiaire d'amour,* p. 54, ll.
3–4).[5] The inferences were clear, and the forced redirection of the bestiary's symbolism was cataclysmic. Originally the function of that symbolism had been unequivocal, its possible interpretations had been finite.
Now fixed symbolism acquired idiosyncratic application. From that moment it was capable of infinite variation at the hands of any enterprising
expositor.

Richard's selection and ordering of the inherited bestiary symbols were
no less individual. The traditional introduction had featured the lion, symbol par excellence of divine domination and majesty. The lion was now
displaced in favor of a previously insignificant farmyard symbol, the cock
(Richard), crowing desperately for attention. Having begun the animal
procession with himself, Richard continued the anticlimactic parody—of
self, of love, and of all previous bestiaries—with four more representations
of futile love: a braying ass, a paralyzed wolf, a useless cricket, and a dying

swan. By these self-deprecatory images of the author-lover, Richard ridiculed both his own past lyricism and the impotence of lyricism itself. The anti-poetry message was reinforced by Richard's rejection of the bestiary's traditional medium: verse. The choice of prose for a bestiary of love was again an abnegation of both bestiary and love traditions.[6] It was simultaneously an affirmation of the various other intellectual interests which, from time to time, would take over Richard's narrative to the point of real digression. Religious typology would in this work be subordinate to Aristotelianism. If *Le Bestiaire d'amour* was in fact an *ars amandi,* its first five exempla were inevitably cautions rather than ideals for love's proper conduct!

The royal introduction had not been lost without trace from Richard's prologue. Richard there labeled his new bestiary a king's "arrière-ban," explaining its necessity by the following simile: "Car *ausi comme uns rois* [emphasis my own], quant il va guerroier fors de son roialme, il en maine de ses melleurs hommes une partie, et s'en lasse encor gringnor partie a sa terre garder; mais quant il voit qu'il ne se puet soufire a tant de gent com il a mené, si parmande tous chiax qu'il a laissiés et fait son ariereban: *ausi me covient il faire*" (emphasis my own)  (p. 7, l. 8–p. 8, l. 1).[7] Since all previous (lyric) resources had proved inadequate, Richard was now issuing an all-out summons to his vassals (members of the animal kingdom) as he campaigned in alien territory (the "domna"). The Lion of Judah had been dethroned so that the cock, Richard, could play master of ceremonies in his own private carnival of the animals.

As if this symbolic prelude were not explicit enough, Richard then proceeded to categorize his unsuccessful love-pleas as dog vomit which he would willingly now bite back if that were possible: "Elas! et si me sui puis tantes fois repentis de chou ke je vous avoie proié, por vostre douce compaingnie perdre. Car se jou puisse faire ausi comme li chiens, ki est de tel nature ke quant il a vomi, k'i repaire a son vomite et le remangüe, jou eüse volentiers me proiere rengloutie cent fois, puis k'ele me fu volee des dens" (p. 14, l. 8–p. 15, l. 2).[8] The image is a graphic confirmation of Richard's categorization of *Le Bestiaire d'amour* as a "contre-escrit" to his previous lyricism (p. 14, l. 4).

It was obvious already that this new symbolism parodied human and not animal behavior. Animal properties had their own preordained inevitability. Their descriptions retained the simple dignity of the original sources. But the human term of each implied comparison was flawed. And if Richard's imagery for his own role was depreciatory, his assumptions about women were not less so.

The brutality of the dog image switched the allegory of love in a new direction: toward the woman. Richard's misogyny became explicit in his interpretation of the wolf's three natures as symbolic of a woman's lubricity, caprice, and deceit: "Toutes ces .iij. natures sont trovees en amour de feme. Car elle ne se poet doner, se toute ensamble non: c'est selonc le primiere nature. Et selonc le second si est ke s'il avient k'elle aime un homme, quant il ert loins de li si l'amera trop durement, et quant il ert pres, si n'en fra ja samblant. Et selonc le tierce nature si est ke s'elle va si avant de parolle ke li homme se perchoive k'ele l'aint, tout ausi ke li leus se vaingne par sa bouce de son pié, si set elle trop bien par force de paroles recovrir et ramanteler chu k'ele a trop avant alei" (p. 16, l. 4–p. 17, l. 2).[9]

Not all imagery was so satiric, but few images were without prescriptive advice. The advice coupled love idealism with patristic misogyny, nostalgic dreaming with Ovidian sniggers at the object of the dream. Richard was the master of the beasts by divine right, but their animal properties exposed the incongruity, impotence, and pathos of his behavior. His "bele, tredouce amie" was, despite all his protestations, similarly demeaned. That woman should, through love's foolishness, have mastery over man in the animal kingdom of love was the ultimate parody.

The image of the lion remained significant, although displaced. The domination metaphor par excellence, the lion was now transposed to a context of dominating love. As the lion will not attack the man who refuses to glance in its direction (since man asserts God's mastery over animals by his features, which reflect the likeness of God), "Amors" can be kept in abeyance by man's refusal to look it in the eyes. If, however, man is rash enough to confront the gaze of Amors, he is drained of his wits, intelligence, and very soul. "Com plus est sages li homme, tant se paine plus Amors de lui esragiement tenir" (p. 25, ll. 7–8).[10] Thus while rationality is specific to man, non-rationality is the specific product of love.

Non-rationality is also a natural property of women, and reason is consequently ineffectual in man's treatment of them. In an unusually scathing outburst of Ovidian misogyny, Richard expressed the opinion that some women appear to have holes in their heads. Information passes through without effecting the proper, or at least, the predicted results (p. 26, l. 5–p. 27, l. 4). Arguing that reason was no ally of love, Richard foreshadowed Jean de Meun once more: "car encore ait raisons tel pooir c'on puist a une damoisele proveir par raison k'ele doie amer, por chu ne li puet on mie prover k'ele aint, ains ne li ara on ja si bien prové k'ele ne puist dire s'i li siet, k'ele n'en veut rien faire" (p. 61, ll. 2–5).[11]

Thus, although rationality is the proper characteristic of man, non-rationality was, in *Le Bestiaire d'amour,* the proper characteristic of love and of women. Animal exempla were not inappropriate, therefore, but their role needs to be understood in Aristotelian terms. They were not intended to promote courtliness, for it was Aristotle's "amor naturalis" rather than the obsessive passion of contemporary love literature that was Richard's *desiderandum*. His most frequent directive to his lady was that she be nurturing—an obvious legacy of Mariology. Several times he assumed the role of her dependent, calling her suggestively "ma douce mere"[12] and urging that she emulate animal species like the swallow, crow, and pelican. Occasionally he too offered nurture, in anticipation of a day when she might need it. With distasteful imagery that anticipated the sentiments of Jean de Meun's La Vieille, he promised that if she would consent to love him now, he would later be willing to care for her as if she were an old hoopoe or an old screech-owl, filthy and incapable of self-care.[13] If Jean de Meun's *Roman de la rose* was "une composition systématiquement ordonné à ridiculiser les théories de l'amour courtois,"[14] Richard de Fournival's *Le Bestiaire d'amour* was its intellectual predecessor.

Thus Aristotelian naturalism converged paradoxically with Mariology. "Courtoisie," on the other hand, had negative connotations, and was named only once, in fact: as the crocodile, eternally obsessed with remorseful tears, will be rent apart and devoured by the hydra, so should Richard's lady suffer for the harm she has inflicted. Such repentance would, according to Richard, be appropriately "courtly." "Car une *courtoise* maniere de vengnance si est repentance, et bel se venge de son anemi ki le maine dusques al repentir" (emphasis is my own) (p. 65, ll. 4–6).[15]

Nevertheless, courtly game-playing persisted ambivalently to the end. Although Richard's initial *sententia* had established that rationality was the property of mankind, and the bestiary itself had established that love deprived mankind of rationality, Richard concluded with a plea *not* for rationality but for the only "sentence" that could be effective in love's world: mercy. "Neporquant, por chu ke nule *raisons* ne me puet vers vous valoir, si ne requier nule riens fors *merci*" (emphasis is my own).[16]

The *Response* to *Le Bestiaire d'amour* was as original as the work that had provoked it, but it too worked within the conventions, bestiary answering bestiary. As with *Le Bestiaire d'amour*, a superficial patina of politeness masked combativeness.

Replicating the structure of *Le Bestiaire d'amour*, the *Response* began its prologue with a *sententia*—of reproach, however! "Hom qui sens et descretion a en soi ne doit metre s'entente ne son tans a cose nule dire ne faire par coi nus ne nule soit empiriés."[17] Richard's assertion of the authority of the ancients was replaced by a reminder of the primacy of Scripture which, however, the author both restated and reinterpreted to new purpose: the defense of woman's dignity. Her new material was cleverly justified by Richard's own dictum that "no one person can know everything" ("nus ne puet tout savoir"). But what for him had justified citation from his classical authorities became an explicit challenge to Richard, "maistre" (mere), expositor of the ancients. Daringly the unknown laywoman cited her own unnamed "autor" for heterodox material of which, she said, he was apparently ignorant. "Car encore ne puisse je savoir tout che que vous savés, si sai je aucune chose que vous ne savés mie" (p. 106, ll. 13–15).[18]

The new theology from her "aucuns actours" (p. 107) was intended to supersede and combat Richard's Aristotelian digressions of which no trace remains in the *Response*. No longer interested in memory or in sense perception, the *Response*'s prologue maintains the superiority of woman's creation and the responsibility of Adam for original sin:

> Dieus, qui par se digne poissanche tout le mont estauli, et premierement fist chiel terre et quanques il est ordené en l'un et en l'autre, aprés fist home pour le plus noble creature qu'il peüst faire; et li plot qu'il le feïst d'une matere qui n'est mie des plus souffissans des autres. Et de cheli matere, selonc aucuns actours, fourma il une feme tele qui mie ne pleut a l'omme que il devant avoit fait. Dont il avint que quant Diex eut l'un et l'autre donné vie, Adans ochist se feme, et Diex li demanda pour coi il avoit che fait. Il respondi: "Ele ne m'estoit rien, et pour che ne le pooie je amer." Dont aprés vint nostre Sires a Adam ou il dormoit, et prist l'une de ses costes, et en fourma Evain dont nous sommes tout issu. Dont li aucun voelent dire que se le premiere feme fust demouree, Adam ne se fust acordés au pechiet pour coi nous sommes tout en paine; mais pour le tres grant amour qu'il eut a cheli qui faite estoit de lui, l'ama il tant comme il parut. Car li amours de li seurmonta le commandement de nostre Seigneur, si comme autre fois avés oï comment il mengerent le fruit qui leur avoit este devees. (p. 107, l. 1–p. 108, l. 6)[19]

The narrative of Creation appeared to reach termination when its author stated her awareness of the need for abridgement: "Mais ceste matere me couvient abregier et metre a che que je le commenchai" (l. 7).[20] She then parodically continued, as had Richard, with further elaboration of the themes she had initiated which derived added piquancy from her more personal application of them: "nous sommes plus noblement crïees que vous, biaus maistres, n'aiés esté" (p. 108, l. 21).[21]

Since Richard's bestiary had converted traditional symbolism to its individual purpose, the author of the *Response* now proceeded systematically to her own reinterpretation of the reinterpretation. It was she who, needing the "arrière-ban" of which Richard spoke, must emulate the wild ass in its desperate call for help. *She* had been rendered powerless, like the wolf surprised by man. *Her* need was prudence, which she could learn from Richard's introductory images of wasted endeavor.

The reinterpretation frequently developed beyond role reversal into minor disputation. The author rejected Richard's view that Love is a crow picking out man's brains through his eyes: "Encore diiés vous que li corbaus ait autre nature pour coi je le doie miex faire; et il me sanle que de tant que vous dites que li corbaus prent l'omme par les iex, et par la em prent il le cervele, que il est contraires a che que vous dites . . . on le doit comparer des iex del cuer a haïne" (p. 113, l. 21–p. 114, l. 5).[22] The animal property remained the given premise of all imagery, but the conclusion derived therefrom lost its inevitability. The author's consistent reworking, example by example, of Richard's themes of love, discretion, reason, and nurture demonstrated the idiosyncrasy of his interpretations. Woman's pride was not reprehensible as a flaw—it was her sole protection against men. Love was not equatable with death—dishonor (of the sort Richard was proposing) was death for a woman. Discretion certainly was desirable—but in true love there was true forthrightness. In the "clerc"-"chevalier" contest, the chevalier was preferable to the "clerc." Love of a "clerc" deprived him of ecclesiastical advancement and the woman of love and support: "Li demoisele aroit .j. chevalier gentil home dont ele seroit a honneur et deportee plus que de chelui qui tel riqueche n'a mie" (p. 135, ll. 3–5).[23] "Clercs" were in fact "oiseaux de proie."

Finally the *Response* put Richard himself in his place by converting his name to "Renart" in a blistering apostrophe: "Ahi Renart, con vous avés le langue traite hors sans raison!" (p. 135, ll. 9–10).[24] Her ultimate "sentence" for Richard was therefore refusal, not mercy as he had requested. The *Response* concludes with a wish for "bon entendant" ("good understanding").

Thus in this duel of bestiaries a particular situation was brought to closure, but wider issues were at stake. Richard had affiliated himself with Aristotle, and contemporary literary vogues had been challenged, although orthodox theology was unscathed. Conversely, the author of the *Response* had affiliated herself with the neo-Platonism of established literary conventions, but had presented a dramatic challenge to orthodox theology. The debate was destined to continue long afterwards in centuries when Aristotelian–neo-Platonic duelling was no longer relevant.

## Notes

1. *Li Bestiaires d'amours di Maistre Richart de Fornival e Li Response du Bestiaire*, ed. C. Segre (Milan and Naples: Riccardo Ricciardi, 1957).

2. See C. Hippeau, ed., Richard de Fournival, *Le Bestiaire d'amour*, p. iv; L. Kukenheim and H. Roussel, *Guide de la littérature française du moyen âge*, p. 102, who call it "un art d'amour"; R. Bossuat, *Le Moyen âge*, p. 191, who describes it as "*un traité d'amour courtois* adressé par l'auteur à sa dame pour tenter une dernière fois de vaincre sa résistance."

3. For a description of the manuscripts, see Segre, pp. lxxix–ccxxvi.

4. See Segre, pp. 88–89.

5. "One may learn the nature of one animal from the nature of another," *Master Richard's Bestiary of Love* and *Response*, trans. Jeanette Beer, p. 19. All English translations are from the above.

6. Pierre de Beauvais and not Richard de Fournival was in fact the first known author to have made this choice for a bestiary in the vernacular.

7. "As a king who goes to wage war outside his kingdom will take with him a group of his best men, leaving an even greater part behind him to guard his territory, but when he sees the number he has taken cannot suffice for his needs, he summons all of those he left behind and makes his arrière-ban, so *I* must do," *Master Richard's Bestiary*, p. 2.

8. "Alas! I have so often since repented that I entreated you and thus lost your sweet company. For if I could have acted like the dog, which is of such a nature that, after vomiting, it can return to its vomit and re-eat it, I would happily have swallowed down my pleading a hundred times, after it flew out through my teeth," *Master Richard's Bestiary*, p. 5.

9. "All these three natures can be found in woman's love. For she cannot give herself in any way but totally. That conforms with the first nature. In conformity with the second, if it happens that she loves a man, she will love him with the utmost passion when he is far away from her, yet when he is nearby she will never show a visible sign of love. In conformity with the third nature, if she is so precipitate with her words that the man realizes she loves him, she knows how to use words to disguise and undo the fact that she has gone too far," *Master Richard's Bestiary*, p. 6.

10. "For the more intelligent the man the more Love strives in passion to hold him," *Master Richard's Bestiary*, p. 9.

11. "For although Reason has such power that one can prove by reason to a young girl that she should love, one cannot for all this prove that she *does* love. On the contrary, however well it may be proved to her, she may still say, if it suits her, that she wants nothing to do with it," *Master Richard's Bestiary*, pp. 21–22.

12. For example, Segre, p. 86.

13. See Segre, pp. 86–88.

14. G. Paré, *Les Idées et les lettres au XIIIᵉ siècle* (Montreal: Bibliothèque de philosophie, 1947), p. 13.

15. "For Repentance is a courtly type of vengeance, and he is well avenged of his enemy who can lead him to repentance," *Master Richard's Bestiary*, p. 23.

16. "Nevertheless, since no rational argument can avail me anything with you, I ask nothing from you but mercy," *Master Richard's Bestiary*, p. 36.

17. "A man who has intelligence and discretion must not employ his time or his attention to say or do anything by which any man or woman may be damaged," *Response*, p. 41.

18. "For although I cannot know all that you know, yet I know something that you do not," *Response*, pp. 41–42.
19. "God who by His dignity and power created the whole world and first made heaven and earth and all that is established in the one and in the other, afterward made man to be the noblest creature He could devise. And it pleased God to make man out of a substance that is not among the most suitable of substances. And from this substance, according to certain authorities, He formed such a woman as did not please the man whom he had previously made. Then it came to pass that when God had given life to the one and to the other, Adam killed his wife and God asked him why he had done this. He replied, 'She was nothing to me and therefore I could not love her.' So Our Lord came to Adam where he slept, and took one of his ribs, and from it fashioned Eve, whence we are all descended. Wherefore some maintain that if that first woman had remained, Adam would never have yielded to the sin for which we are all in pain. But for the very great love Adam had for the woman who was made from him, he loved her in the way that became apparent. For that love for her took precedence over the commandment of Our Lord, as you have heard on other occasion how they ate the fruit that had been forbidden them," *Response*, p. 42.
20. "But I must abridge this matter and attend to what I began," *Response*, p. 42.
21. "We are created of nobler stuff than you were, fair master," p. 43.
22. "You say further that the crow has a second nature by which I am bound to be improved. It seems to me that inasmuch as you say that the crow seizes man through his eyes and through them it extracts his brain, this is in contradiction with your words . . . one must with the eyes of the heart compare it to Hate," *Response*, p. 45.
23. "The maiden could have had a knightly gentleman who would give her more happiness and honor than the cleric, who has no comparable wealth," *Response*, p. 45.
24. "Ah! Reynard, how far out your tongue is hanging!" *Response*, p. 57.

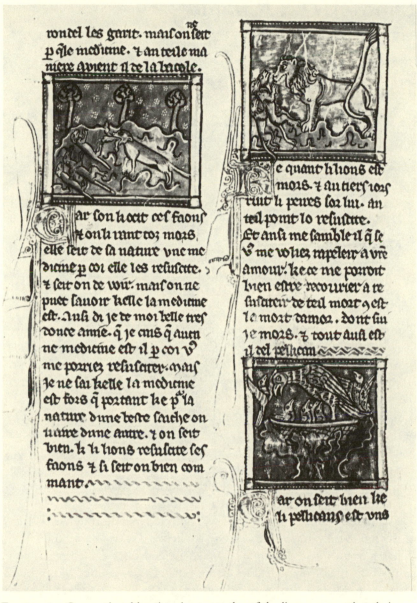

FIGURE 6.1. Conventional bestiary iconography of the lions resurrecting their young and the pelican in her piety are interpreted in this text in terms of the lover Richard and his lady. Richard de Fournival, *Bestiaire d'amour:* Oxford, Bodleian Lib. MS Douce 308. (Photo: Bodleian Lib.)

# Lilian M. C. Randall

## 7. An Elephant in the Litany: Further Thoughts on an English Book of Hours in the Walters Art Gallery (W. 102)

*ne est rien en ce munt*
*Ki essample ne dunt*
*Kil savreit demander*
*Enquere es epruver.*

—Philippe de Thaon, *Bestiaire,* v. 2541

Florence McCulloch spent part of the summer of 1960 at the Walters Art Gallery working on books of hours to be included in a comprehensive catalog projected at the time.[1] In the process, her attention was drawn to an early English example of this type of personal prayerbook, a product of the so-called Court school of illumination assigned to the late thirteenth century (MS W. 102).[2] Despite the loss of the calendar and the beginning of the opening Office of the Hours of the Virgin, it could be established that the Office of the Dead and the litany were for the use of Rome. In 1963 McCulloch published a ground-breaking article on Walters 102, reconstructing the original order of the radically misbound contents and reviewing its remarkable textual and pictorial features.[3]

Her special interest in beast epic was reflected in a thorough exposition of the longest illustrative sequence in Walters 102, inspired by the tale of Renart's death in the *Roman de Renart*. Evidence for the current popularity of the theme on both sides of the Channel was pointed out through reference to mimes of the narrative stages in 1300 in Paris, where it served to demonstrate publicly King Philip the Fair's antagonism toward Pope Boniface VIII. In the Walters Hours, the episode is the subject of a cycle depicted in the lower margins of seventeen consecutive folios. The solemn procession of animal participants extended from the last leaf of the Office of the Dead to Sext in the next Office of the Hours of Christ Crucified, a rare Latin and French version of the Hours of the Cross.[4] Renart, the "hero" of the occasion, was shown at a midway point in the cortège, lying, with tail hanging limp, on a litter borne by Brichemer the Stag and Tibert the Cat. The profile view of the fox with his eye open was intended to signal his regaining of consciousness from the death-like faint into which he had fallen after being defeated at chess by his archenemy, Ysengrin the Wolf. The subtle artistic detail of the open eye presages the next turn of events, the leap from the litter and escape from the grave, which form paradigms for Christ's triumph over death, anticipated in the accompanying devotional text.

The love of contrast and sense of drama exemplified in the structuring of the cortège are traits that find particularly vivid expression in the secondary decoration of the Walters Hours. A consistent feeling for alternating visual rhythms is also demonstrated in the sequence of marginal motifs that follow the extended example of Renart's fraud. In the canonical hours of None and Vespers, single figures are shown in a staccato rhythm, individually or on facing pages. Engaging in armed combat, wrestling, and suicide, they are personifications of ire and cowardly despair, a series of vices associated with delinquents of the faith.

At Compline, a second and more refined illuminator introduces generic symbols of sin in the form of energetic hybrids in line fillers. The work entrusted to this collaborating artist in the Walters Hours reflects the influence of contemporary drama, most forcibly so in a jewel-like rendering of the Tree of Jesse in the initial to Compline in this Office (Fig. 7.7). The unusual positioning of this theme was the result of a carefully calculated omission of Christ before Pilate at Lauds in the Passion cycle at preceding major openings. Space was thus created in the initial at Compline for a culminating visual reminder of sin and redemption. Allusion to the former is made through inclusion of Adam and Eve in the "wings" formed by the outline of the initial. Center stage is occupied by traditional New Testament figures and prophets. In the right foreground, the rarely depicted figure of Balaam on an ass marks a borrowing from a dramatic tradition initiated in the twelfth-century Anglo-Norman *Jeu d'Adam*, a semi-liturgical drama presented at the onset of Lent as a forceful reminder of penance.[5] Pose and gesture of all participants are notably animated. Even Jesse is brought into the action. Instead of being shown asleep, as was customary in this setting, he is awake and pointing to the word *creator* in the opening hymn.[6] The constricted space available was no deterrent to the proliferation of detail for dramatic effect. The latter was a natural consequence of the common source of inspiration in a pseudo-Augustinian sermon for the visual formulation of the Tree of Jesse and the representation of the *Ordo prophetarum* in either its independent Latin form or the vernacular version preserved in the *Jeu d'Adam*.[7]

The refined style of the illuminator of the Tree of Jesse initial has led to identification of his contributions in several other manuscripts of the Court school.[8] In the Walters Hours, he collaborated with the artist of Renart's funeral procession in every aspect of the decoration, from the thirty-three extant major initials to marginalia and line-fillers. The last form of secondary decoration includes in the litany an extraordinary series of eleven large designs, whose interpretation forms the subject of this essay.

Thematic illustrations in a liturgical text are in themselves an anomaly in the history of medieval illumination.[9] These eleven themes form a unique two-part cycle, which deviates from contemporary norms most strikingly in a set of images placed beside standard hagiographic divisions of Roman use. In this section of the text there are relatively few examples of the currently fashionable form of line-endings otherwise consistently adopted in the volume. The lively animals and hybrids that elsewhere disport themselves en masse at the ends of short lines of text belong to a breed exemplified centuries before in the Book of Kells.[10]

The first six exceptions appear on the first two folios of the litany in scalloped or straight-edged panels set in the lengthy spaces provided at the right by the brevity of the names cited at the left (Figs. 7.1–7.4). The images occupy from four to seventeen lines at the right of the nineteen-line text, extending about halfway across its breadth. In the subsequent five-part visual sequence among the petitions, the proportions of the three- to five-line heights are less startling (Figs. 7.5, 7.6). Both series reflect a delight in exaggeration and distortion that are hallmarks of contemporary English illumination. This exaggeration in line-fillers, well represented in Walters 102, finds parallels beside certain verses of psalms and canticles in the Windmill Psalter (New York, Pierpont Morgan Library, MS M. 102), the prime example of the Court style around 1300.[11]

Judicious curtailment of the six standard hagiographic divisions in the litany of the Walters Hours facilitated the creation of a mnemonic tabula that leaves an indelible impression on viewers to this day.[12] The strong response is triggered to a certain extent by the panache exhibited in the juxtaposition of sacred and ostensibly profane images. An aura of hidden meaning heightens the fascination exerted by the mysterious, very large line-fillers, even though the individual entities are readily recognizable as an elephant, Adam, a nimbed male head, a chess game, Romulus and Remus, and an ape riding a bear. To paraphrase Bernard of Clairvaux's famous diatribe,[13] what are these curiosities doing in a liturgical text? This question has not yet been addressed, despite repeated published references to the intriguing cycle since 1942, when it was first brought to public attention.[14] The fullest description to date appears in Florence McCulloch's above-mentioned article on Walters 102. It is thus fitting that the following observations are dedicated to her memory.

The unlocking of the riddle of all eleven themes requires two turns of a key for the primary six-part sequence, and only one for the five topics distributed less concentratedly among the petitions. The first turn opens an initial level of understanding, established through more or less literal reference to the text beside the top of the line-filler. A second, more consequential turn reveals a broader insight into the cultural milieu which inspired the program. Each of the eleven images is thus endowed with a literal sense, which in the first six images serves as an ideological springboard to references pertaining to salvation and its attainment through penance. The scheme is fully in harmony with the recitation in the litany of the Christian hierarchy and ensuing invocations for protection and mercy in petitions and prayers. The penitential content of the litany is emphasized by its position in the Walters Hours after the seven Penitential Psalms; it is followed by the fifteen Gradual Psalms. The appending of the litany to the Penitential Psalms was standard, although the inclusion of the Gradual Psalms is relatively rare in books for private devotion.

The pictorial sequence in the litany opens on a positive note with a painting that attests to the enduring popularity of illustrated copies of the bestiary, especially among the English upper classes. One of the traditional illustrations for the bestiary's compilation of animal tales, with their Christian meanings, became the model for a design in the first major line-filler: an elephant bearing a castellated howdah (Fig. 7.1).[15] The animal's quizzical expression and orange color contribute to the humorous effect of this variant representing its legendary strength in military exploits. Instead of the customary group of armed soldiers in the howdah, a single defenseless youth leans out to blow his horn in the face of an ape with crossbow. The inefficacy of the assault by the *figura diaboli* is underscored by its diminutive size, seated position, and upward glance. A variant prototype for this ludicrous attack appears in the lower margin of the opening page of Proverbs in a slightly earlier manuscript of the Court school, a Bible completed

c. 1280—1290 (Paris, Bibl. Nat. MS lat. 15472, fol. 225), in which an elephant is attacked by a small nude archer.[16]

According to the bestiary, physical strength also enabled a young elephant to lift a fallen older member of the species back on its feet, an action symbolically equated with the salvation of mankind by Christ. This sense may underlie the portrayal of a winsome young elephant pointing its trunk at the opening words of the canticle *Te Deum* in the Windmill Psalter (Fig. 7.9). Images such as these in the secondary decoration of manuscripts of the Court school may well perpetuate the memory of an African elephant, the first of its kind ever seen in Britain, which was presented to King Henry III by King Louis IX of France in 1255.[17] The gift was recorded by the St. Albans chronicler Matthew Paris, who made several likenesses of it from life before the celebrated beast, which occupied the Tower of London, succumbed to the rigors of the British climate in 1258.[18] A ceremonial burial in Westminster concluded this episode, so interesting for members of the court, doubtless including the young prince Edward (b. 1239, r. 1272—1307). If the Windmill Psalter of c. 1300 was created for Edward's use, as has been proposed,[19] a subtle reference to a memorable event of his youth, through the elephant in the line-filler beside the *Te Deum,* would have been most apt.

The solitary existence of the elephant in the royal menagerie did not afford an opportunity for observing its inclination toward chastity as proclaimed in the bestiary. However, this virtue of the elephant establishes a rationale for the choice of theme in the first litany line-filler, which is aligned at the top with a triple invocation to the Virgin. Allegedly, the elephant could overcome his state of innocence only by traveling east toward Paradise and sampling the fruit of the mandrake plant that grew there. This association of ideas leads directly to the view of Adam after the Fall in the next large line-filler on the verso (Fig. 7.2).

Guilt and repentance forge a double bond between the succeeding figure of Adam, a visual reminder of disobedience to God, and the denial of Christ by Peter, the first of the apostles and disciples cited in the text at the left. Adam's striking figure comes to life as light glistens on the surface areas of the white impasto applied to his body, which is subtly shaded in gray. Covering his shame, he holds the fateful apple, to the obvious delight of the gaily striped red and green serpent coiled like an additional stage prop around the trunk of the Tree of Knowledge. By chance or design, the melancholy post forms a pictorial counterpart to the gist of a stage instruction in the *Jeu d'Adam.* Before beginning the lament after the Fall, the actor impersonating Adam is directed to assume the very attitude depicted in the Walters Hours: *maximum simulans dolorem*.[20] An artistic comparison has been drawn between Adam in Walters 102 and a monumental sculptural figure which forms part of a typological program completed about 1260 for the south transept of Notre-Dame in Paris.[21]

The literal and figurative turn of Adam's back to the apostles and disciples in Walters 102 brings him into a direct relationship with the subjects of two line-fillers on the facing page. These constitute the ideological centerpiece of the six-part cycle (Fig. 7.3). At the top, set against a deep red ground, a male head with blue halo enclosing a gold cruciform rises from shoulders clad in blue. A bleeding wound establishes an immediate connection with the lapidation of St. Stephen, who, as the first Christian martyr, heads the group of saints listed at left. Equally apparent is the similarity of the visage to earlier English representations of the Veronica Veil, or Vernicle, a favored illustrative motif for the devotional text composed in 1216 by Pope Innocent III after witnessing a miraculous reversal of the sacred relic.[22] Preserved at St. Peter's in Rome, the veil was periodically displayed publicly. Its exhibition during the jubilee year of 1300 attracted such throngs of pilgrims that at least one person, an English Benedictine monk, was killed in the crush.

The conflated Stephen-Christ visage in the Walters Hours directs the stern gaze of its gray-blue eyes at the viewer. Its import, however, issues from hitherto unrecognized implications of the scene below. The lower picture is an obvious reference to chess, which complements the scene of Renart's sham death after losing at chess, noted earlier in the marginal cycle of the Hours of Christ Crucified. Here in the litany the chess match can be related quite directly to the adjoining citation of St. Silvester, who heads the list of popes, confessors, and doctors of the Church. The season of the feast-day of St. Silvester on December 31 was traditionally celebrated with revels, among them games of chance.[23]

The tense poses and differentiated attires of the two chess players leave little doubt that more is at stake than merely winning a game. Fear is conveyed by the defensive attitude of the bald man, who is clad only in underdrawers, and who clutches a small black sack. His opponent is fully clothed in an orange robe with shoes to match, a color with possibly evil connotations.[24] The clothed man reaches forward confidently for the last game piece on the board, toward which the ashen protagonist also extends his hand. The chess move alluded to is an English technicality termed "covered check," by which a player could try to save the game after his opponent had said "Check!"[25] This move, and the sack held by the bald player, are key elements for comprehension of the motif.

The move and the sack form part of an anonymous and untitled moral- ized treatise on chess which was composed in England or France about the middle of the thirteenth century; its first extant transcription is in a com- pilation datable between 1307 and 1327 (British Library MS Harley 2523).[26] The principal idea of the text was doubtless popular in oral tradition be- fore being written down, and is one of a host of allegories and anecdotes on the theme of chess. The opening lines of this brief moralization set the stage for what follows by comparing the world to a chess board. The white squares are said to represent life and grace, the black ones death and guilt. Humans issue from a maternal womb, assume their ranks and stations, only to be leveled by Death and buried in a grave. Chessmen experience a similar fate. They are removed from a sack, take their prescribed places on the board, and are returned to a sack when the game is done: *sicut de uno sacculo exierunt ita iterum reponuntur*. The leveling process for chessmen occurs in the sack in which the pieces are stored. Here the king, being the heaviest, may find himself beneath even the lowly pawn. A list of game pieces and their moral attributes is followed by a closing reminder that the Devil says "Check!" to sinners of all ranks. The only hope of escape from his clutches is to "cover one's check" through immediate penance.

This is the lesson so vividly imparted in the litany of the Walters Hours. The stern visage serves as a reminder of the seriousness of the satanic warn- ing issued below. Hope of salvation for the would-be penitent at the left is implied by his position on the side traditionally reserved for the Blessed in medieval representations of the Last Judgment. A different fate apparently awaits an analogous near-nude chess player in the Rutland Psalter, who is depicted in the margin below repeated condemnations of the faithless (London, British Library MS 62925, fol. 78ᵛ: Psalm 77: 10—20).[27] The scantily clad figure sits at the right of the gameboard and dangles a red cord. This cord is probably a reference to the drawstring which closes the bag in which the chess pieces were stored. The Rutland Psalter, of c. 1260, is approximately contemporary with the moralization in the British Li- brary treatise, and this miniature is an early illustration of the moralization which occurs also in later copies of the treatise.[28]

The chess moralization echoes a theological concern with penance, which was given impetus by the institution, at the Lateran Council in 1215, of annual private confession to one's parish priest.[29] The impact of this concern with penance on the visual arts in France is reflected in several scenes in the vast pictorial repertory conceived in the second quarter of the thirteenth century for the renowned *Bible moralisée*. An example of particular relevance in the present context accompanies the reprimand in Proverbe 6: 9 to delinquents in faith.[30] The illustration in the *Bible moralisée* for the accompanying moralization shows a preacher with an open book, pointing to a vision of Christ in Judgment above the two men seated behind a game board and accompanied by a woman holding a drinking vessel: *Hoc significat quod predicator debet monere peccatorem ut peniteat . . . si quis peccator differt penitentiam deus accelerat vindictam*. Form and content of the composition offer a unified precedent for the two essential ingredients of the call to penitence issued in the litany of the Walters Hours. No purse or sack appears in this illustration of the *Bible moralisée,* although the motif is sometimes included in its other gaming scenes.[31]

The theme of penance was also not necessarily stressed in depictions of chess or moralizations of that theme. Human folly was, however, a common point of reference for both. In this connection, a thirteenth-century Anglo-Norman poem consisting of forty-eight verses is of special interest, because one of its sequences is structured along the same lines as a litany.[32] By way of prelude, the first game of chess is said to have pitted Adam against the Devil, who tricked the white king into making a series of disastrous moves that lost him the game. A return match was promptly initiated by God, who installed a white line-up, with Christ as king, the Virgin as queen, the rooks as apostles, the *aufins* (present-day bishops) as confessors, and the pawns as ordinary men. Adam's defeat by the Devil at chess must already have been a current topic in the twelfth century. No better evidence could be found than that preserved on a French ivory rook, a chessman equated in the poem cited above with an apostle. The sides, ends, and top of the piece are carved with the Temptation and Fall, a joust representing the conflict between good and evil, and a bridled bear symbolizing lust.[33]

Extant examples, as well as descriptions of still another medieval chess piece, offer witness to the shape of the *aufin* (bishop) as an elephant with howdah in elaborate sets destined for Western European medieval rulers.[34] This design, echoed in the first line-filler in the litany of Walters 102, originated in India but was transmitted to the West mainly through Arabic intermediaries. Medieval chess sets for men of lesser rank included an *aufin* designed by two horn-like projections, which originally may have represented abstract references to elephant tusks. By the thirteenth century, this idiosyncratic detail had become associated with the miter attribute of a bishop, who was represented by this piece.[35] This piece's oblique move on the board led in the *sacculum* moralization to an attribution of cupidity not only to bishops, but also to prelates whose horn attributes were noted as differing from those of Moses.[36] It would be interesting to know the shape of the *aufin* in either the ivory or the crystal and jasper set documented as having been owned by King Edward I about the time that the design of Walters 102 was created.[37] The king's enjoyment of chess as a young man was linked with an anecdote about his miraculous escape from death, when an immense rock fell on the seat he had just vacated beside the gameboard.[38] If the *aufin* in his set was in the shape of an elephant with howdah, an added entertaining allusion to a contemporary anecdote may be imbedded in the first large line-filler in the litany. The evidence provided by the actual chess game in the litany and the hidden allusion in the Renart cycle suffices to show that the patron, and presumably also the designer, had a special penchant for chess and allegories related to it.

The chess topos is abandoned in the fifth major line-filler, where one of the rare extant medieval representations of Romulus and Remus refers to Rome,[39] seat of the papacy and fountainhead of the Christian faith, exemplified in the leading founders of monastic and hermetic orders cited in the text at left (Fig. 7.4). Several details in the rendering of the she-wolf suggest allusions rooted in bestiary lore. The account of the wolf's nature describes how the nocturnal beast turns its gleaming eye on its prey in a manner used by the Devil to ensnare souls.[40] The licking of the hindmost twin recalls the method used by the bear-mother to shape her formless newborn cubs.[41] The fraternal twin on whom the she-wolf confers favor is doubtless Romulus, whose capacity for evil, this image seems to say, was nurtured by the adoptive mother. The murder of Remus was termed in Augustine's *Civitas dei* the worst disaster in the history of Rome, an example of the Earthly City turned against itself, and thus a parallel to the enmity between the Earthly and Heavenly Cities symbolized by the first murder on earth, that committed by Cain against Abel.[42] The equation of Romulus with evil, while not commonly referred to in later medieval sources, was occasionally mentioned in contexts such as the *Policraticus,* completed by John of Salisbury in the mid-twelfth century.[43] In the visual arts, the Augustinian corollary of the biblical and classical fratricides provided special inspiration in the second half of the fourteenth century to pictorial programs in French copies of the *Cité de dieu.*[44]

It is conceivable, though remotely so, that a reference to the biblical fratricide is implied by the Romulus-Remus image in the litany. The

Romulus-Remus theme is so rare in the Middle Ages that some special reason must have occasioned its choice. Latent anti-Semitism through reference to Cain as the prototype for Jews who killed Christ may have played a part in the thematic selection,[45] especially since this bias finds obvious expression in the Walters Hours in viciously caricatured Jews in several episodes of the Passion cycle.[46] The force of this sentiment was still very much in evidence in the decade following the Jews' expulsion from England in 1290.[47]

Another possible motivation for emphasis on Rome may have been provided by the declaration of the year 1300 as a jubilee year. Previously mentioned events that occurred in 1300, namely the recreation of Renart's funeral procession in Paris and the extraordinary magnetism of the Vernicle in Rome, are depicted in Walters 102. Perhaps they indicate a date for the manuscript not at the end of the thirteenth century, the period usually assigned to it, but in 1300 or shortly thereafter. An indication that the patron may have gone on an extensive journey is provided by a number of prayers at the end of the volume for protection during travel, including one to St. Julian the Hospitaller, patron saint of travelers. The destination of such a journey could well have been the Continent in 1300. Needless to say, however, the highlights of the year could have been integrated into the pictorial program without the patron's leaving home. Elsewhere in the manuscript are portrayals of what can be presumed to be relatives of the patron, figures who add a personal picture-album dimension to the contents of the devotional volume. These pictures could well have been intended to provide comfort to the owner during an extended absence from his family.[48]

No deep, ulterior meanings lurk behind the representation of an ape astride a bridled bear in the sixth major line-filler (Fig. 7.4). The pejorative connotations of these beasts, which include lewdness and lust,[49] make this a particularly outlandish companion piece for the final hagiographic group, the female saints. The first name cited leads one to a point of reference: the moral depravity of Mary Magdalene before her conversion by Christ. His bridling of her sensual passion and the reward of salvation achieved through penance and devotion are implied in the immobilization of both ape and bear, since the latter is firmly tethered to a post. The six-part cycle thus concludes as it began, with positive motifs bracketing the more foreboding intermediate elements.

Less effort is required to understand the secondary five-part sequence of enlarged line-fillers in the Hours of Christ Crucified. More obvious, literal associations obviate the need to delve into a reservoir of culturally relevant topoi. Only the first of these line endings reflects the general predilection of the period for risqué allusions, found especially in marginal motifs.[50] The petition for denial of the spirit of fornication was chosen as the theme for the first large line-filler, which is occupied by a half-length nude man adopting a gesture typical of Jesse to emphasize the meaning of the words *Per misterium incarnationis* (Fig. 7.5). The next two petitions, *Per adventum tuum* and *Per nativitatem tuum,* are juxtaposed to a gold star and hooded head that form appropriate visual cues to the Nativity of Christ and the Annunciation to the Shepherds. References to death, burial, and resurrection in petitions on the verso are also aptly illustrated by a somewhat ambiguous figure representing St. Margaret or Jonah, shown issuing with hands clasped from the jaws of a dragon-like creature (Fig. 7.6). The sequence of petition ends on the opposite recto with the plea, *Ut nos exaudire digneris / Fili dei,* the urgency of which is underscored by the pointing gesture of a hybrid monk with exaggeratedly large hands. The appended invocations conclude with a design by the less refined illuminator of Walters 102. This is an exception to the usual rule of literal word association, for here reference is made to the cyclical nature of birth and death as a spotted quadruped rises from the mouth of a dog and turns to sink its teeth in the dog's hindquarters.

The litany ends with the texts of Psalm 69 and four collects, for which the use of standard one-line fillers consisting of animals and hybrids is resumed. The only illustrative detail of note appears in the two-line initial to the first collect, *Omnipotens sempiterne deus misere famulo tuo ministro nostro.* The bearded, frontal head of a monk seen here may represent the patron's spiritual advisor. In any event, the depiction provides visual evidence that the first owner had a connection of some kind with a monastic institution, indicated by intermittent textual references to *fratres* and *frères.* Identification of the order in question is precluded by the loss of the calendar, the generalized nature of extant liturgical evidence, and the non-specific habits worn by clerics depicted in historiated initials.[51] Florence McCulloch suggested a possible affiliation with the Hospital of St. Catherine near the Tower of London, basing her conjecture on the rare nine-lesson Office of St. Catherine and a prayer to St. Julian Hospitaller included at the end of the prayerbook.[52] A provenance in or near London is indeed indicated for Walters 102 on stylistic grounds, as well as by the sophistication of the textual and illustrative contents.

The last include a formidable array of laypeople depicted in attitudes of

prayer in twelve extant three- to seven-line initials at primary text divisions. All figures are shown in unadorned apparel colored deep blue and
red, and, less often, orange, tan, and white. Identification of any of the
three ladies depicted in ten of the initials, or of the praying older and
younger men shown in two others, is precluded by the absence of heraldry.
It can be assumed that these individuals were related to the first owner,
who, to judge from the number of female figures presented, may have been
a woman. If so, she remains to be picked out from among the three types
of ladies depicted. One, represented four times, is distinguishable by her
white veil; another, shown twice, wears a snood caught in a bandeau.[53]
The third, the likeliest candidate for patroness because of her prominent
and diverse representations, seems younger and wears her long blonde hair
uncovered.

As the volume presently exists, incomplete at the beginning, the blonde
woman makes her first appearances at Prime in the Hours both of the Virgin and of the Holy Spirit. She is seen once more in a two-line initial to the
antiphon at Lauds in the Office of the Dead. The most imposing version of
this figure fills the large initial to the final prayer in a sequence devoted to
Christ Crucified. Here a man, presumably her husband, kneels behind her
to receive the blessing pronounced by a standing figure of the Christ
Child. Punchwork tooling of the burnished gold ground and frame signal
the importance both of this initial and of the final view of the blonde
woman, which shows her alone before Christ at the beginning of a prayer
fully contained on a recto (Fig. 7.8). Since the verso of the leaf marks the
beginning of the Hours of St. Catherine, the patroness may have been
named for this saint. In the opening letter "C" of the prayer, *Clementissime
deus qui omnium occultorum es cognitor . . . ,* she is shown in unprecedent-
edly large scale, kneeling before Christ. Directing his attention toward her,
the Savior is shown with right hand raised and left hand resting on a book
turned so that the inscription *Dominus tecum* faces the worshipper, imply-
ing that she is literate. The personal blessing is in sharp contrast to inscriptions of the first words of the accompanying text found on books held by
clerics depicted at other major liturgical openings.[54]

Directly below the initial showing the blonde woman before Christ is
one of several scribal changes that have not previously been noticed, some
care having been taken to make them unobtrusive. Slight variations of ink
color and letter forms show that the Latin word for "supplicant" has been
altered from the male to the female gender at the beginning of line 7, and
again on line 11. The original word *peccatore* now reads *peccatrici*. Since the

use of the male form for supplicant was not uncommon, even in books of devotion designed for female patrons, the original reading does not contradict the visual evidence provided in the initial. The figure here, as indicated by scientific examination, has not undergone an analogous sex change.[55] Ultimate proof for the patron's gender has regrettably been eradicated at the center of line 11. The Christian name which must have been inscribed here was erased. In its stead were entered the inconsequential, non-committal words *quod est,* followed by a hyphen. The conclusion to be drawn is that the name of the first owner was as objectionable to a subsequent female owner as the male form of reference for "sinner" ( *peccator*) would have been. The image in the initial was not tampered with, and the worshippers in previous initials were also spared.

The textual alterations in the prayer seem to have been made fairly early in the history of the book. One indication is the resemblance of the script here to that of two psalm verses initially omitted but added in the margins of a quire containing the Gradual Psalms.[56] Each of these additions is attached to a rope and "hauled into place" by a lay figure, who points to the section of the text where the verse belongs. The spirit and style of these decorated corrections suggest that no more than a decade or two elapsed before they were introduced along with the changes in the prefatory prayer to the Hours of St. Catherine.

As noted earlier, circumstantial evidence warrants a conjecture that the Walters 102 prayerbook originated in 1300, the year of the grand jubilee declared by Pope Boniface VIII. Specific related events of international import appear to be alluded to pictorially in the margins and litany line-fillers. They include a cortège of Renart similar to the propagandistic, anti-papal one in Paris, and an emphasis on Rome through reference initially to the relic of the Veronica Veil at St. Peter's. The focus of international attention on Rome in 1300 made the depiction of the Holy City's founders doubly appropriate in the litany, providing an explanation for the selection of a theme rarely depicted in medieval art.

At home or abroad, the admixture of sacred and profane images would have enhanced the owner's pleasure in reciting her devotions (assuming the owner to be a woman). The design of the pictorial program provided spiritual and worldly edification, to be enjoyed by the patron in the privacy of her chamber, at chapel, or in the company of favored individuals portrayed in the initials of her prayerbook. The spirit of her time so vividly captured in its contents found superb expression in the cycle of the elephant and his multivalent companions in the litany.

## Notes

1. The Walters Art Gallery, *Twenty-Eighth Annual Report* (Baltimore, 1960), p. 23: "Florence McCulloch of Wellesley College . . . was able to identify the calendars and liturgical 'uses' of 68 of our French Books of Hours. This was an important and much appreciated contribution toward the preparation of a definitive printed catalogue of the manuscripts." Although this project could not be realized as anticipated, the results of McCulloch's labor have proved most useful in the preparation of a two-volume catalog of French medieval and Renaissance manuscripts in the Walters Art Gallery, of which the first is in press at the Johns Hopkins University Press and the second in progress. This undertaking was made possible by generous grants from the National Endowment for the Humanities and the Samuel H. Kress Foundation.

2. 105 fols., 264 × 185 mm, justification 164 × 116 mm; nineteenth-century red velvet binding; purchased by Henry Walters from Paul Gruel, Paris, about 1930. Seymour de Ricci and William J. Wilson, *Census of Medieval and Renaissance Manuscripts in the United States* (New York: W. J. Wilson Co., 1935) I, p. 784, no. 169. See Lucy Freeman Sandler, *Gothic Manuscripts 1285–1385* (London and Oxford: Harvey Miller-Oxford University Press, 1986) II, no. 15; *The Age of Chivalry: Art in Plantagenet England 1200–1400*, London, Royal Academy of Arts, 6 November 1986–6 March 1988 (London: Royal Academy of Arts, Weidenfeld and Nicolson, 1987), no. 359; Roger S. Wieck, et al., *Time Sanctified: The Book of Hours in Medieval Art and Life*, Baltimore, Walters Art Gallery, 23 April–17 July 1988 (New York: Braziller, The Walters Art Gallery, 1988), no. 111.

3. "The Funeral of Renart the Fox in a Walters Book of Hours," *Journal of the Walters Art Gallery*, 24/25 (1962–63), 9–27. The contents of Walters 102 are misbound as follows: Hours of the Virgin, use of Rome, beginning imperfectly in Lauds (fols. 87–90$^v$, 86$^{r-v}$, 92–93$^v$, 16$^{r-v}$, 91$^{r-v}$); Advent Office of the Virgin (fols. 17–21$^v$, identified by Judith Oliver); Hours of the Holy Spirit (fols. 22–26$^v$, 85$^{r-v}$, 35$^{r-v}$, 41–42$^v$); Seven Penitential Psalms (fols. 43–48$^v$, 40$^{r-v}$, 27$^{r-v}$); Litany and collects (fols. 28–30$^v$, 36–38$^v$); Fifteen Gradual Psalms (fols. 39$^{r-v}$, 31–34$^v$, 49–50$^v$); Office of the Dead, use of Rome (fols. 51–73); Hours of Christ Crucified (fols. 73$^v$–84$^v$, 2–3$^v$); Prayers to Christ Crucified (fols. 4–11$^v$); Prayer, Hours of St. Catherine, miscellaneous prayers (fols. 12–15$^v$, 94–105).

4. The text for Lauds is reprinted in McCulloch, "The Funeral," p. 27. Two other examples of this text in English Books of Hours, one earlier and one later, are cited in the description of Walters 102 in Clare M. Baker, "The Early Development of the Illustrated Book of Hours c. 1240–1350," diss., University of East Anglia, 1985, no. 8; the relevant manuscripts are London, British Library, Egerton MS 1151, and Norwich, Castle Museum MS 158.926.4f; see, respectively, Nigel Morgan, *Early Gothic Manuscripts*, II, 1250–1285 (London and Oxford: Harvey Miller/Oxford University Press, 1988), no. 161; and Sandler, *Gothic Manuscripts 1285–1385*, no. 47.

5. Willem Noomen, "Le *Jeu d'Adam*. Etude descriptive et analytique," *Romania,*

89 (1968), p. 188; Lynette R. Muir, *Liturgy and Drama in the Anglo-Norman Adam,* Medium Aevum Monographs, n.s. III (Oxford: Basil Blackwell, 1973), pp. 24–25, 102–103; Steven Justice, "The Authority of Ritual in the *Jeu d'Adam,*" *Speculum,* 62 (1987), 853–854; on the significance of Balaam in the *Jeu d'Adam,* see also M. F. Vaughan, "The Prophets of the Anglo-Norman *Adam,*" *Traditio,* 39 (1983), 86, 90.

6. A wakeful Jesse is seated in the midst of the full-page Tree of Jesse on the Beatus page of the Windmill Psalter, Morgan Library MS M. 102; M. R. James, *Catalogue of Manuscripts . . . Library of J. Pierpont Morgan* (London: Chiswick Press, 1906), color pl. opp. p. 41; Adelaide Bennett, "The Windmill Psalter: The Historiated Letter E of Psalm One," *Journal of the Warburg and Courtauld Institutes,* 43 (1980), pl. 11a, also p. 59, n. 24, for references to near-contemporary English representations of Adam and Eve in this context. Examples of the wakeful Jesse in English manuscripts of the first quarter of the fourteenth century are illustrated in George Warner, *Queen Mary's Psalter* (London: British Museum), pl. 119; James, *Catalogue . . . Morgan,* ill. opp. p. 13 (MS M. 107, Tiptoft Missal); the poses of Jesse are discussed in Arthur Watson, *The Early Iconography of the Tree of Jesse* (London: Humphrey Milford, Oxford University Press, 1934), pp. 47–52.

7. Watson, *The Early Iconography,* pp. 10–36. For the sermon attributed in the Middle Ages to Augustine, entitled *Contra Iudaeos paganos et Arianos sermo de symbolo,* see J. P. Migne, *Patrologia latina,* 42: 1117–1130; on this sermon and the dramatization of the *Ordo prophetarum,* Karl Young, *The Drama of the Medieval Church* (Oxford: Clarendon Press, 1933) II, pp. 126–171; see also Noomen, "Le Jeu," p. 152.

8. Oxford, Bodleian Library MS Auct. D.3.2, and Cambridge, Trinity College MS O.4.16; Sandler, *Gothic Manuscripts 1285–1385,* nos. 13, 14.

9. Cf. Malibu, Getty Museum Ludwig MS IX.3, a north French book of hours of the early fourteenth century; Joachim M. Plotzek in Anton von Euw and J. M. Plotzek, *Die Handschriften der Sammlung Ludwig,* II (Cologne: Schnütgen Museum, 1982), pp. 74–83. The predilection for thematic programming of line-fillers in English Gothic manuscripts is noted with special reference to the litany in Lucy Freeman Sandler, *The Peterborough Psalter in Brussels and Other Fenland Manuscripts* (London: Harvey Miller, 1974), p. 35.

10. Cf. Carl Nordenfalk, "Katz und Maus und andere Tiere im Book of Kells," *Zum Problem der Deutung frühmittelalterlicher Bildinhalte,* ed. Helmuth Rith, Veröffentlichungen des Vorgesch. Seminars der Philipps-Univ. Marburg a. d. Lahn 4 (Sigmaringen, 1986), pp. 212–214; for the interpretation of a hybrid man with fish tail in the Book of Kells (fol. 201) as possible clue to production, see Carl Nordenfalk, "Another Look at the Book of Kells," *Festschrift Wolfgang Braunfels,* ed. F. Piel, J. Traeger (Tübingen: Ernst Wasmuth, 1977), p. 278.

11. Lilian M. C. Randall, "Humor and Fantasy in the Margins of an English Book of Hours," *Apollo,* 84 (1966), 68, figs. 2, 20–24; for the contents and further bibliographical references to Morgan 102, see Sandler, *Gothic Manuscripts 1285–1385,* no. 4.

12. For relevant references regarding literacy among female members of the En-

glish upper classes in the mid-thirteenth century, Michael Camille, "Seeing and Reading: Some Visual Indications of Medieval Literacy and Illiteracy," *Art History*, 8 (1985), 41–42.

13. *Apologia ad Guillelmum Sancti Theoderici Abbatem*, Migne, *Patrologia latina*, 182: 915–916; English translation in Elisabeth G. Holt, *Literary Sources of Art History* (Princeton: Princeton University Press, 1947), pp. 17–19.

14. Dorothy Miner, *Illuminated Books of the Middle Ages and Renaissance*, exhib. cat. Baltimore Museum of Art, 27 Jan.–13 March (Baltimore: Trustees of the Walters Art Gallery, 1949), no. 153, pl. LVIII (fol. 28ᵛ).

15. See G. C. Druce, "The Elephant in Medieval Legend and Art," *The Archaeological Journal*, 76, 2nd ser. (1919), 1–73; Florence McCulloch, *Mediaeval Latin and French Bestiaries* (Chapel Hill: University of North Carolina Press, 1960), pp. 115–119; M. R. James, *The Bestiary* (Oxford: Oxford University Press, Roxburghe Club, 1928), pl. VII (fol. 7); further discussion of this manuscript in Morgan, *Early Gothic Manuscripts*, I, no. 2; for an artistically related example see M. R. James, *A Peterborough Psalter and Bestiary of the Fourteenth Century* (Oxford: Oxford University Press, Roxburghe Club, 1921), pl. 10.

16. Paris, Bibl. Nat. MS lat. 15472, fol. 225; Sandler, *Gothic Manuscripts 1285–1385*, I, no. 6; II, fig. 8.

17. Suzanne Lewis, *The Art of Matthew Paris in the Chronica Majora* (Berkeley, Los Angeles, London: University of California Press, 1986), pp. 212–216.

18. Michael Evans, "An Illustrated Fragment of Peraldus' Summa of Vice: Harleian MS 3244," *Journal of the Warburg and Courtauld Institutes*, 45 (1982), 41–42.

19. Bennett, "The Windmill Psalter," 52–67.

20. *Le Jeu d'Adam (Ordo representacionis Ade)*, ed. Willem Noomen (Paris: Honoré Champion, 1971), p. 41.

21. On the kinship between the Adam figure in Walters 102 and the sculpted stone counterpart in the Musée Cluny, Paris, see Dieter Kimpel, "Die Querhausarme von Notre Dame zu Paris und Ihre Sculpturen," diss., Bonn, 1971), pp. 121–122, figs. 188, 189; this reference was kindly called to my attention by Adelaide Bennett.

22. Lewis, *The Art of Matthew Paris*, pp. 126–130; the impact of the relic on a Croatian pilgrim is described in Dante's *Paradiso*, Canto XXVI. See also Flora Lewis, "The Veronica: Image, Legend, and Viewer," *England in the Thirteenth Century: Proceedings of the 1984 Harlaxton Symposium*, ed. W. M. Ormrod (Grantham: Harlaxton College, 1985), pp. 100–106.

23. For condemnation of this form of entertainment as a pagan practice in Augustine's sermons for Christmas and New Year's days, see Migne, *Patrologia latina*, 38: 1015–1017, 1021–1024.

24. Cf. Ruth Mellinkoff, "Judas's Red Hair and the Jews," *Journal of Jewish Art*, 9 (1982), 31–46; the orange elephant in the opening line-filler in the litany of Walters 102 indicates that this color did not necessarily bear evil connotations.

25. Harold J. R. Murray, *The History of Chess* (Oxford: Oxford University Press, 1913), pp. 533–534.

26. Murray, *The History of Chess*, pp. 530–534, Latin text on pp. 560–561. The brief

tract is a vastly reduced offshoot of moralizations in major thirteenth-century chess treatises such as Jacobus de Cessolis's *Liber de moribus hominum et officiis nobilium,* ed. E. Köpke (Mittheilungen aus den Handscriften der Ritter Akademie zu Brandenburg a.H., 1879); earlier medieval interest in chess is discussed in Helena M. Gamer, "The Earliest Evidence of Chess in Western Literature; the Einsiedeln Verses," *Speculum,* 29 (1954), 734–750. For symbolic attributes assigned to the game by the twelfth century, William Tronzo, "Moral Hieroglyphics: Chess and Dice at San Savino in Piacenza," *Gesta,* 15: 1 (1976, *Essays in Honor of Sumner McKnight Crosby*), 15–26. Monastic interest in chess moralizations is reflected in an example in a compilation recorded in a late fifteenth-century library catalog drawn up at Cîteaux: "Ludus scacorum moralisatus; de corpore Christi cum multis exemplis utilibus; casus Senece et aliorum circa leges civitatum . . ." *Catalogue générale des manuscrits des bibliothèques publiques de France,* V (Paris: E. Plon, 1889), p. 424, no. 850.

27. Eric G. Millar, *The Rutland Psalter* (Oxford: Oxford University Press, Roxburghe Club, 1937), p. 53.

28. Murray, *The History of Chess,* pp. 559–560.

29. E. Hamann, "La pénitence privée," *Dictionnaire de théologie catholique,* 12, 894–914; on the rise of penitential literature and practices in thirteenth-century England, G. R. Owst, *Preaching in Medieval England* (New York: Russell & Russell, 1965), pp. 38–60.

30. Paris, Bibl. Nat. MS lat. 11560, fol. 45$^v$; A. de Laborde, *La bible moralisée conservée à Oxford, Paris, et Londres,* II (Paris: SFRMP, 1913), pl. 269.

31. Cf. other gaming scenes in the *Bible moralisée,* refer to Genesis 1: 9; Job 7: 1–6; Psalm 61: 1–2; Psalm 79: 1–2; Proverbs 23: 20; and Jeremiah, Lam. 4: 6; see Laborde, *La bible moralisée,* I (1911), pl. 3; II, pls. 213, 241, 246, 276; III (1913), pl. 399; representing, respectively, Oxford, Bodleian Library MS Bodley 270b, fols. 3$^v$, 213$^v$, and Paris, Bibl. Nat. MS lat. 11560, fols. 17$^v$, 22, 52, 175$^v$.

32. Oxford, Corpus Christi College MS 293B, fols. 15$^v$–16; printed in Oesten Södergard, "Petit poème allégorique sur les échecs," *Studia Neophilologica,* 23 (1950/51), 133–134. I am indebted for this reference to Christine Butler of Corpus Christi College.

33. Hans and Sigfried Wichmann, *Schach: Ursprung und Wandlung der Spielfiguren in Zwölf Jahrhunderten* (Munich: Georg D. W. Callway, 1960), p. 289, figs. 31, 32; for an analogous symbolic joust in an early twelfth-century English manuscript, Otto Pächt, C. R. Dodwell, Francis Wormald, *The St. Albans Psalter* (London: The Warburg Institute, 1960), pp. 162–163, 206, pl. 41.

34. An early ivory example in Paris, Bibl. Nat., Cabinet de Médailles, was long believed to form part of a set given by Sultan Harun al Raschid to Charlemagne; for the latter's donation of an ivory chess set to the royal abbey of Saint-Denis, see Wichmann, *Schach,* p. 281, fig. 1. The commission by King Alfonso X of Spain of an *aufin* in the shape of an elephant with howdah is recorded in an instructive manual on games completed in 1283; Murray, *The History of Chess,* pp. 568–569, 769.

35. For illustrations of medieval examples, Wichmann, *Schach,* figs. 35 (with horns), 43 (mitered bishops); see also Murray, *The History of Chess,* pp. 765–769.

36. Murray, pp. 530, 560.

37. The royal English wardrobe accounts for 1299–1300 record that the crystal and jaspar chess set was preserved in a coffret (Murray, *The History of Chess*, p. 449).

38. Nicholas Trivet, *Annales VI regum Angliae . . .*, ed. Thomas Hog (London: English Historical Society, 1845), p. 282; for another miraculous escape from death by Edward I, see Bennett, "The Windmill Psalter," p. 65. Reference to loyal vulnerability was implied in the *sacculum* moralization by the reminder of the possible location of the king at the bottom of the sack in which the pieces were stored. Such an allusion may be intended by the exaggerated size of this object in a thirteenth-century scene of a chess game in a stained-glass window donated to Chartres Cathedral by a royal chamberlain; see Yves Delaporte, *Les vitraux de la cathédrale de Chartres* (Chartres: E. Houvet, 1926), III, pls. 212, 213. It is noteworthy that the king's potential place at the bottom of the chess sack was mentioned in a moralizing treatise written for the French king Charles VI (1368–1422) by his tutor; *Philippe de Mézieres . . . Le Songe du vieil pélerin*, ed. G. W. Coopland (Cambridge: Cambridge University Press, 1969) II, p. 201.

39. For an Italian thirteenth-century representation of Romulus and Remus beside the inscription *Roma caput mundi*, see John White, "The Reconstruction of Nicola Pisano's Perugia Fountain," *Journal of the Warburg and Courtauld Institutes*, 33 (1970), 70–83.

40. McCulloch, *Mediaeval Bestiaries*, p. 189.

41. Cf. Eric G. Millar, *A Thirteenth Century Bestiary in the Library of Alnwick Castle* (Oxford: Oxford University Press, Roxburghe Club), pl. XXXVI; McCulloch, *Mediaeval Bestiaries*, p. 9.

42. Book III, ch. 6, and book XV, ch. 5; Migne, *Patrologia latina*, 41: 82–83, 411–412. The special interest in the *Civitas dei* among Franciscans and Dominicans at Oxford in the thirteenth century is discussed in Beryl Smalley, *English Friars of Antiquity in the Early Fourteenth Century* (Oxford: Basil Blackwell, 1960), pp. 51–65; her only reference to Romulus and Remus pertains to a mention of the theme in a fourteenth-century Italian sermon (pp. 41, 277).

43. *The Statesman's Book of John of Salisbury . . . Policraticus*, trans. John Dickinson (New York: Russell & Russell, 1963), I, p. 410; for an early medieval artistic prototype of Romulus and Remus, see Alfred Becker, *Franks Casket* (Regensburg: Hans Carl, 1973), pp. 55–63.

44. Notable examples dating from the 1370s are Paris, Bibl. Nat. MS fr. 22913 and Cambridge, Massachusetts, Houghton Lib. MS Typ 201H; see, respectively, Sharon Off Dunlap Smith, "Illustrations of Raoul de Praelles' Translations of St. Augustine's 'City of God' between 1375 and 1420 (Volumes I and II)," diss., New York University, 1974, pp. 62, 203, 271; Roger S. Wieck, *Late Medieval and Renaissance Manuscripts*, exhib. cat. Harvard University, Houghton Library, 15 March–3 June 1983 (Cambridge: Harvard College Library, 1983), no. 2, ill. opp. p. 4.

45. A symbolic reference to Cain and Abel may underlie the representation of Romulus and Remus at the foot of the cross of the Crucifixion in an Italian

ivory diptych tentatively assigned to the tenth century; see Danielle Gaborit-Chopin, *Ivoires du moyen âge* (Fribourg: Office du Livre, 1978), p. 93, fig. 116. On the imposition of eternal penance on Cain in the Anglo-Norman twelfth-century *Jeu d'Adam*, see Muir, *Liturgy and Drama*, p. 92; cf. Stephen Spector, "Anti-Semitism in English Mystery Plays," *The Drama of the Middle Ages*, ed. C. Davidson, C. J. Ginakaris, J. H. Stroupe (New York: AMC Press, 1982), p. 333.

46. Distinctive examples, including Jews wearing winged headdresses, are the Flagellation and the Carrying of the Cross in the Hours of Christ Crucified (fols. 74, 76), and a martyrdom of St. Lawrence added early in a pen drawing on the verso of the last folio of the Walters Hours (fol. 105ᵛ); cf. Ruth Mellinkoff, "Demonic Winged Headgear," *Viator*, 16 (1985), 367–381.

47. Cecil Roth, *A History of the Jews in England*, 3rd ed. (Oxford: Clarendon Press, 1964), pp. 76–90.

48. See below, n. 53.

49. On the sexual connotations of the ape and bear, Horst W. Janson, *Apes and Ape Lore in the Middle Ages and the Renaissance* (London: The Warburg Institute, 1952), pp. 222–226, pl. XLVIb; cf. an early thirteenth-century German depiction of an ape holding an apple and riding a bear in Hanns Swarzenski, *The Berthold Missal* (New York: The Pierpont Morgan Library, 1943), p. 45, pl. LIVd; reference to the Fall is made via a comparable image in a late fourteenth-century French copy of Bartholomaeus Anglicus's *De proprietatibus rerum* (Paris, Bibl. Nat. MS fr. 9141, fol. 303ᵛ); see Millard Meiss, *French Painting in the Time of Jean de Berry: The Fourteenth Century* (London: Phaidon, 1967), pp. 73, 94, 221. I would like to thank Sandra Hindman for examining this image in situ. The appearance of the more common medieval symbol of lust, a he-goat, in a late fifteenth-century French illustrative cycle for the Penitential Psalms, is discussed by William V. Voelkle, "Morgan Manuscript M. 1001: The Seven Deadly Sins and the Seven Evil Ones," *Monsters and Demons in the Ancient and Medieval Worlds, Papers Presented in Honor of Edith Porada*, ed. A. E. Farkas, P. O. Harper, E. B. Harrison (Mainz: Philipp von Zabern, 1987), pp. 106–107.

50. McCulloch, "The Funeral of Renard the Fox," fig. 4; Randall, "Humor and Fantasy," figs. 4, 5.

51. Hours of the Holy Spirit, Matins: two clerics before altar, foremost with open book inscribed with first words of text (fol. 22); Penitential Psalms, opening initial: cleric standing before seated Christ and holding up open, uninscribed book (fol. 43); Office of the Dead, Matins, and Lesson I, respectively: two clerics chanting (fol. 51); two clerics, one with book inscribed with opening words of text, officiating at funeral service attended by two laymen (fol. 55).

52. McCulloch, "The Funeral of Renard the Fox." A Franciscan connection for the litany is not clearly established by the sequence of monks and hermit saints, which is headed by Benedict and further includes Francis, the hermit-saint Anthony, and Dominic; cf. Sandler, *Gothic Manuscripts 1285–1385*, p. 25.

53. The portrayals listed below incorporate the following abbreviations: blonde,

bareheaded lady = bb; lady wearing bandeau attached to snood = b; lady wearing white veil = wv; grounds are burnished gold (g), punched burnished gold (pg), and blue or rose with white-dot patterns (bwd, rwd). Figures are shown in prayer, with hands folded or in orant position: Hours of the Virgin, Prime: lady bb, bwd (fol. 88$^v$); Terce: lady with open book, bg (fol. 92$^v$); Sext: lady before altar, wv, bwd (fol. 16). Hours of the Holy Spirit, Prime: lady bb, rwd (fol. 24$^v$); Terce: young man (fol. 25$^v$); Sext: lady b, rwd (fol. 26$^v$); None: lady wv, g (fol. 85$^v$); Vespers, misrubricated ad nonam: lady wv, pg (fol. 35$^v$); Compline: lady wv, bwd (fol. 42). Office of the Dead, Vespers: youth and older man, g (fol. 70); antiphon to Lauds: lady bb (fol. 67). Last prayer in sequence to Crucified Christ, rubricated conclusio: man and lady (bb) blessed by standing Christ-Child, pg (fol. 9). Prayer introducing Hours of St. Catherine: lady bb before seated Christ with open book inscribed *Dominus tecum,* pg (fol. 12).

54. See above, n. 51.
55. The technical examination was carried out by Melanie Gifford, Associate Curator, Conservation Department, Walters Art Gallery.
56. McCulloch, "The Funeral of Renard the Fox," figs. 5, 6.

FIGURE 7.1. Elephant bearing a howdah (Walters Art Gallery MS W. 102, fol. 28). (Photo: courtesy Walters Art Gallery)

FIGURE 7.2. Adam after the Fall (Walters Art Gallery MS W. 102, fol. 28ᵛ). (Photo: courtesy Walters Art Gallery)

FIGURE 7.3. St. Stephen-Christ visage (top); chess game (bottom) (Walters Art Gallery MS W. 102, fol. 29). (Photo: courtesy Walters Art Gallery)

FIGURE 7.4. Romulus and Remus suckled by the she-wolf (top); ape
riding bear (bottom) (Walters Art Gallery MS W. 102, fol. 29ᵛ). (Photo:
courtesy Walters Art Gallery)

FIGURE 7.5. Nude man pointing at text (top); hooded head before star (bottom) (Walters Art Gallery MS W. 102, fol. 30). (Photo: courtesy Walters Art Gallery)

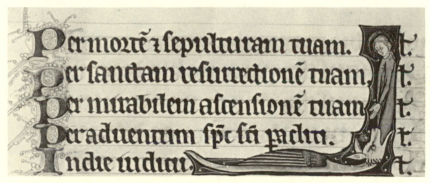

FIGURE 7.6. St. Margaret or Jonah emerging from creature's mouth (Walters Art Gallery MS W. 102, fol. 30ᵛ). (Photo: courtesy Walters Art Gallery)

FIGURE 7.7. Tree of Jesse (Walters Art Gallery MS W. 102, fol. 1). (Photo: courtesy Walters Art Gallery)

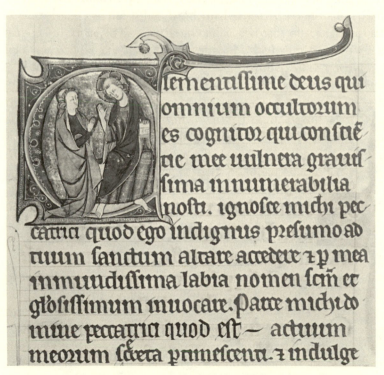

FIGURE 7.8. Manuscript owner before Christ (Walters Art Gallery MS W. 102, fol. 12). (Photo: courtesy Walters Art Gallery)

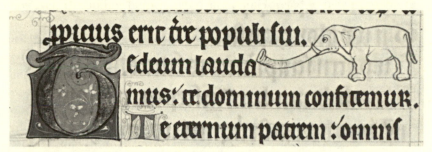

FIGURE 7.9. Elephant (New York, Pierpont Morgan Library MS M. 102, fol. 162). (Photo: courtesy Pierpont Morgan Library)

# Meradith T. McMunn

## 8. *Bestiary Influences in Two Thirteenth-Century Romances*

There is considerable scholarly interest in the study of Latin and vernacular bestiary manuscripts, but less attention has been paid to assessing the contribution of this important tradition to the study of other medieval genres.[1] The Greek and Latin *Physiologus* established the bestiary tradition by providing information about real and imaginary animals, and about their value as moral and theological symbols. This text was primarily a teaching device whose entertainment value was secondary. Beginning in the twelfth century, however, vernacular translations made the bestiary available to audiences with different tastes and more varied requirements than formerly. By the thirteenth century, there is clear evidence of borrowing from the bestiary tradition by authors of popular and courtly literature. The present study is an examination of bestiary influence in two such works composed for the Flemish court in the later thirteenth century, the *Chevalerie de Judas Macabé* and the *Roman de Kanor*.[2] I have chosen to focus on the lion figure because of the variety of lion iconography in the bestiary tradition and the heraldic associations of the lion with the court for which the two romances were produced.

The essence of the bestiary genre lies in the relation between iconography and symbolic interpretation. Each of these elements operates on both the verbal and the pictorial levels, a fact that was recognized explicitly by medieval authors themselves. Hugh of Fouilloy in his *De avibus,* which resembles the bestiary in literary structure and popular appeal, wrote:

> Columbam cuius pennae sunt deargentatae et posteriora dorsi eius in pallore auri pingere, et per picturam simplicium mentes aedificare decrevi . . . et quod vix poterat auditus percipiat visus. Haec tantum columbam volui formando pingere, sed etiam dictando describere, ut per scripturam demonstratem picturam.[3]

At the beginning of his *Bestiaire d'amour,* Richard de Fournival commented in a similar vein on the importance of language and painting.[4]

Latin and French bestiaries until Richard de Fournival's *Bestiaire d'a-mour* always began with the description of the lion, and the lion chapter became one of the longest and most complex in the bestiary. This elaboration of verbal material was matched pictorially by an increase in the number and subjects for the illustration of the lion.[5]

In the Latin *Physiologus,* and later the Old French bestiaries, the lion was said to have three natures or characteristics. It covers its tracks with its tail to escape hunters; it sleeps with its eyes open; and its cubs are born dead and on the third day they are revived by the parents' licking, breathing, or roaring life into them. Thus, the lion was an obvious Christ-figure and also a model of the Christian knightly hero. Later bestiary versions, B-Isidore and Pseudo-Hugh of St. Victor, introduced the notion that lions had three temperaments, indicated by their physical appearance. Timid lions had short bodies and curly manes, fierce lions had longer bodies and straight hair, while the third temperament was not described. Their strength was visible in their chests, firmness in their heads, and courage in their foreheads and tails. They were afraid of hunters, spears, the noise of wheels, fire, and the white cock. Scorpions and snake venom were said to be deadly to lions, and sick lions became healthy by eating monkeys. The Third Family bestiary version introduces the notion that lions mate like humans and that they have five cubs the first year and one fewer each succeeding year. A lion will attack a man if he observes it eating its prey.[6] Philippe de Thaon adds the detail in his *Bestiaire* that a hungry lion treats other animals, especially the ass, ferociously. He also states that the lion uses its tail to draw a circle on the ground from which its prey cannot escape.[7]

Both *La Chevalerie de Judas Macabé* and *Le Roman de Kanor* have considerable lion imagery as well as other bestiary features. Both were produced at the Flemish Court for Gui Dampierre or perhaps another member of his family, several of whom were important patrons of literature and art. The emphasis on lions and lion imagery in *Kanor* and *Judas Macabé* may be explained in part by the fact that the heraldic device of Gui and his son included a lion; these references thus compliment the patron.[8]

Other literary references or works connect the Dampierre court with the two romances. Baudoin de Condé mentions the popularity at this court of *romans d'aventures* and in particular of the *Sept sages de Rome,* to which *Kanor* is a sequel.[9] A version of the *Roman de Kanor* is dedicated in 1292 to Gui's son-in-law, Hugh II of Châtillon, Count of St. Pol.[10] Moreover, several manuscripts containing bestiaries or the *Bestiaire d'amour* also include works known to have associations with this court, either during

Gui's lifetime or those of his mother and aunt.[11] The quarrels of the Dampierre and Avesnes families, in which Gui took part, were recreated in plots about fictitious emperors of Rome and Constantinople, and satirized in the beast-fable, *Le Couronnement Renart*. Interest in the Maccabees is shown by the commissioning of the first translation of the first book of Maccabees into French and the introduction of these heroes into romances composed for the court.[12]

When it is used in other genres, bestiary material may either be quoted directly or alluded to indirectly. These two principal ways of using bestiary material are represented in the two romances to be examined here.

The anonymous version of *La Chevalerie de Judas Macabé* exemplifies the use of direct visual and verbal quotation from the bestiary tradition. It exists in a unique manuscript dated 1285 and dedicated to a "seigneur Guillaume," who is thought to have been the eldest son of Gui Dampierre. The manuscript is in the hands of two scribes and is illustrated by 128 miniatures and several historiated initials, six of which illustrate animals in the bestiary tradition. In the romance, the narrative of Judas Maccabee and his brothers becomes medieval propaganda advocating the renewal of crusading efforts in the Holy Land. Incorporated into the fabric of the narrative are selections from the bestiary for the lion, antelope, elephant, wild boar, domestic pig, and ass, which are explicated in terms of the story of the Maccabees.[13]

The lion in *Macabé* is said to have five natures which are also applied by the narrator to the psychology and actions of Judas Maccabee, illustrating the medieval belief that states of mind are externalized in physical acts. The lion section in the romance is introduced by the sage of the Syrian prince Seron who tells him:

> . . . tu Judas as comparé
> Au lion, s'as bien asené,
> Car lions est il, bien le sai,
> En maniere ke te dirai.[14]

The general characteristics of the lion, designated king of beasts by God, are then enumerated. He is gentle, noble, courtly, worthy, brave, cruel, wise, strong, subtle, and confident. These anthropomorphisms are next applied to the human hero Judas, and the five natures of the lion, drawn from the bestiary tradition, are interpreted in terms of the personality of Judas. They are: (1) the lion is not easily provoked, but when he is, he is relentless in devouring his enemy; (2) lion cubs are born shapeless and are given form by the licking of their parent who revivifies them by roaring (the application to Judas concerns his noble parentage and his metaphorical "shaping" by the tongue of his father Matathias); (3) the lion is singleminded once he has made a decision; (4) the lion does not like to be looked at by a man while he is eating his prey and will attack the man (the application to Judas concerns reactions to his victories and criticism which he will not allow); and (5) the lion covers his tracks with his tail when chased by hunters (when Judas makes a mistake, he corrects it). It will be seen at once that bestiary material has been selected to conform to the need to describe the qualities of a military and political leader in stressful times. Strength, even harshness, and pragmatism are emphasized. The lion's other traits of sickness, indigestion, and insomnia are not even hinted at.

One isolated miniature in *Macabé* (Fig. 8.1) has the lion as its subject (fol. 10) and a series of five miniatures (Figs. 8.2–8.6) illustrate the lion passage discussed above (fols. 19a–21d). In this first miniature a lion watches a group of humans from a distance. In the series a lion and a lioness mate (Fig. 8.2), a lion and lioness form their cubs by licking a lump of flesh into their own likeness (Fig. 8.3), a lion attacks a bull (Fig. 8.4), a lion turns a man upside down in order to look him "ens el viaire" (Fig. 8.5), and a lion attacks an ass (?) (Fig. 8.6). These scenes have nothing to do with the literal story of the Maccabees, but the interpolated bestiary illustrations and bestiary texts together provide a symbolic elaboration on the main narrative.

Though it is somewhat difficult to identify the specific bestiary source or sources for this romance, there are many similarities between the lion material in *Macabé* and French bestiary sources such as the bestiary of Pierre de Beauvais or Philippe de Thaon, who is the source for certain details such as the lion devouring the man who watches him eat his prey. Jean-Robert Smeets, the editor of *Macabé*, suggested Vincent de Beauvais' *Speculum naturale* or Pierre de Beauvais as sources.[15] The two illustrated manuscripts of Philippe de Thaon, Oxford, Merton College MS 249, and Copenhagen, Royal Library MS 3466, have seven drawings of the lion, which include the scenes of the lion attacking an ass, standing over a man (or animal), covering its tracks with its tail, and standing by a dead cub, all of which are illustrated in *Macabé*.[16] However, the only extant illustrated bestiary text which includes all the less usual features included in *Macabé*— the lion attacking a bull, lions mating, and the lion mauling an ass—is the

manuscript of Richard de Fournival's *Bestiaire d'amour* in Paris, Bibliothèque Ste. Geneviève, MS 2200. These distinctive miniatures form the
subject of another more extended study, and I will not deal further with
them here.

The use of the bestiary material by the author of *Macabé* is similar to
that of Richard de Fournival. Each preserves the text of the bestiary description of the animal but substitutes a moral drawn from secular society,
though the feudal crusading culture described in *Macabé* is markedly less
sentimental than the courtly society of the *Bestiaire d'amour*.

A second use of bestiary material is the allusion or echo, often without
any direct quotation of bestiary words or pictures. The bestiary associations are used to enrich the polysemy of the narrative. This type of association may account for certain juxtapositions of texts in manuscripts, or even
interpolations or otherwise not obviously associated texts one within another, such as the insertion of some 6,200 lines of Chrétien de Troyes'
*Yvain*, with its prominent lion episodes, into an incomplete text of Gautier
de Belleperche's version of *La Chevalerie de Judas Machabée* in Princeton
University Library, Garrett MS 125.[17] In these works bestiary material is
not extensively, or even necessarily, quoted, but references to an animal's
features such as the lion and his tail or his ferocity and nobility, could
stimulate bestiary associations for the audience familiar with their use in a
bestiary context and thus provide a subtext to the work. Another complex
and sophisticated example of bestiary allusion is the fourteenth-century
*Dit dou lyon* by Guillaume Machaut.[18] In the *Dit* the lion is the protagonist,
the lover of a courtly lady. Machaut uses the bestiary associations of the
lion as king of beasts, noblest of all animals, an ideal monarch, and a symbol of trust, and he suggests that these are also the attributes of the ideal
lover, animal or human.[19]

The second use of bestiary material, that of allusion or association, is
demonstrated in the *Roman de Kanor*. In fact, *Kanor* functions as a *summa*
of lion imagery in medieval literature, encompassing topoi from classical,
biblical, courtly, and popular sources. Into the interwoven plots of this
complex work, the author incorporated allusions to the motifs of Daniel in
the lion's den.[20] Judas Maccabee "who roared like a lion,"[21] the lion as
companion of the saint and the hero whom it mourns,[22] the lion as holy
messenger,[23] the lion as guardian,[24] the beast-fable lion who acts like a
courtly hero,[25] the fiercely attacking lion,[26] and the hunter lion.[27] The figure of the lion also appears as an allegorical symbol of courage and king-
ship as well as of vice and violence. It appears in two allegorical dreams in

the text and is used by several characters as a general image of menace, viciousness, and evil.[28] There are a number of allusions to bestiary lore, such as the belief that a lion will attack a man if the man looks at it. Besides the bestiary, other possible literary sources for lion imagery in *Kanor* include Chrétien's *Yvain*, Ovid, *Androcles,* and *Renart*. Nevertheless, bestiary associations or echoes underlie each lion episode in *Kanor*.

The lion character in *Kanor* was first introduced in earlier romances in the *Sept sages de Rome* cycle as a companion sent from God to protect the hermit-emperor Cassidorus and his family.[29] The lion avenges Cassidorus's death and afterward continues to serve his quadruplet infant sons (Kanor and his three brothers). It carries off the infants and protects their mother while providing food for her and the holy hermit, Dieudonné, with whom she stays. This lion is reminiscent of both the lion which carried off the children of St. Eustachius and the companion of saints Jerome, Nicolas of Lycia, Anthony, and Mary the Egyptian.

Another example of lion-related iconography in *Kanor* can be shown to have been associated with the bestiary subject in thirteenth-century bestiary texts. In an illustration in Cambridge, Fitzwilliam Museum MS 254, fol. 15, an episode from the Androcles story, called Andronicus in the text, is illustrated by the lion licking a man tied to a stake.[30] The incorporation of the Androcles material in this thirteenth-century bestiary shows the close association of this text with the bestiary subject, an association which could also have influenced the *Kanor* author. Moreover, the Androcles bestiary version may be the inspiration for the *Kanor* lion with no need to postulate another version of the classical narrative.

An obvious literary antecedent of the lion in *Kanor* is the lion companion in Chrétien de Troyes' *Yvain*. As in *Yvain,* the lion in *Kanor* functions as the knight's companion and, beast-fable-like, as a courtly hero. The author even postulates dialogue for it: "conme se il vaustist dire. . . ."[31] The lion's courtliness, restraint, and humility are emphasized. It seeks out the empress, widow of its former master Cassidorus, at court in order to bring her to her sons at the hermit's cave. It refuses the offer of beastly food (raw mutton), and bows to the empress when it enters the hall. It is also a source of humor when it strokes the empress gently with its tail in order to persuade her to follow it in search of her sons.

The hermit Dieudonné, the serving-girl Nicole, and the lion bring up the quadruplets in a cave on a mountain in the middle of a dense forest. When the boys are seven years old, they wander farther than usual into the forest, and, in a scene which the author explicitly compares with a similar

Perceval episode, they meet knights who are hunting a white stag.[32] The boys are thrilled by the knights, horses, and dogs, the first that they have ever seen. The knights, in their turn, are amazed and delighted by the beautiful, intelligent children dressed in wild animal skins, and ask to be taken to meet the hermit, their guardian. The knights are driven off, however, by the return of the lion. The boys then go back to the hermitage where the lion saves their pet stag from the hunters' hounds, killing several and badly frightening their handlers.

In this episode, the naive boys use the term "lion" to refer to any animal except the stag. The lion hunts "other lions" and brings them back as food for Nicole, though the author elsewhere calls the meat *venoison*. The hunting dogs are "little lions," which the boys prefer to their "ordinary" lion. In fact, they treat the real lion like a dog, pulling its mane and ears, and the King of Hungary later remarks that the lion behaves with them like any *levrier*, a reversal of the proverb that "every dog is a lion at home." The author uses the contrast between the adults' and the children's reactions to the lion to create humor at the knights' expense, while emphasizing the boys' child-like egocentricity and lack of experience. The bestiary iconography of the lion as hunter and hunted is illustrated in a number of bestiary manuscripts.[33] The lion as hero and guardian in these episodes seems closely linked to the bestiary as well as the beast-fable tradition of the *Roman de Renart*.

Another use of lion imagery in *Kanor* is in dream allegory. Here the lion functions neither as a real beast nor as a character in the narrative, but rather as a symbol. The Empress Nera, widow of the Emperor Helcanus, has just given birth to a son. Her jealous sister, the Queen of Aragon, manages to have a low-born baby substituted for the royal heir. The empress, suspecting from the baby's changed manner that something is wrong, dreams that after her baby is born she holds a lion in her arms. Later, the lion is changed to a malicious wolf. The lion in the dream symbolizes the bold, noble child she gave birth to, and the wolf the low-born changeling. The dream thus allegorizes her subconscious fears and premonitions. This allegorization and moralization is, of course, typical of the bestiary procedure.

In each of these episodes the author includes material whose allusions to the bestiary descriptions of the lion must have been easily recognizable to a contemporary audience—the lion's use of its tail to cover its tracks, its fierceness, bravery, and nobility.

My discussion of the romances of *La Chevalerie de Judas Macabé* and *Le*

*Roman de Kanor* has focused on verbal lion imagery to demonstrate quotation of and allusion to bestiary material in another medieval genre. These examples furnish only a few instances of the lively interaction of genres within a single court and constitute only the preliminary step in an attempt to document precisely the importance of the bestiary as a source of material for the medieval romance and for other genres as well.

## Notes

1. My interest in bestiary material, and this essay in particular, are due in large part to Florence McCulloch, as a result of both her published research, including her fundamental study, *Mediaeval French and Latin Bestiaries*, rev. ed. (Chapel Hill: University of North Carolina Press, 1962), and her gracious generosity in private communications. Like the bestiary lion, she gently but firmly shaped inchoate scholars who came within the circle of her influence.

2. *La Chevalerie de Judas Macabé,* ed. Jean-Robert Smeets (Assen: Van Gorcum, 1955), and *Le Roman de Kanor,* ed. Meradith T. McMunn, in *"Le Roman de Kanor:* Edition critique d'un texte en prose du xiii<sup>e</sup> siècle," diss., University of Connecticut, 1978. The anonymous *La Chevalerie de Judas Macabé* exists in a unique copy, Paris, Bibl. Nat. fr. 15104. *Kanor* is preserved in four manuscripts: London, Brit. Lib. MS Harley 49803; Brussels, Bibl. Roy. MS 9245; Paris, Bibl. Nat. fr. 93; and Paris, Bibl. Nat. fr. 22550; an abridged version exists in Paris, Bibl. Nat. fr. 1446.

3. Prologue I, Migne, *Patrologia latina,* 177, 14. "I have decided to paint the dove with silver wings and a back of pale gold, and by a picture enlighten the minds of the simple folk—I wish not only to paint the dove by modeling it, but also to outline it by words, so that through writing I may set forth a picture." I am indebted to Professor Willene B. Clark for this reference.

4. *Li Bestiaires d'amours di maistre Richart de Fornival e li response du bestiaire,* ed. Cesare Segre (Milan and Naples: Riccardo Ricciardi, 1957), pp. 3–4. "Toutes gens desirent par nature a savoir. . . . Et pour chu Diex, ki tant aime l'omme qu'il le velt porveoir de quant ke mestiers lui est, a donne a homme une vertu de force d'ame ki a non memoire. Ceste memoire si a .ij. portes, veir et oir, et a cascune de ces .ij. portes si a un cemin par ou on i puet aler, che sont painture et parole. Painture sert a l'oel et parole a l'oreille." Professor Beryl Rowland discusses this passage in relation to the art of memory in her essay in this volume.

5. The following discussion is greatly indebted to the summary of lion bestiary material in Florence McCulloch's *Mediaeval Latin and French Bestiaries,* pp. 137–140.

6. McCulloch, p. 138.

7. McCulloch, pp. 138–139. A thirteenth-century illustration of the scene with the ass occurs in Oxford, Merton College MS 249, fol. 1<sup>v</sup>; the lion is depicted making a circle with its tail to enclose other animals in Paris, Bibl. Nat. fr. 1941, fol. 31<sup>v</sup>.

8. M. Alison Stones, "Secular Manuscript Illumination in France," *Medieval*

*Manuscripts and Textual Criticism,* ed. Christopher Kleinhenz (Chapel Hill: University of North Carolina Press, 1976), p. 87.

9. Mary D. Stanger, "Literary Patronage at the Medieval Court of Flanders," *French Studies,* 11 (1957), 224.

10. Joseph Palermo, "A la recherche du 'seigneur devant nomme' du roman de *Kanor,*" *Romance Philology,* 12 (1959), 243–251.

11. For example, Paris, Bibliothèque de l'Arsenal MS 3516, contains a bestiary of Pierre de Beauvais, Gautier de Belle-Perche's *Livre Machabeus,* and the *Roman des sept sages de Rome.*

12. Stanger, pp. 220, 224.

13. Smeets, p. xi. See also Jean Bonnard, *Les traductions de la Bible en vers français au moyen âge* (Paris: Imprimerie Nationale, 1884), pp. 177–180.

14. *Macabé,* ed. Smeets, p. 61, ll. 2100–2103.

15. *Macabé,* ed. Smeets, pp. xlvii–xlix.

16. McCulloch, pp. 138–139.

17. Robert L. McGrath, "A Newly Discovered Illustrated Manuscript of Chrétien de Troyes' *Yvain* and *Lancelot* in the Princeton University Library," *Speculum,* 38 (1963), 583–594, discusses this text and illustrations. It is not the same work as the anonymous *Macabé* which I discuss here as an example of quotation of bestiary material.

18. *Oeuvres de Guillaume de Machaut,* ed. Ernest Hoepffner, 3 vols. (Paris: Société des Anciens Textes Français, 1908–1921), vol. 2, pp. 159–237.

19. For further discussion of the lion and narrator in the *Dit dou lyon,* see William Calin, *A Poet at the Fountain: Essays on the Narrative Verse of Guillaume de Machaut* (Lexington: University of Kentucky Press, 1974), pp. 75–91.

20. *Kanor,* ed. McMunn, p. 8, l. 240: "Ha! Souverains Sauvierres, qui sauvastes Danyel en la fosse au lion," and p. 10, ll. 309–312: "Vrais Deux, . . . qui sauvas Jonas ou ventre de la balainne et Daniel en la fosse au lyon."

21. *Kanor,* ed. McMunn, p. 26, ll. 829–830: "conment il rungoit aussi conme le lyon qui sa proie chace."

22. *Kanor,* ed. McMunn, p. 4, ll. 103–110: "Dont il avint a l'endemain que le lyon vint el chastel aussi humblement conme se il fust prive, et dont il finent voie les uns et les autres tant que il vint en l'eglisse de Saint Nicholas . . . si vint droit sus la tombe a l'empereeur et conmença ilec a gemir et a plaindre," and p. 148, ll. 4765–4766.

23. *Kanor,* ed. McMunn, pp. 8–9, ll. 247–250: "selonc le glorieus miracle que Nostre Sire me moustre ci entroit de ces nobles enfans, que je voi que ceste beste mue m'a ci aporté a l'avoiement de Nostre Seingneur."

24. *Kanor,* ed. McMunn, p. 135, ll. 4344–4347. This is a typical episode in which the lion protects the boys upon the arrival of strangers in the forest.

25. *Kanor,* ed. McMunn, p. 16, ll. 491–496.

26. *Kanor,* ed. McMunn, p. 3, ll. 70–76; the lion attacks the wicked châtelaine and later it attacks her accomplice who plotted to kill Emperor Cassidorus.

27. *Kanor,* ed. McMunn, p. 128, ll. 4121–4126.

28. *Kanor,* ed. McMunn, p. 101, ll. 3253–3264: the prophetic dream of the canon about the woman "qui aportoit .i. lyon entre ses bras" of whom the whole city

was afraid. This refers to the future emperor. The second prophetic dream is that of the Empress Fastige who dreams that after her son is born her friend the duchess comes and tells her that he has become a lion "le plus fier et le plus orgueilleux du monde."

29. Besides *Kanor* the prose sequels of the *Roman des sept sages de Rome* which include the lion are: *Le Roman de Cassidorus*, 2 vols., ed. Joseph Palermo (Paris: Société des Anciens Textes Français, 1963–1964); *Le Roman de Helcanus*, ed. Henri Niedzielski (Geneva: Librairie Droz, 1966); and *Le Roman de Pelyarmenus*, which has not yet been published. A partial edition of the last was prepared by Lorna Bullwinkle Brodtkorb, "*Le Roman de Pelyarmenus:* A Preliminary Study and Partial Edition of an Unpublished Thirteenth-Century Prose Romance," diss., Yale University, 1965.

30. McCulloch, p. 140.

31. *Kanor,* ed. McMunn, p. 16, ll. 492–493 (fol. 52$^v$).

32. For a fuller discussion of this episode, see Meradith T. McMunn, "Psychological Realism and the Representation of Medieval Children in the *Roman de Kanor*," in *Studies on the Seven Sages and Other Essays in Medieval Literature Dedicated to the Memory of Jean Misrahi,* ed. Henri Niedzielski, Hans R. Runte, and William Hendrickson (Honolulu: Education Research Associates, 1978; reprinted 1984).

33. The lion as hunter appears in Paris, Bibl. Nat. fr. 15213, fol. 66$^v$; the lion is the object of the hunt in Cambridge, Corpus Christi College MS 53, fol. 189.

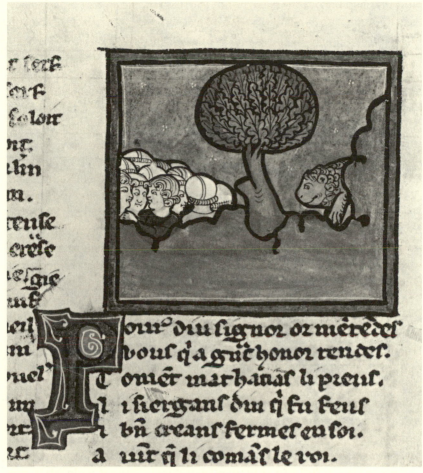

FIGURE 8.1. Lion watches people (Paris, Bibl. Nat. MS fr. 15104, fol. 10). (Photo: Bibl. Nat.)

FIGURE 8.2. Lion and lioness mate (Paris, Bibl. Nat. MS fr. 15104, fol. 19ᵛ). (Photo: Bibl. Nat.)

FIGURE 8.3. Lion and lioness lick shapeless cub into their likeness (Paris, Bibl. Nat. MS fr. 15104, fol. 19ᵛ). (Photo: Bibl. Nat.)

ne lecouuent anoient

esal q̃ mie ne urlent

ace celi entreplusiors

esa foure vil viēt lecourf

es entre celef leur predie

de cou ne nest mic aapredie

raus fire rois tout autretes

di de iudas machabes

este nature de lyon .

FIGURE 8.4. Lion attacks a bull (Paris, Bibl. Nat. MS fr. 15104, fol. 20). (Photo: Bibl. Nat.)

En auват lïu v conseue
L apſtair q̃ nus nereqиite
ſ us hom q̃ deconaur q̃ faire
Cꝛ il les garde en mi lems
d econ ⁊ meruelle abaubis
Cꝛ muour a de son uisage

Car a la forme ⁊ a l'image
Est formes de son creatour
h onte a saciez dauoir mor
S icort ſeure p̃ voir celuy

FIGURE 8.5. Lion looks man in the face (Paris, Bibl. Nat. MS fr. 15104, fol. 20^v). (Photo: Bibl. Nat.)

FIGURE 8.6. Lion attacks an ass (Paris, Bibl. Nat. MS fr. 15104, fol. 21). (Photo: Bibl. Nat.)

# Michael J. Curley

## 9. Animal Symbolism in the Prophecies of Merlin

The appearance of Geoffrey of Monmouth's *Historia regum Britanniae (HRB)* c. 1136 aroused considerable attention, much of it unflattering, among Geoffrey's contemporaries. William of Newburg (c. 1198) gibed that Geoffrey acquired the name Arthur because of his role in promoting the fictional British hero of that name to the rank of a historical character.[1] Gerald of Wales seldom passed up the opportunity to take Geoffrey down a peg or two. In his *Journey Through Wales* (1191), Gerald observed that whenever the Welsh prophet Meilyr was harassed by unclean spirits, he would take up St. John's gospel, and thereby compel the demons to flee like so many birds. If Geoffrey's *HRB* were placed in his lap, however, the malevolent spirits would immediately alight on him and linger longer than usual on his book.[2] If Arthur's presence in what pretended to be a serious historical work offended William of Newburg's scholarly standards, Merlin's prophecies in *HRB* VII rankled even more. William claims that Geoffrey spread abroad Merlin's false predictions with even greater boldness (*etiam majori ausu*), since while translating them into Latin, Geoffrey did not hesitate to add many prophecies of his own invention to those of the boy-prophet.[3] Gerald of Wales claimed to have discovered a manuscript of the true Welsh prophecies of the Caledonian Merlin at Nevin on the Llyn Peninsula during his circuit through Wales in the retinue of Archbishop Baldwin in 1188. Unhappily for students of political vaticination, Gerald never lived up to his promise to restore the corrupt text of these predictions to their original purity, and to translate them from their "rude British idiom into the light of the Latin language."[4]

Not all respected scholars during the Middle Ages were predisposed to dismiss Geoffrey's version of the prophecies of Merlin. The Abbot Suger, for one, praised them for truly and eloquently predicting events in Henry I's reign.[5] Not one word, not one iota of what the wild prophet (*agrestis vates*) had uttered about Henry's reign, claimed Suger, varied from the facts.[6] Alan of Lille, Matthew of Paris, Caesar of Heisterbach, and a number of anonymous commentators on Geoffrey's prophecies of Merlin all shared Suger's viewpoint. And as the later history of these sometimes obscure predictions shows, Geoffrey established a vogue for Merlin's prophecies that was to continue unabated down to the sixteenth century and beyond.

Rupert Taylor was the first to characterize as "Galfridian" the kind of political prophecy that represents men and nations as animals.[7] This is perhaps overestimating Geoffrey's influence on the genre, however, since the prophetic books of the Old Testament relied on precisely this kind of symbolism. In Daniel's prophetic vision of the four beasts arising from the sea (Daniel 7), the Babylonians, Medes, Persians, and Greeks were respectively represented by the lion with eagle's wings, the bear, the four-headed winged leopard, and the ten-horned creature with great iron teeth. The successors of Alexander the Great were symbolized in Daniel's vision by the ten horns on the last of these beasts, the one small horn standing specifically for the Seleucid monarch Antiochus Epiphanes. Similarly, the Medo-Persian Empire and the person of Alexander were represented in Daniel's vision by the ram and the he-goat (Daniel 8). Moreover, the dense allegorical imagery of Revelation provided Christians with a familiar cast of apocalyptic *dramatis personae,* some of whom were represented zoomorphically. The anticipated redeemer-king of Revelation 5: 5 was known as the Lion of the Tribe of Judah, an epithet which probably derived from a messianic interpretation of Genesis 49: 9 ("Judah is a Lion's whelp"), while the red dragon of Revelation 12 was explicitly identified in the text as Satan (Revelation 12: 9; cf. also Revelation 17: 3). Again, the tetramorphic figure of Revelation 4: 6–8, as well as its prototype in Ezechiel's vision on the bank of the River Chebar (Ezechiel 1: 4–10), was commonly interpreted during the Middle Ages as a symbol of the Four Evangelists. It is probable that such biblical passages influenced not only Geoffrey, but also Dante in composing the *veltro* prophecy of *Inferno* I: 100–105.[8]

If Daniel and Revelation provided Geoffrey with convenient models of prophetic rhetoric in which men and nations were represented as animals, Virgil's *Aeneid* supplied him with a model of prophecy's function in a historical work. Like the oracular sixth book of the *Aeneid,* book VII of the *HRB* stands apart from the main narrative both formally and substantively as a kind of meditation on history itself. Just as *Aeneid* VI marks a critical juncture in the turbulent fate of the wandering Trojans, providing them with a galvanizing vision of the glorious civilizing mission that awaits their progeny, so, too, *HRB* VII proclaims that the sovereignty of the island will once again be returned to the descendants of Brutus. Moreover, Aeneas's *kataplus,* with all the conventional apparatus of the classical underworld journey, occurs at the center of the poem and signals an end to the hero's wandering and a beginning to his foundation mission in Italy. Similarly, *HRB* VII is placed at the center of Geoffrey's work to mark the end of Vortigern's notorious reign and to announce the rebirth of British hopes in the coming of Arthur, the new Brutus.

Whether we look beyond Geoffrey's refashioning of Nennius's story of the boy-prophet's confrontation with the wicked king to Daniel's conflict with Nebuchadnezzar, or to similar Celtic legends such as the Welsh *Hanes Taliesin,* the *HRB* VII, as Geoffrey himself admits, interrupts the main narrative line, and draws attention to itself as a passage of special importance. Geoffrey learned from Virgil how to heighten the gravity of his historical matter by projecting its scope through the use of prophecy far beyond the temporal framework of the history, down to and even beyond the audience's own period. While animal symbolism, of course, played no part in Virgil's oracular book, its presence in biblical prophecy lent an air of authority and seriousness to Merlin's utterances.

Geoffrey himself claimed only to have translated the prophecies from their original "British" language at the urging of Alexander, Bishop of Lincoln. In his prefatory letter to Alexander, Geoffrey states that he reluctantly left off writing his history and turned to Merlin's prophecies because they had recently begun to arouse a flurry of interest among his contemporaries, and he found himself beseeched from many quarters to publish (*edere*) them.[9] Whether this was simply another of Geoffrey's private jokes, arising from the fact that he himself had previously circulated *HRB* VII as a pamphlet which was the cause of so much public attention, need not concern us here. While his parallel claim that the rest of his history too was simply a translation from "a certain very ancient book written in the British language" has met with understandable skepticism over the centuries, there is less room to doubt that he availed himself of the Welsh Myrddin poems when compiling the *HRB* VII, the book of Merlin's prophecies. Political prophecies attributed to Myrddin are known to have circulated in Welsh as early as the mid-tenth century and appear to have had a particular vogue during the bitter resistance in Wales to Norman incursions in the mid-twelfth century.[10] Merlin's prediction that an alliance between Cadwaladr and Cynan would result in a return of the island of Britain to its exiled Celtic inhabitants is closely paralleled in the Welsh *Armes Prydein* (*The Prophecy of Britain*, c. 930), the earliest work in which Myrddin clearly appears as a prophetic authority.[11]

Yet it would be untrue to claim that Welsh predictive poetry relies very heavily on the kind of animal symbolism found in the *HRB* VII. Admittedly, in the *Armes Prydein* Cynan and Cadwaladr are called *deu arth* ("two bears"),[12] and the Welsh host battling against the Saxons is said to be *mal arth o vynyd* ("like a bear from the mountain").[13] But the only other example of animal symbolism to be found in the surviving Welsh Myrddin prophecies occurs in the *Oianau* ("Little Pig") where Myrddin foretells that "two whelps of the line of Rhys" (*dev kenev . . . o hil Ris*) will rout the English at a place called Cymerau in the vicinity of Carmarthen.[14] These animal epithets, however, probably found their way into Welsh prophecy from Welsh heroic poetry where they are fairly common;[15] in themselves they could scarcely have suggested to Geoffrey the rather extensive use of animal symbolism as it is found in *HRB* VII. It is always possible, of course, that such symbolism regularly figured in twelfth-century Myrddin predictions known to Geoffrey but subsequently lost. For example, Gruffydd ap Cynan's anonymous biographer cites the following otherwise unattested Old Welsh englyn-prophecy to show that Gruffydd's illustrious career was foreseen by Myrddin:

> Llyminauc lletfer a daroganer,
>   Anaeth diarvor dygosel.
> Llegrur y enw, llycraut llawer.

The biographer also gives the Latin prophecy: "Saltus ferinus praesagitur; uenturus de mari insidiaturus cuius nomen corruptor, quia multos corrumpet" (A wild leaping one is foreseen who will come from the sea, and lie in ambush. His name will be the destroyer since he will destroy many men).[16] The Old Welsh form of the prophecy indicates that it in all likelihood pre-dated Geoffrey's *HRB* VII and originally applied to a person other than Gruffydd. The term *llyminauc lletfer* ("fierce leaping one"), however, does not have in Welsh the animal associations of the odd Latin translation "*saltus ferinus.*" Yet aside from the fact that the *saltus ferinus* may not be an animal epithet at all, there is the further problem that this passage may date from as late as 1171, and, therefore, might possibly have been influenced by the imagery of *HRB* VII.

In addition to the Myrddin poems, it is quite possible that Geoffrey knew the Welsh pedigrees closely related to those found in Harleian MS 3859 and elsewhere. It is not widely known, however, that these genealogies preserve not only the names and descent of famous men, but also their traditional epithets, and that among these there are a number of animal appellations. In the pedigrees published by P. C. Bartrum, the following persons with their animal epithets can be found: Rhirid *Blaidd* ("Wolf"), Cillin *Y Blaidd Rhudd* ("The Red Wolf"), Cynwal *Carnhwch* ("Sow's Foot"), Cynan *Y Cwn* ("Of the Dogs"), Rhydderch *Eryr* ("Eagle"), Meilir *Eryr Gwyr Gorsedd* ("Eagle of the Men of the Gorsedd"), Anarawd *Gwalch-crwn* ("Sturdy Hawk"), Elgan *Gwefl-hwch* ("Sow's Lip"), Idwal *Iwrch* ("Roe-buck"), Bywyr *Llew* ("Lion"), Selyf *Sarffgadau* ("Serpent of Battles"), Siwyrder *Sur* ("Sow"), and Brochwel *Ysgithrog* ("Tusked One").[17]

That Geoffrey was aware of the Welsh practice of bestowing epithets on illustrious men can be demonstrated in *HRB* VII, where Merlin foretells that "A king who is blessed [*rex benedictus*] will fit out a navy and will be reckoned the twelfth in the court among the saints." The context in which this prophecy occurs leaves no doubt that it applies to Cadwaladr, son of Cadwallo (Welsh Cadwallon), who in the closing episodes of the *HRB* VII gathers together a fleet during his exile in Brittany and prepares to return to Britain. He is dissuaded, however, by an angelic voice which tells him that the time for a return is not yet at hand and commands him to go to Pope Sergius in Rome where he will be "numbered among the blessed." Cadwaladr obeys the angel's command, journeys to Rome where he is confirmed by the pope, and later dies of the plague: "He was then attacked by a sudden illness and in the six hundred and eighty-ninth year after Our Lord's Incarnation, or the twelfth day of the Kalends of May, he was released from the corruption of the flesh and so entered the hall of the Kingdom of Heaven."[18] As is well known, Geoffrey is here confusing the Welsh Cadwaladr with the West Saxon King Caedwalla, who died a pilgrim in Rome in 689. Nevertheless, both Cadwaladr and his more illustrious father Cadwallon were known to the Welsh as "the blessed" (*Vendigeit*), and Cadwaladr is so named in numerous Welsh genealogies.[19] It does not seem too daring to propose, therefore, that among the sources that may have suggested to Geoffrey the use of animals to represent men in the prophecies of Merlin, were the animal epithets which he may have found in the Welsh pedigrees. Thus, his claim that the *HRB* VII was merely a translation from a "British" source may contain a half-truth. As we have seen, the alliance of Cadwaladr and Cynan was indeed a theme of the Welsh Myrddin prophecies, and if knowledge of the Welsh genealogies encouraged Geoffrey in his use of animal symbolism in *HRB* VII, they too might legitimately be counted among the "British" sources of that part of his history. Moreover, in order for Geoffrey to have used this kind of material, he need not have had more than a cursory knowledge of Welsh vocabulary, which even the most skeptical scholars are willing to accord him.

Apart from the Bible and various Welsh sources, Gildas's excoriating indictment of the five British tyrants probably also served as a model for the animal symbolism of the *HRB* VII. Gildas's own reliance on such symbolism was part of his attempt to rival the hortatory style of the Old Testament prophets, as he called back his wayward contemporaries to the path of righteousness. Constantine was a "tyrant whelp of the filthy lioness of Dumnonia," Aurelius Caninus was a "lion-whelp," and Vortipor was "like a leopard . . . spotted with wickedness." He taunts Cuneglas, (whose name means "gray wolf" or "gray hound") with the derogatory epithet *lanio fulve,* "tawny butcher," and calls him a "bear who had been rolling in the filth of his wickedness since youth."[20] This metaphor appears to have arisen from Cuneglas's control of "the Bear's Stronghold," possibly to be identified with Dinarth (= Welsh *din* "fortress" and *arth* "bear"), a fortress located near the town of Llandudno in North Wales.[21] Gildas's most bitter reproach, however, was reserved for the great Welsh leader Maelgwn (= "Hound-Prince") Gwynedd, whom he branded the "dragon of the island" (*insularis draco*), perhaps referring to Maelgwn's traditional base of power in Aberffraw on the island of Anglesey.[22] In accepting the religious habit, Gildas states, Maelgwn seemed to escape the nets that entrap "fat bulls" like him. Having been a raven, he became a dove and avoided the talons of the swift hawk. Yet the wolf turned lamb was snatched from the fold by the cunning wolf. Finally, like an uncontrollable foal who could resist no novelty, Maelgwn renounced the religious life and was swept away over the wide fields of crime.[23]

Taken in its context along with Gildas's other animal epithets, *insularis draco* could be interpreted only as a term of reproach probably intended to associate Maelgwn with the dragon of Revelation 12. For Welsh readers of Gildas, however, this term may have appeared doubly sardonic. First, it suggested that Maelgwn's authority did not extend over all of North Wales (Gwynedd), but only over the isle of Anglesey. And perhaps more important, it contained a play on the literary use of the Welsh *draig* "dragon," meaning "war leader," as in the name Uthyr Bendragon, that is, Uthyr "Foremost Leader" or "Chief of Warriors." Given the heroic associations of the term *draig* in Welsh, Gildas's Latin epithet *insularis draco* reflected his view that Maelgwn had perverted his true calling as a leader of his people (*draig*) to become their enemy (*draco*).

Another possible source of Geoffrey's extended animal imagery in the Merlin prophecies may be Nennius's story of the battle between the red and white dragons in chapter 42 of the *Historia Brittonum*. In Nennius, the boy-prophet Embreis Guletic (Ambrose the Overlord) interprets the conflict of the dragons, which he alternately calls *vermes* and *dracones,* to signify that the newly arrived conquerors (the white dragon) would occupy the island almost from sea to sea, but would ultimately be routed by the native Britons (the red dragon). As for Vortigern, continues Embreis, he will never be able to build on the site of the dragon pool near Snowdon, but must flee over many provinces before finding a suitable location for his stronghold. Vortigern heeds Embreis's advice, grants the lad control over Snowdon along with the kingdoms of the western part of Britain, and flees with his retinue of wizards and soldiers to the north where he builds a city called Caer Gwrtheyrn.[24] If Geoffrey borrowed this story from Nennius, he changed the boy-prophet's name to Merlin, and appended Merlin's elaborate sequence of prophecies as an extension to the interpretative prophecy based on the battle between the red and white dragon.

As with the animal imagery in the main body of Merlin's prophecies in *HRB* VII, the prophecy of the dragons probably arose as an amalgamation of various traditions. How long before Nennius (ninth century) the story took its present form is impossible to say; however, in the *Historia Brittonum* it forms a subplot to the larger anti-Vortigern framework of the visitation of St. Germanus to the shores of Britain. Taken together, Vortigern's two conflicts with Germanus and Embreis Guletic form a single unit demonstrating the British king's spiritual and political vacuity. Nennius, and later Geoffrey, probably also intended the battle of the dragon to be a reflection of the story of Aaron's rod in Exodus 7. In the biblical story, God instructs Moses and Aaron, the prophet, to confront Pharaoh and demand that the people of Israel be set free from their bondage:

> So Moses and Aaron went to Pharaoh and did as the Lord commanded; Aaron cast down his rod before Pharaoh and his servants, and it became a serpent. Then Pharaoh summoned the wise men and the sorcerers, and they also, the magicians of Egypt, did the same by their secret arts. For every man cast down his rod, and they became serpents. But Aaron's rod swallowed up their rods. Still Pharaoh's heart was hardened, and he would not listen to them; as the Lord had said. (Exodus 7: 10–13)

In both Nennius and Exodus 7, the confrontation between the prophet and the wizards takes place before a king whose heart has been hardened against the Lord. In addition to his political misdeeds, Vortigern had married Hengest's sister, the pagan princess whom Geoffrey named Renwein, and had conceived a child by incest with his own daughter. Responsibility for the captivity of the Lord's chosen people (the British) is his alone. In both narratives, the prophet bests the king's wizards as dramatic proof of the king's loss of favor with God, and as a warning of the inevitable consequences of incurring his wrath. There is also a prophetic foreshadowing in Exodus 7 of the liberation of a people held in unjust servitude when Aaron's rod swallows the rods of the wizards. Pharaoh and Egypt were punished with ten plagues; Vortigern is burned to death in his tower with his retinue, and then swallowed up by the earth. Perhaps as Aaron's confrontation with Pharaoh is but one incident in the greater contest between Moses and Pharaoh, so the boy-prophet's conflict with Vortigern in Nennius reflects the larger conflict between St. Germanus and the king. The story of the red and white dragon appears, at least, to have reminded the author of the Middle-Welsh prose tale *Cyfranc Lludd a Llefelys* (early thirteenth century) of Exodus 7, for he called the place where the dragons were buried *Dinas Ffaraon Dande,* that is to say, "fortress of the fiery Pharaoh," or perhaps "fiery fortress of the Pharaoh."[25]

Yet while the *vermes* and *dracones* of Nennius and Geoffrey clearly are symbols of the British and Saxon races, the *colubri* of Exodus 7 represent not so much the Jewish and Egyptian peoples per se, but rather divine as opposed to earthly power, God's authority as opposed to man's. The dragon, however, may well have been known in post-Roman Britain as a more concrete symbol of the British people. The dragon pennant appears to have been introduced into the Roman army sometime during the second century A.D. where it is represented on Trajan's column. Whether it originated in Scythia, as Arrian states,[26] or came in with Sarmatians enrolled in Roman cavalry units, as Graham Webster maintains,[27] need not concern us here. By the fourth century, the dragon standard was a common device in the Roman legions. Vegetius (fourth century A.D.) says that one was carried by each cohort, and that the bearer was known as the *draconarius,* though he implies that this was a new title in his day.[28] The dragon *signum* figured in a number of fourth-century depictions of imperial *adventus* ceremonies, suggesting that it may have had some association by that time with the person of the emperor. The Arch of Constantine, for example, shows the dragon standard being carried aloft in front of the imperial chariot during Constantine's entry into Rome in A.D. 312.[29] Similarly, Ammianus records its colorful presence in Constantius's *adventus* into Rome in A.D. 357:

And behind the manifold others that preceded him he was surrounded by dragons, woven out of purple thread and bound to the golden and jewelled tops of spears, with wide mouths open to the breeze and hence hissing as if roused by anger, and leaving their tails winding in the wind.[30]

Arrian also stresses the striking impression made by the vividly colored bits of cloth of which the dragon standard was constructed, and by its life-like quality as it cavorted and hissed in the wind like a snake.[31]

In his description of Julianus Caesar's campaign against the Alamanni in A.D. 357, Ammianus explicitly identifies the dragon as an imperial *sig-num*. Having learned that his cavalrymen were in retreat, Ammianus states, Julianus set out for the battlefield to meet them. Their retreat was brought to an abrupt halt when they were struck with awe upon recognizing the emperor by his "purple ensign of a dragon fitted to the top of a very long lance as though spreading out the slough of old age." The emperor skill-fully exhorted them to return to battle and to share in the glory of the approaching victory. This they agreed to do, we are told, and the fortunes of battle soon turned their way.[32] In describing the impression that Julia-nus's standard made on his troops, Ammianus alludes to the well-known habit of the snake's periodic sloughing of its skin. The transfer of this at-tribute of the snake to the dragon is easily explained since the Latin *draco* can refer to a serpent as well as to the legendary winged reptile. Ancient and medieval authorities on natural history comment on the self-regenerating powers of the snake as exemplified by its shedding. These comments prob-ably account for the animal's being considered sacred to Hippocrates and to Hygeia, the goddess of healing.[33] The sacred symbol of Asclepius, the Greek god of medicine, was also the snake. Given the context of Am-mianus's allusion to the dragon's *exuviae,* and its well established status as a symbol of regeneration for the ancients, it is difficult not to conclude that he was using the dragon standard in this passage, whatever its historical value, as an emblem of renewal, symbolizing the rebirth of military valor that Julianus kindled in his dispirited cavalrymen.

The importance of all this for Nennius's and Geoffrey's story of the red and white dragons is threefold. First, if Vegetius is right in saying that the dragon standard was carried by every Roman cohort and that its bearer even held the special title of *draconarius,* we can reasonably assume that the standard was known in Britain during the fourth century, though admit-tedly corroborating evidence for this assumption is lacking, since the rec-ord of this period of British history is notoriously thin. As we have seen, the brilliant coloration of the fabric of the standard was a feature which strongly impressed Arrian and Ammianus and may suggest the origin of the dragons' colors in Nennius. Second, as a military and imperial emblem, the dragon, as much as the eagle, stood for Roman civilization itself, and upon the departure of the legions, may have been adopted by the Romano-British as a symbol of their Roman character. The fact that Britons in the post-Roman centuries continued to identify with their Roman past is demonstrated by the number of important dark-age British families that traced their ancestry back to Roman officials such as Maximus.[34] In Nennius, Embreis Guletic reveals to Vortigern that his father was "one of the consuls of the Roman people" and identifies the red dragon as "our race" (*gens nostra*).[35] We need not interpret this passage to indicate the presence of a Roman and an anti-Roman faction in sixth-century Britain, but rather that Embreis was reminding Vortigern in this encounter of the dual heritage, Roman *and* British, they had in common, and that he was reproaching him for falling under the sway of the pagan *barbari*. Finally, the regenerative attributes of the dragon/snake made the animal a particularly apt emblem of Romano-British Christianity in the wake of increasingly aggressive Saxon expansion, especially during the fifth and sixth centuries. Like Julianus's disheartened cavalry in the battle against the fierce Alamanni, the red dragon, though temporarily routed, would return one day in accord with his nature, reinvigorated, to claim the final victory.

If my interpretation is correct, the story of the red and white dragons originated as a complex interaction of biblical narrative, animal lore, and Roman military symbolism. Whether Nennius alone was responsible for this amalgamation of traditions or he was merely recording an established legend is impossible to know. Nor are we likely to find incontrovertible evidence to show that the Roman dragon standard was indeed taken over by British leaders in the post-Roman period. But Embreis Guletic's Roman parentage, combined with his identification of the red dragon as "our race," tend to support the theory that the dragon was viewed in Nennius's day as a symbol closely connected with the Roman past. Again, Exodus 7: 10–13 is a fairly close literary analogue to Nennius's account of the confrontation of Embreis and Vortigern, but there are significant differences between the two narratives. An examination of the animal symbolism in Geoffrey's *HRB* VII appears, as we have seen, to demonstrate a similar admixture of scriptural and native sources.

Since no essay in honor of Florence McCulloch would be complete without reference to the bestiary tradition, it seems fitting to point out that Geoffrey's Merlin, like Nennius's Embreis Guletic, was no stranger to animal lore from this popular source. Among Merlin's prophecies, the following concerns the city of Winchester:

> A Hedgehog loaded with apples shall re-build the town and, attracted by the smell of these apples, birds will flock there from many different forests. The Hedgehog shall add a huge palace and then wall it round with six hundred towers. . . . The Hedgehog will hide its apples inside Winchester and will construct hidden passages under the earth.[36]

Whatever historical allusion, if any, stands behind this prophecy, the hedgehog's supposed ability to carry fruit on its quills was well known to ancient and medieval naturalists and was surely not one of Geoffrey's inventions. The creature's behavior is described as follows in *Physiologus:*

> The hedgehog does not quite have the appearance of a ball as he is full of quills. Physiologus said of the hedgehog that he climbs up to the grape on the vine and then throws down the berries (that is, the grapes) on to the ground. Then he rolls himself over on them fastening the fruit of the vine to his quills, and carries it off to his young and discards the plucked stalk.[37]

As far as we know, no citizen of Winchester has ever claimed to be the hedgehog described in Merlin's prophecy. And for good reason. The hedgehog, *Physiologus* informs us, is a type of the devil who lies in wait to scatter our spiritual harvest and leave our souls empty and barren like a tendril without its fruit.

*I would like to thank Professor Brynley F. Roberts of the National Library of Wales, Aberystwyth, for taking the time to read and offer suggestions on an earlier version of this essay.*

## Notes

1. *Historia rerum Anglicarum Willelmi Parvi . . . de Newburgh,* ed. Hans Claude Hamilton (London: Sumptibus Societatis, 1856), 1: 4.
2. Gerald of Wales, *The Journey Through Wales and the Description of Wales,* trans. Lewis Thorpe (Penguin Books: Harmondsworth, 1978), pp. 117–118.
3. *Historia rerum Anglicarum Willelmi Parvi,* 1: 4.
4. *Giraldi Cambrensis opera,* ed. J. S. Brewer, et al., RS 21 (London: Longman and Co., 1861–91), 3: 46.
5. *Oeuvres complètes de Suger,* ed. Albert Lecoy de La Marche (Paris: J. Renouard 1867), pp. 54–57.

6. Ibid., p. 54.

7. Rupert Taylor, *The Political Prophecy in England* (New York: Columbia University Press, 1911), p. 4.

8. Dante Alighieri, *The Divine Comedy: Inferno,* trans. Charles S. Singleton (Princeton: Princeton University Press, 1970), pp. 8–9. "Molti son li animali a cui s'ammoglia, / e più saranno ancora, infin che'l Veltro / verrà, che la farà morir con doglia. / Questi non ciberà terra nè peltro, / ma sapienza, amore e virtute, / e sua nazion sara tra feltro e feltro." (Many are the beasts with which she mates, and there will yet be more, until the Hound shall come who will deal her a painful death. He will not feed on earth or pelf, but on wisdom, love, and virtue, and his birth shall be between felt and felt.)

9. Geoffrey of Monmouth, *The History of the Kings of Britain,* trans. Lewis Thorpe (Penguin Books: Harmondsworth, 1966), p. 170, hereafter cited as *HRB.* For the Latin text, see *The Historia regum Britanniae of Geoffrey of Monmouth,* ed. Acton Griscom (London: Longmans, Green and Co., 1929), p. 383.

10. The best general surveys of the Welsh Myrddin poems and their political content are Margaret Enid Griffiths, *Early Vaticination in Welsh with English Parallels,* ed. T. Gwynn Jones (Cardiff: The University of Wales Press, 1937), and A. O. H. Jarman, "The Welsh Myrddin Poems" in *Arthurian Literature in the Middle Ages: A Collaborative History,* ed. Roger S. Loomis (Oxford: Clarendon Press, 1959), pp. 20–30.

11. *Armes Prydein: The Prophecy of Britain from the Book of Taliesin,* ed. Sir Ifor Williams, trans. Rachel Bromwich (Dublin: The Dublin Institute for Advanced Studies, 1972), esp. ll. 1–16, 28–44, 87–98, 163–170, and 182–185.

12. Ibid., p. 13, l. 170.

13. Ibid., p. 9, l. 113.

14. *Llyfr Du Caerfyrddin gyda Rhagymadrodd, Nodiadau Testunol a Geirfa* (Cardiff: The University of Wales Press, 1982), p. 32.

15. See Kenneth Hurlstone Jackson, *The Gododdin: The Oldest Scottish Poem* (Edinburgh: Edinburgh University Press, 1969), esp. p. 41, for a list of heroic animal epithets. Also, J. Vendryes, *La poésie galloise des xiiᵉ–xiiiᵉ siècles dans ses rapports avec la langue* (Oxford: Clarendon Press, 1930), pp. 12–13.

16. *Historia Gruffud Vab Kenan,* ed. D. Simon Evans (Cardiff: University of Wales Press, 1977), pp. 5 and 57–59.

17. *Early Welsh Genealogical Tracts,* ed. P. C. Bartrum (Cardiff: The University of Wales Press, 1966), esp. pp. 225–228, "Index of Epithets."

18. *HRB,* pp. 283–284.

19. *Early Welsh Genealogical Tracts,* see pp. 36, no. 1; 38, no. 1; 47, no. 22; 50, no. 51; 59, no. 11; 91, no. 28a; 95, no. 1a; 109, no. 28.

20. Gildas, *The Ruin of Britain and Other Works,* ed. and trans. Michael Winterbottom (London: Phillimore and Co., 1978), pp. 29–32 (chs. 28–32); Neil Wright, "A Note on Gildas's '*lanio fulve,*'" *The Bulletin of the Board of Celtic Studies,* 30 (1983), 306–309.

21. *Trioedd Ynys Prydein: The Welsh Triads,* ed. and trans. Rachel Bromwich (Cardiff: The University of Wales Press, 1978), p. 437.

22. Ibid., pp. 437–441.

23. Gildas, *The Ruin of Britain,* pp. 32–36 (chs. 33–36).

24. Nennius, *British History and the Welsh Annals,* ed. and trans. John Morris (London: Phillimore and Co., 1980), pp. 29–31 (chs. 40–42).

25. *Cyfranc Lludd a Llefelys,* ed. Brynley F. Roberts (Dublin: The Dublin Institute for Advanced Studies, 1975), pp. xxxvi–xxxvii, 5: "Sef ffuruf y gelwit y lle hwnnw gwedy hynny Dinas Emreis, a chyn no hynny Dinas Ffaraon Dande."

26. Arrian, *Tactica,* ed. A. G. Roos (Leipzig: B. G. Teubner, 1928), 35, 3.

27. Graham Webster, *The Roman Imperial Army of the First and Second Centuries A.D.* (New York: Barnes and Noble, 1979; 2nd ed.), p. 36.

28. Vegetius, *Epitoma rei militaris,* ed. A. Lang (Leipzig: B. G. Teubner, 1885), 2, 13 and 2, 7.

29. See Sabine G. MacCormack, *Art and Ceremony in Late Antiquity* (Berkeley: The University of California Press, 1981), pl. 13; M. P. Speidel, "The Master of the Dragon Standards and the Golden Torc: An Inscription from Prusias and Prudentius' *Peristephanon,*" *Transactions of the American Philological Association,* 115 (1985), 283–287.

30. Ammianus Marcellinus, *The History,* trans. John C. Rolfe (Cambridge: Harvard University Press, 1963), XVI, 10, 7.

31. Arrian, *Tactica,* ed. Roos, 35, 4–5.

32. Ammianus Marcellinus, *The History,* XVI, 12, 38–39.

33. See Aristotle, *History of the Animals,* trans. A. L. Peck (Cambridge: Harvard University Press, 1965), 5.17.549b, 8.17.600b; Pliny, *Natural History,* trans. H. Rackham (Cambridge: Harvard University Press, 1947–63), 8.41, 59; Aelian, *On the Nature of Animals,* trans. A. F. Scholfield (Cambridge: Harvard University Press, 1958), 9.16, 66.

34. See Bartrum, *Early Welsh Genealogical Tracts,* p. 201 (Macsen Wledig), and Bromwich, *Trioedd Ynys Prydein,* pp. 452–453.

35. Nennius, *British History,* p. 31 (ch. 42). The connection between the Roman dragon standard and Nennius was pointed out by Sir Ifor Williams, *Cyfranc Lludd a Llevelys* (Bangor: Jarvis a Foster, 1922), p. xvii. On its political significance for the Romano-British, see A. W. Wade-Evans, *Nennius's History of the Britons* (London: Society for Promoting Christian Knowledge, 1938), p. 64, and Wade-Evans, "Prolegomena to a Study of Early Welsh History," in *The Historical Basis of Welsh Nationalism,* ed. A. W. Wade-Evans (Cardiff: Plaid Cymru, 1950), pp. 1–41. For the dragon standard in medieval miniatures representing Arthur and Merlin in battle, see Roger Sherman Loomis and Laura Hibbard Loomis, *Arthurian Legends in Medieval Art* (New York: Modern Language Association of America, 1938; repr. 1966), figs. 224, 236.

36. *HRB,* pp. 178–179.

37. *Physiologus,* trans. Michael J. Curley (Austin: University of Texas Press, 1979), pp. 24–25.

# Mary Coker Joslin

## 10. *Notes on Beasts in the* Histoire ancienne jusqu'à César *of Rogier, Châtelain de Lille*

The Old French *Histoire ancienne jusqu'à César,* compiled in the early years of the thirteenth century for Rogier, Châtelain de Lille, the patron mentioned in the unknown author's verse prologue, exhibits an abundance of both fantastic and familiar beasts. Although a complete reading of the Genesis portion of the *Histoire* provides us a comprehensive acquaintance with its biblical beasts, an initial sampling of marvelous creatures described in its unpublished sections, based on stories found in antique romances, reveals this author's breadth of beastly interest. These beasts are not merely natural inhabitants of earth, sea, and air, nor well-known quadrupeds in the service of pastoral people of the biblical Genesis; they include legendary creatures that appeal to the imagination of those curious about the unfamiliar, as was the medieval person of literary taste.[1]

In the *Histoire*'s stories of Thebes, of Aeneas, and of Alexander, legends familiar to contemporary devotees of medieval romances, we encounter semi-human creatures, monsters of Eastern lands, wild beasts who become friends of hearth and chamber, and great war elephants of India. In the author's version of the tale of Thebes, Oedipus confronts a sphinx "mout hisdose e grande e parcrue" (91c) who, though possessing "cors e visage de demoiselle cruel e espoentable" (91b), according to the text, demonstrates a manly posture and bearded visage in the accompanying miniature (fr. 20125). The minotaur, "moitié hom e moitié tors, plus crueus que nulle beste," is quickly passed over by Rogier's historiographer in the section which Paul Meyer calls "Le Minotaure, Les Amazones, Hercule" (*Romania,* 14, 41). However, the story is told in greater detail in the Aeneas section (fols. 158–159).

The beasts of the Alexander story in the *Histoire* are so numerous and varied as to require a special study. Examples include the crested serpent which kills with venom thrown from its mouth (238d); the three-horned *dent-tirant* which, according to Indians of the Region, chases away all serpents and other beasts (239a); mice the size of foxes; and blue owl-like birds who do no harm when allowed to fish in peace (239b, c). Especially interesting is the deadly double-headed beast which threatens Alexander's forces in the *senestre partie* of India (241d). It emerges from marshes full of reeds. This creature seems to be a conflation of two denizens of the Nile described in succession by Isidore (*Etymologiae*, xii.6.19–21). According to the *Histoire ancienne*, its heads are those of the *hypotamien* and the *calcatrix*, its teeth are huge, its back harder than stone. The *Histoire's hypotamien* corresponds to Isidore's *hippopotamus* and Brunetto Latini's *ypotame*. The *calcatrix* of Rogier's history is similar to Isidore's *crocodillus* and Brunetto's *cocodril* which, according to *Li livres dou tresor*, is also called *caucatrix*. Rogier's clerk, however, uses the word *emolue*, which implies a blade sharpened against a haystack, as the instrument incapable of harming his two-headed beast.[2] All three writers remark on the teeth of the *hypotamien*. Isidore and Brunetto compare them to those of a wild boar.[3] Though Rogier's historiographer does not mention the teeth of a boar, the identical heads of the fr. 20125 miniature illustrate such tusks (Fig. 10.1).

There are two particularly appealing domesticated wild animals in Rogier's *Histoire:* the tiger of Thebes and the stag of Laurentia. The compiler of this history embellishes elements found in the *Roman de Thèbes*, with his own description of the wild tiger and with bestiary lore.[4] The tiger, transported from Ethiopia as a cub, is trained by the king Eteocles and his sisters to be a household pet.[5] The author introduces the wild tiger with which he assumes his audience to be unfamiliar: it is beautiful, graceful, and swift; its behavior, though ordinarily cruel, can be transformed into sweetness so that other beasts are attracted by its fragrant breath.[6] The gentle tiger, nourished at the court of Thebes, has no more wrath than a lamb or any other small beast. It is greatly loved in the city, so much that King Eteocles would not sell it for a great sum. It becomes the innocent cause of a fierce combat (112a) when it is killed while investigating the noisy army of Adrastus and Polynices outside the city walls. The illustration in fr. 20215 of the tiger alone against a schematic background was probably influenced by a bestiary illustration (112b; Fig. 10.2).[7]

The original story of the second domesticated beast in the *Histoire ancienne* to be discussed here is found in the *Aeneid*, though a detail in common with the *Roman d'Eneas* reveals that Virgil may not be the only source. A gentle deer owned by Sylvia, daughter of Tyrrhus, is a creature that allows its horns to be interwoven with chaplets of flowers and leaves, and its coat to be combed and smoothed. Patiently bearing lighted candles attached to the branches of its horns, it makes itself useful by illuminating the dinner table.[8] This kind beast dies most pitifully from an arrow wound inflicted by Ascanius while hunting. Its death causes a battle, as did that of the tiger of Thebes, this time between Tyrrhus and the Trojans (162c).

The texts related to two miniatures of fr. 20125 mention elephants used for military purposes: the first is in Alexander's encounter with Porus (234d; Fig. 10.3); the second in Pyrrhus's battle with the Romans (260d). The latter described "li olifans dou regnes d'Inde sor quoi il avoit tors de fust faites faire, grandes assés e merveillables e chevaliers mis par dedens. por assaillir e por defendre." Although the war elephant is in bestiary illustrations, the war-like function of this beast does not figure in bestiary descriptions of the elephant.[9] The miniature on fol. 235[r] (Fig. 10.3) depicts elephants comparable to the one on fol. 8 of the bestiary in British Library MS Harley 4751.[10]

The opening portion of this history, called the Genesis by Paul Meyer, is not dependent on the Vulgate Bible as its principal source. Though unified by the biblical story, the author's account uses more material from the Latin Josephus and Petrus Comestor than from the biblical Genesis story. For his secular material, the compiler depends upon Eusebius's chronological tables, and upon liberal borrowings from Orosius, Isidore, Bede, and others. He puts his own stamp on familiar stories by including legends and bits of advice apparently from his own mental reserve.[11]

Generally, the *Histoire ancienne*'s author treats the Genesis beasts as useful actors in his story, describing their habits rather than their symbolic function: the dove is trustworthy (97: 21–27); the deer is swift (87: 6–9); the serpent is *viseuse* (84: 10–11); the desert beast of the Joseph story is *crueuse* (225: 19–20). Many of the animals of Rogier's Genesis plod along predictably, carrying travelers and their burdens in the migrations of the patriarchs, just as any reader of the biblical Genesis, Josephus, or Petrus Comestor would expect.[12] Nonetheless, there is a medieval ambience as one reads this Genesis, an atmosphere that enriches the author's sources and calls upon his personal information. For example, one senses the clear distinction among the various types of horses referred to by Rogier's cleric. The *destrier* is prominent in the battle between Hercules and the Amazons. The same type of horse, "si trés grant e si trés pesant . . . sans faillance," figures in the Genesis section where the author recounts the battle against Babylon of King Ninus of Assyria, a contemporary of Abraham. The war horses of Ninus were large, but few men rode them, says the *Histoire*, because humans at this time were even larger in proportion.[13] The *palefroi* is the horse of ladies and of the peace mission. Jocasta and her daughters depart on their *palefroi* as peace emissaries from Eteocles to Polynices and Adrastus (fol. 113), though in the *Roman de Thèbes* Jocasta rides a mule (vv. 4105–4106). In the story of Troy, Paris and Antilogus mount "sor lor palefrois" and leave without arms, supposedly to meet Priam and Hecuba in a conference at which their daughter Polixene is proposed to be exchanged for peace terms (140b). The same sort of swift steed is pictured in the pursuit of the eleven brothers by Joseph's emissaries who seek to recover the hidden cup in Benjamin's grain sack. The *Histoire* says, "Si virent venir mout durement de gens a chevau une grande route a desroi, quanqu'il pooient, l'un avant l'autre" (255: 29–31). Here the author dramatizes the words of Josephus, his source, who says simply, "a troop of horsemen encompassed them" (*Antiquities*, II.v.7). The biblical version is sparser still (Genesis 44: 6). In the same episode as the finding of Benjamin's cup, the *somier* plays its role: "aroutee lor bestes qui les grans fais portoient" (255).

Some of the historiographer's most interesting personal contributions are his description of biblical animals in contemporary or personal terms. The creatures of nature may be moralized, but in cultural terms without Christian references such as those found in the bestiaries. The author's source, Petrus Comestor, says the raven that Noah sent out to find dry land settled on the cadaver of a drowned animal and failed in its mission. The *Histoire*'s version does not compare the faithless bird to the backsliding Christian, as does Isidore of Seville, but rather to the unreliable envoy of a distinguished man. Contemporaries of the author refer to this faithless emissary as a "*message corbin*."[14]

The personified beast appears vividly in the Fall of Man story of the *Histoire*. "Cil deables," who originally bore the medieval name Lussiabel, puts himself in the form of a serpent to tempt first Adam and then Eve. He has changed from an angel, "plus bel de toz les autres" to one "d'orrible figure" and finally to "la plus viseuse beste que lors fust fete."[15] That Cain is mistaken for a *beste sauvage* by his blind descendant Lamech and killed by Lamech's arrow is a symbolic transmutation for which Rogier's compiler has called on Petrus Comestor. Moreover, the author changes and embroiders his source's story.[16] The *Histoire ancienne* departs from the Joseph story's source, Josephus, to include Jacob's poetic lament over Joseph's bloodstained coat. This *plainte Jacob* differs from other similar laments, such as that of the six-syllable Joseph story or that found in the Malkaraume Bible, in that Jacob addresses the cruel beast in the second person: "Bestes sauvages, por quoi devoras tu mon fiz Joseph e coment fus tu si crueuse?"[17] (225: 19–20). Thus, Lussiabel assumes an animal form out of jealousy in order to destroy the first couple's happy life. Cain is killed by appearing to be a wild beast to be hunted, while Jacob raises to human status the desert beast, who supposedly destroyed his favorite son, as though to imply that the deed was humanly inspired.

A look at the miniatures of two Crusader copies of the *Histoire ancienne* suggests the illustrators' awareness of the implications of this text for a medieval society. The author describes Joseph being carried through the city upon Pharaoh's command in "son riche car a .iiii. roes sor quoi li rois Pharaons aloit par sa terre." Although this sort of chariot is described also in scenes of impressive military victories (125: 24), the distinction of riding in a cart was equivocal to anyone acquainted with Lancelot's disgrace as told in *Le Chevalier de la Charette*. For a reader turning the pages of the fr. 20125 copy of the *Histoire ancienne,* the depiction of a lone man seated in a cart driven by a small person with a whip in hand, a driver who is looking back at his passenger (Fig. 10.4), may have conjured up Lancelot's humiliation, such as that pictured in Morgan 806 (Fig. 10.5).[18] A curious illustration of Joseph's triumph in the copy of the *Histoire* preserved at Dijon (Bibl. Mun. MS 562) shows Joseph mounted upon a white horse which itself is borne upon a horse-drawn chariot (Fig. 10.6). Could the atelier supervisor at Saint-Jean d'Acre have decided to thus elevate his passenger to the more honorable position of chevalier, while still illustrating the biblical scene?

Rogier's cleric seems particularly interested in the ceremonial significance of animals. His stress upon "le jor de la delivrance Ysaac" is an example. Though the story of the sacrifice of Isaac is largely taken from Josephus (with the Vulgate providing the dramatic direct address of the intervening angel), the compiler takes pains to draw from Petrus Comestor the special tribute to the ram which figures in Isaac's deliverance by providing itself as substitute sacrifice. The author writes:

> Le jor que Ysaac fu ensi par Nostre Segnor rescous e delivrés dient li Juif que ce fu le premerains jors de setembre. E si le claiment e noment "le jor de la delivrance Ysaac" encore. E si en funt mout grant feste e cornent e buisinent en la memoire dou mouton qui ot grans cornes e en la remembrance. (165: 4–9)

The importance of beasts in conveying dignity to a military victory is noticeable in the author's elaboration of the biblical account of Abraham's rescue of Lot, which states only that he returned home with Lot, his goods, his women, and his people (Genesis 14: 16). Rogier's imaginative compiler of history has the conquering Abraham freeing Lot on a brilliant, sunny morning, after collecting a booty of "tentes e chevaus, or e argent, e mainte riche vaisselamente, e chameaus e oriphans e autres bestes dont on ne saureit mie dire le numbre" (144: 20–24).

Medieval vocabulary colors Genesis stories in this history as we would expect. Words derived from the chivalric tradition describe scenes and designate societal rules familiar to the contemporary listener. Though Rebecca, on her way to meet her future husband, Isaac, is mounted on a camel, she and her party "chevaucherent qu'il trespasserent Mesopotanie" (171: 5–6). Phutiphares, who buys Joseph from the Ishmaelite merchants, is not only *seneschaus* and *conestables* of Pharaoh, but also chief of all of his *chevalerie* (230: 5–6). *Chivaliers, dames, puceles, e borgois e marcheant* all attend "une haute sollempnites por veir les jus" and thus leave the lady free to attempt the seduction of Joseph (233: 10–13).

A bit of practical information about animals which is not in the biblical record, but which is found in Petrus Comestor (*Patrologia latina*, 198: 1124), is the ingenious idea of Esau's father-in-law, Anah, to breed mules from mares and asses: "E ce fu cil qui premerains fist les asnes metre e assembler avec les jues por ce que li mulet nasquissent e venissent" (215: 32–34). Animal-breeding stories seem to fascinate this author. After recounting how Jacob determined the color of Laban's and his own new lambs by the use of peeled wands (the details of the story are from Petrus Comestor), the writer assures us of the truth of his information. Different types of sheep could be separated because of the large pastures available at the time (196: 34–197: 1). He further offers proof of the determination of the color of offspring by giving an exemplum of a black baby born to a white couple because of the image of a *more* in their chamber (198: 24–199: 18).

Author and illustrator of thirteenth-century copies of the *Histoire ancienne* seem particularly interested in fantastic animals of the romance tradition, although the beasts in the miniatures of the fr. 20125 copy are not always recognizable in their text descriptions. Most of the creatures of the Genesis section would be familiar to one acquainted with the biblical tradition, as well as to the medieval person, who was so much more dependent on animals for existence than we are today. We notice, however, that Rogier's historiographer takes pains to select for inclusion in his compilation unusual stories about animals that are not found in the scriptural Genesis. A medieval overlay on biblical and secular history is evident in the author's and in the illustrator's treatment of animals. A comparison with

Latin source material reveals that the compiler of this first French prose chronicle has clothed his descriptions of classical and biblical animals with local color and has invested some of the creatures in his stories with his own symbolic content. He allows his beasts a dignity and a liveliness that reflect the interest of the public which this history was intended both to inform and to entertain.

*Notes*

1. For more about the Genesis text as found in Paris, Bibl. Nat., fr. 20125, see my transcription, *The Heard Word* (University of Mississippi: Romance Monographs, 45, 1986). Quotations of the unpublished portions of the *Histoire ancienne* are drawn from this manuscript. Quotations from the Genesis section are noted here by page and line numbers from *The Heard Word*.

   For a description and discussion of unpublished portions of the *Histoire ancienne,* see Paul Meyer, "Les premières compilations français d'histoire ancienne," *Romania,* 14 (1885), 36–75; Brian Woledge, *Bibliographie des romans et nouvelles en prose française antérieure à 1500* (Geneva: Droz, 1954), and D. J. A. Ross, "The History of Macedon in the 'Histoire ancienne jusqa'à César,'" *Classica et Mediaevalia,* 24 (1963), 181–182.

   Some of the earliest surviving copies of this history composed for the court at Lille, including the manuscript quoted in these notes, were probably produced at Acre. See H. Buchthal, *Miniature Painting in the Latin Kingdom of Jerusalem* (Oxford: Clarendon Press, 1957), pp. 66–87, and Jaroslav Folda, *Crusader Miniature Illumination at Saint-Jean d'Acre: 1275–1291* (Princeton: Princeton University Press, 1976), esp. pp. 95–102.

2. Of the two-headed beast, Rogier's cleric says, "ele avoit le dos si dur qu'ele ne cremoit nulle esmolue tant fus trenchans ne afilee, e si avoit .ii. testes, l'une semblant a hypotamien et l'autre a calcatrix. Ambes estoient enarmees de grant denteure" (241d).

   Isidore: "Crocodillus . . . dentium et unguium inmanitate armatum, tantaque cutis duritia ut quamuis fortium ictus lapidum tergo repercutiat." Jacques André, *Isidore de Séville: Etymologiae XII, des animaux* (Paris: ALMS, 1986), p. 193.

   Brunetto: "Dou cocodril c'on apele caucatrix . . . armés de grans dens et de grandes angles; et son quir est si dur k'il ne sentira ja cop de piere." Francis J. Carmody, ed., *Li Livres dou tresor de Brunetto Latini* (Berkeley: University of California Press, 1948), p. 128.

3. Fr. 20125 (241d); André, p. 195; Carmody, p. 131.

4. *Le Roman de Thèbes,* ed. Guy Raynaud de Lage, t. 1 (Paris: CFMA, Librairie Honoré Champion, 1966), pp. 141–142, vv. 4511–4544. The *Roman* calls this beast a *guivre,* a word that usually means serpent, but is associated with the tiger in Pierre de Beauvais' *Bestiary.* See Florence McCulloch, *Mediaeval Latin and French Bestiaries* (Chapel Hill: University of North Carolina Press, 1960), p. 177 and n. 167.

5. "Cele tigre estoit eslongee mout de sa nature por ce qu'ele estoit norie ens es

sales le roi e es chambres as puceles tres ce qu'ele avoit esté petite aportee dou regne d'Ethiope e dou regne d'Egypt" (112a, b).

6. ". . . grande de cors come sers parcreüs en boscage, legiere e forte e isnele autant come nulle autre beste sauvage. Jambes e pies a de lion e coe ausi semblable. . . . Le poil cler e luisant solong sa nature e bien samble d'oree tant par est clere e resplandissans de fresche d'oreüre . . . bestes sauvages . . . vienent a li por flairer et sentir la trés grant dousor de s'alaine" (112b). In the Latin Bestiary, the sweet breath that draws the other animals is an attribute of the panther. See McCulloch, p. 149.

7. Buchthal, *Miniature Painting*, pp. 76 and 151ff. J. Folda, *Crusader*, p. 99, has remarked on the "tapestry-like background of stars and graceful fleurs-de-lys" of this miniature, which distinguishes it from *tigre de Thèbes* illustrations in other Crusader copies of the *Histoire ancienne*. These show ground-line and trees like Buchthal's example from the bestiary (London, B.L. MS Royal 12 F. XIII).

8. "Li cers estoit entre les gens devenus si privés qu'il sofroit que la demoiselle le penoit e aplagnoit a sa main e qu'ele li faisoit capeaus de flors e de fuelles en ses cornes. E si tenoit ausi sor les rains de ses cornes les chandeles toz cois e en pais a la table devant son segor e devant toz les autres" (162c, d). The author of the *Histoire ancienne* has added the detail of the chandelier to the information on Sylvia's stag of the *Aeneid* (VII.vv. 664–673ff.). This detail is in the *Roman d'Eneas,* ed. J.-J. Salverda de Grave, t. 1, 3552–3555.

9. G. C. Druce, "The Elephant in Medieval Legend and Art," *Archeological Journal,* 76 (March–December 1919), 1–73. See also McCulloch, pp. 115–116, for Latin bestiaries that mention elephants with wooden-tower howdahs.

10. McCulloch, p. ivb.

11. For a more precise indication of source material for the Genesis, see Joslin, *The Heard Word,* pp. 33–43. Though Rogier's historiographer claims to translate literally from his Latin sources, his skill as a writer is apparent in his selection for dramatic effect from the materials at his disposal and in his rearrangement and embroidery of these episodes. He is himself author of intercalated verse moralizations that survive most completely in the text of fr. 20125. His claim to absolute fidelity to the sources is a convention of the early vernacular chronicler, as is pointed out by W. J. A. Sayers in "The Beginnings and Early Development of Old French Historiographer," diss., University of California at Berkeley, 1966, pp. 279–280. See the author's own statement of his intent in his verse prologue (79–80: 260–268).

12. Animals mentioned in Rogier's Genesis are: *agnel* (88: 3), *asnes* (215: 33), *berbis* (197: 27), *bous* (224: 24), *bues* (243: 29), *cers* (87: 7), *chamel, chameaus, chameu* (171: 15, 144: 21, 168: 33, 167: 3), *cheval, chevaus* (125: 19, 29, 30), *chavreaus, chavrot* (186: 7, 228: 6), *colons* (97: 17), *corbel* (97: 9), *faon* (197: 22), *germes* (208: 8), *jues* (215: 34), *mul, mule, mulet* (215: 34, 36), *oiseaus* (81: 8, 147: 28), *oriphans* (144: 21), *poissons* (81: 8), *serpent* (84: 11). The *dragons* is mentioned, but as the figurehead of Triptolemus's ship (217: 4). Verbs like *trossier* (163: 8), *deschargier* (169: 23), *faoner* (197: 22), *garder* (90: 29), *abrever* (180: 28), *amener* (180: 27), *manoir* (90: 29)—as related to beasts—describe the events of animal husban-

dry or travel. Nouns like *fais* (167: 28), *somes* (167: 28), *harnois* (265: 35) characterize descriptions of the accoutrements of journeys.

13. "Poi d'omes chevauchoient, car il erent si trés grant e si trés pesant qu'a paines les portast nulle beste. Li pluisor dient que ausi erent li cheval grant encontre. Grant erent il sans faillance, mes n'erent mi si tres grant ne si fort a lor endroit come li home estoient" (125: 17–21).

In attempting to coordinate his chronology of biblical and secular events, Rogier's historiographer returns to Ninus after the story of Aeneas and before he begins his major section on Rome (177b, 178c).

In writing about Ninus in the Genesis section, the author is probably using Eusebius-Jerome *Chronici canonis* as a means of coordinating biblical and secular events. This intercalation of non-scriptural history recorded by Eusebius is to be found in other universal histories both before and after this one, histories by such diverse writers as Freculphus of Lisieux, Walter Raleigh, and Bossuet.

14. "Si mist fors le corbel por ce qu'il alast veoir e savoir s'il ja trouveroit terre descouverte. Li corbeaus s'en vola e ala tant qu'il trova une charoigne d'une beste morte flotant sor l'aigue. Si s'assist por mangier par deseüre ne ne repaira onques dedens .vii. jors a cels qui l'atendoient e regardoient en l'arche. E por ce dist on encore, quant uns haus hom envoie quanquesoit son message e il ne revient tost e repaire, 'c'est des messages corbin. Il ne reviendra mie'" (97: 8–15).

For Isidore's commentary, see *Questiones in Vetus Testamentus*, Migne, *Patrologia latina*, 83: 233. For raven iconography see Milton McC. Gatch, "Noah's Raven in Genesis A and the Illustrated Old English Hexateuch," *Gesta*, 14/2 (1975), 4–8.

15. *Histoire*, 83–84. Also see Joslin, *The Heard Word*, note for 84: 13, p. 284, for details on how greatly this author is expanding on his source, the Vulgate.

16. For the *Histoire*'s version, see 91, 92. For partial source, see Petrus Comestor, Migne, *Patrologia latina*, 198: 1079.

17. For the *plainte Jacob* of the six-syllable Joseph story, see Ernst Sass, *L'Estoire Joseph, Gesellschaft für romanische Literatur,* Band 12 (Dresden, 1906), pp. 50–51. For Malkaraume, see Jean Bonnard, *Les Traductions de la Bible en vers français au moyen âge* (Paris: Imprimerie Nationale, 1884; rpt. Geneva: Slatkin, 1967), p. 58.

18. I am indebted to Professor D. J. A. Ross of the University of London for calling my attention to the resemblance of the Joseph in triumph illustration of fr. 20125 to Lancelot and the cart illustrations.

il la proucherent. Quant li rois
alixandres vit quil empirer ne
le poroient as espious trenchans

FIGURE 10.1. The two-headed beast (Paris, Bibl. Nat. MS fr. 20125, fol. 242). (Photo: Bibl. Nat.)

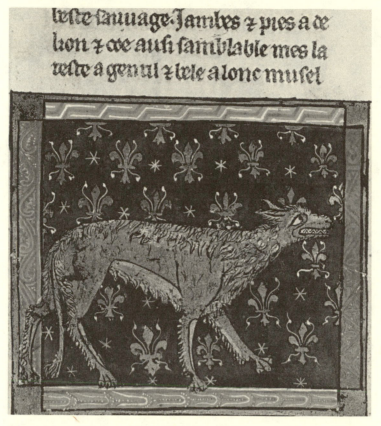

FIGURE 10.2. The tiger (Paris, Bibl. Nat. MS fr. 20125, fol. 112). (Photo: Bibl. Nat.)

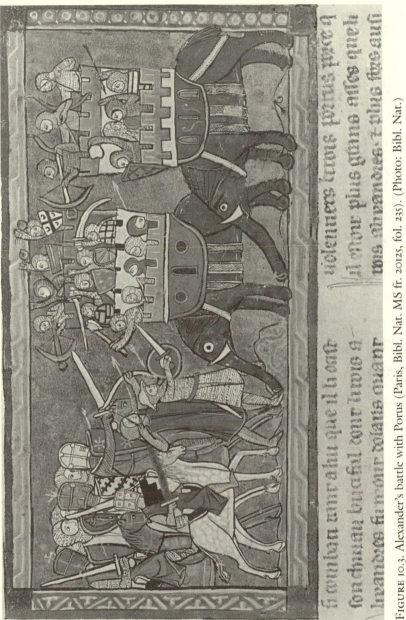

FIGURE 10.3. Alexander's battle with Porus (Paris, Bibl. Nat. MS fr. 20125, fol. 235). (Photo: Bibl. Nat.)

> oseph fust secuns sues ⁊ comā
> dewes en tor ⁊ par tor son roiaume.

FIGURE 10.4. Joseph conveyed in Pharaoh's *car* (Paris, Bibl. Nat. MS fr. 20125, fol. 68ᵛ). (Photo: Bibl. Nat.)

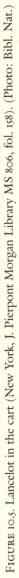

FIGURE 10.5. Lancelot in the cart (New York, J. Pierpont Morgan Library MS 806, fol. 158). (Photo: Bibl. Nat.)

FIGURE 10.6. Joseph conveyed in Pharaoh's *car* (Dijon, Bibl. Pub. MS 562, fol. 51). (Photo: Dijon, Bibl. Pub.)

# John B. Friedman

## 11. *Peacocks and Preachers:*
## *Analytic Technique in Marcus of Orvieto's*
## Liber de moralitatibus, *Vatican lat.*
## MS 5935

One of the most elaborate preaching handbooks of the Middle Ages is the *Liber de moralitatibus,* or *De proprietatibus moralizatus,* or *Liber septiformis*—for the titles vary—compiled about 1290 by a Franciscan, Marcus of Orvieto, who is otherwise unknown.[1] Some measure of the work's popularity may be gained from the fact that there are twelve extant manuscripts of this lengthy compendium. The late Morton Bloomfield's *Incipits of Latin Works on the Virtues and Vices*[2] signals nine of these; there are three others not mentioned by him. These twelve manuscripts are Oxford, New College 157; Paris, Bibliothèque Nationale lat. 3332; Burgo d'Osma Cathedral Library 123; Barcelona, Biblioteca de Catalunya 5.f.1; Munich, Staatsbibl. clm 8809; Cologne, Hist. Arch. W. 4.375; Wolfenbüttel, Landesbibliothek 3292, 130; Bologna, Univ. Bib. 1099; Rome, Angelica Q. 5.26.(750); Assisi, Bib. Communale 243; Padua, Antoniana 388; and Rome, Vatican lat. 5935. All, to my knowledge, have no indication of author, with the exception of the last manuscript, which bears a subscription naming the compiler as Marcus of Orvieto. The majority of the codices are Italian, ranging in date from the late thirteenth century to the early fourteenth; Munich is dated 1426 and Burgo d'Osma is from the fifteenth century.

The *Liber de moralitatibus* arranges moralized science in a format intended to aid the preacher in sermon composition and is representative of the reference works which were one of the chief contributions of the mendicant orders in the late thirteenth century.[3] It contains both old and new elements, showing how books of this type developed according to the needs of their users. As an early scholar's handbook, it is important to us in the historical development of text divisions and visual cues designed to make books accessible to their users and to enable them to be rapidly searched.[4] The purpose of the present study is to focus on some of Marcus's techniques of analysis and to examine his contribution to the reference book's development. As the *Liber de moralitatibus,* which I shall call simply *LM,* is so vast, I shall consider here only one aspect of it, the division devoted to the peacock.

That the *LM* was an outstanding member of the whole class of preachers' compendia is made clear by Pierre Bersuire, who remarks that after finishing his enormous *Reductorium morale*

> a work called [*Liber de moralitatibus*] came into my hands. This volume does not moralize all of the books of the *De proprietatibus rerum* [of Bartholomaeus Anglicus] but only some properties from them. In addition, it seemed to me elegantly written and I read it with great attention. Finding there things I had not already made use of, I determined to introduce them in their appropriate places.[5]

Though Bersuire does not point this out, the *LM* incorporates only books 4, 8, 12, 13, 16, and 17 of the nineteen-book encyclopedia of scientific lore, *De proprietatibus rerum,* by the Franciscan Bartholomaeus Anglicus.[6] As the *LM* is a moralized adaptation of this encyclopedia, it might at first seem that Marcus is merely abridging the work of his predecessor, but this is not necessarily the case.

Bartholomew probably finished his work by 1260 and perhaps as early as 1230. The older Franciscan's encyclopedia was well known in Italy, and Salimbene's *Cronica* (1221–1288) mentions it as enjoying a considerable reputation there.[7] The *De proprietatibus rerum*'s nineteen books surveyed the topics of God, man, and the universe. Bartholomew touched on the nature of Godhead, angels, the soul, the body and its infirmities, the heavens, the constellations, planets and their astrological influences, solar and lunar time, the calendar, the four elements and things pertaining to air, such as winds and rainbows. Books 12 through 19 deal with a large amount of geography, topography, and natural history drawn chiefly from Pliny and Aristotle, as well as with colors and the arts of men.

The author's purpose, and the limits of his intention, are well expressed in the prologue:

> By the help of God this work is compiled, profitable to me and, I hope, to others who do not know the natures and properties of things that are dispersed widely in the books of holy saints and philosophers, to understand riddles and dark scriptural meanings. . . . Thus in these nineteen books the

properties of natural things are summed up and briefly presented, just as the
ears that escape the hands of the harvesters may come into my own hands.
In this work I have put of my own little or nothing, but all is taken from
the authentic books of the holy saints and philosophers arranged in brief
compass.[8]

This prologue indicates the primarily informational content of the
work; spiritual enlightenment is hoped for, but secondary. The two intentions were more equally balanced by Vincent de Beauvais, who produced
the most remarkable encyclopedia of the Middle Ages, in eighty books and
nearly ten thousand chapters. Vincent was born about 1190 and died in
Beauvais in 1264. He had become a Dominican in the convent of Saint-
Jacques in Paris, and his patron was Louis IX, whom he served as a lector.
Louis financed the enormous *Speculum majus,* issued between 1256 and
1259. There are three divisions of this work, the *Naturale,* the *Doctrinale,*
and the *Historiale.* Vincent excerpted hundreds of passages from a great
variety of ancient and medieval authors, arranging them, at least in the
*Naturale,* in a hexameral format which is that followed by Marcus of
Orvieto.

Vincent's prologue is much more elaborate and sophisticated than that
of Bartholomew and gives us a sense of how he regarded his work.

Since the vast number of books, the shortness of human life and the weak-
ness of memory are such that no one person can know all that has been written, I, the least among my brothers, pondering the books of many authors,
concluded that I could order and arrange certain choice passages in one volume. And moreover, it seemed to me that I should benefit my studies and
those of others to collect examples in one volume which relate to the development of our Christian faith, the improvement of morals and the exposition of the mystical meanings of scripture.[9]

Thus Bartholomew's subject matter and the moral purpose of Vincent
as expressed in his prologue were to influence Marcus of Orvieto in the
composition of his own encyclopedic compendium.

Though Bersuire had called attention to it in the Middle Ages, the *LM*
has attracted relatively little interest from modern scholars.[10] Probably because it was concerned with "scientific" material, it has not, for example,
been mentioned by the Rouses in their thorough study of florilegia.[11]
Besides Bloomfield's notice of it, the *LM* has been briefly discussed by
Glorieux in his work on Parisian masters of theology,[12] by Engels and
Samaran in their studies of Bersuire,[13] and by R. E. Kaske, in a manual on
the sources of medieval literary imagery.[14]

The only extended treatment of the *LM* was by Léopold Delisle, who in 1888 discussed it in his article on medieval encyclopedias in the *Histoire littéraire de la France*,[15] and there he was mainly concerned to dispute a recent attribution of the work to Giles of Rome, made by Henry Narducci.

Delisle classed the *LM* with the encyclopedias we have already mentioned, and by a lengthy series of parallels corroborated Bersuire's observation in the preface to the *Reductorium*—that the *LM* adapted the scientific content of the *De proprietatibus rerum* to moral ends. Although the mendicant encyclopedias Delisle discussed contained a certain number of *moralitates,* their emphasis was on natural history; their presumed audience included not only preachers but also literate laymen curious to know more about the natural world. Like the *Historia naturalis* of Pliny, which provided so much information on animals for the Middle Ages, the works of Bartholomew, Thomas of Cantimpré, and Vincent de Beauvais could be read for information or searched and used for the *materia praedicandi,* while the factual content of the *LM* was of secondary importance. Let me clarify this distinction. A preacher was less likely to read it for the pleasure of its lore than he was to search it for specific information or applications useful in the development of thematic sermons. It is precisely the vast allegorical structure of the *LM,* in a post-scholastic milieu we tend to think of as uninterested in allegory, which is so striking. Indeed, the *LM*'s allegories of Bartholomew's natural history are a type of *defloratio patrum,* providing preachers with moralizations of natural phenomena. Thus while these allegories do not reach the proportions and have the narrative structure we find in many exempla collections, the matter of the *LM* is specifically shaped for incorporation into sermons and as we shall see, it comes complete with forms of signposting that allow the preacher to find the excerpts he needed quickly and efficiently.

Until recent years, the critical history of the *LM* has mainly been one of attributions made and denied (we have already mentioned Giles of Rome); Thomas Walleys (c. 1300–1348) and Gaetanus of Thienis (1387–1465)[16] were other candidates for authorship, and, presumably out of desperation, Delisle posited an anonymous Franciscan author. Oddly enough, however, considerable information, which we have no reason to dispute, about the work's composition and authorship appears in the *LM.* As this information is fullest in Vatican lat. MS 5935 and Assisi, Bib. Communale 243, and because these manuscripts are perhaps the earliest ones of the work that we have, I shall concentrate my attentions on them.

In the brief prologue which opens the first chapter of the first *tractatus* in the Assisi example, the compiler tells us that he was invited by Benedict,

Cardinal Deacon of St. Nicholas, to compose the work. "By [this] venerable father and lord I was instructed, taught and informed frequently and in many ways."[17] This is Benedict Guatani, given the title of Cardinal Deacon by Martin IV in 1281. Benedict was to become Pope Boniface VIII in 1291, and he died in 1303, giving us a *terminus post* and *ante quem* for the dedication. By this dating the dedication allows us to rule out Giles, Thomas, and Gaetanus. It is, indeed, difficult to see why these attributions continued to be mentioned as long as they did.

We know Boniface VIII from his appearance, while still alive, in Dante's circle of the Simoniacs in Canto 19 of the *Inferno,* and he seems to have been chiefly responsible for the poet's exile and banishment from Florence. Nothing in Dante's portrait makes him a patron of learning.[18] Interestingly, this dedicatory sentence to Benedict also occurs in the middle of the prologue in the Oxford, Padua, Munich, and Rome manuscripts, but not in the others. Possibly it was deleted by the scribe who copied Vatican lat. MS 5935 and Assisi 243 or the scribes of the archetype from which the other half-dozen manuscripts were copied.

Such a dedication suggests that Marcus, completed book in hand, sought preferment by the use of flattery. There is no reason to suppose that Benedict would have commissioned this work in advance, yet the presence of several copies of the book in the papal library at Avignon implies some interest in the *LM* on the part of the hierarchy.[19]

In the epilogue to the *LM* in Vatican lat. MS 5935 we find a fairly conventional submission of the work for correction by the writer's betters.

> If men of sense, astrologers, physicians, philosophers, theologians, if scholars of authority find additions and corrections to be made to my work, I beg them, I the compiler of this work, Brother Marcus of Orvieto, of the Order of Friars Minor, the poorest of the poor, to make them without hesitation. For I have undertaken the work without any pretension and I accept and solicit the improvement which men more instructed than myself can bring to my writing.[20]

The Oxford, Paris, Munich, Assisi, Padua, Bologna, Cologne, Wolfenbüttel, and Calaluñya manuscripts omit the name and status of Marcus, saying merely, "ego pauperculus compilator," while the entire colophon has been scratched out after the *explicit* in Rome, Angelica.[21] Vatican lat. MS 5935, therefore, seems to be the best witness to the identity of the author. Possibly the copyists felt that by giving his name, Marcus had violated the last of the "common denominators" of mendicant preaching tools—anonymity.[22]

Two words in the epilogue or colophon are worthy of some comment. These are *compilator* and *pauperculus*. We have seen in the prologue to Bartholomew's encyclopedia that the author uses the verb "compile" in reference to his work. The term *compilator* had by the end of the thirteenth century a precise technical meaning. It distinguished a person who gathered material from earlier writers, *auctores*, or *auctoritates*, and arranged that material according to his own plan, from a man who wrote either commentaries on original work or original work himself.[23] St. Bonaventure in the *Sentences* had said about the four methods of making books that the scribe merely copies the work of another, neither adding nor changing, but the *compilator* "aliquis scribit aliena addendo, sed non de suo."[24] Such compilations, though not original, derive their value from the appropriateness of the sources, the *auctoritates*, and the *ordinatio* by which the *auctoritates* are arranged. Thus by identifying himself as a *compilator*, Marcus invites us to look at his sources and his arrangement in evaluating his work.

The second term of interest is *pauperculus*, which at first glance we might dismiss as being applicable only to a Franciscan and with no further resonance. In fact, the word is that used by Thomas of Ireland about 1306 with sufficient elaboration to give us a sense of how Marcus must have meant it. The phrase from Ruth 2: 3 "and she went and gleaned after the reapers" is one which provided a metaphor by which many compilers described their works. We have already seen a hint of the idea in Bartholomew's view of himself as one who picks up "ears that have escaped the hands of the harvesters." Thomas of Ireland elaborates this much further:

> Abiit in agrum et collegit spicas post terga metancium Ruth II. Ruth paupercula non habens mesem propriam ad colligendum, agrum intravit alienum, ut spicas colligeret post terga metancium. Sic ego pauperculus non habens copiam scriptorum nec originalium aceruum, agrum intravi Booz.[25]

Since all we know of Marcus beyond this sense of his role is his name, no conjectures can be made about his life. But the structure of his book is very revelatory. As the alternate title *Liber septiformis* would suggest, the work's hexameral format connects specific divisions of natural history with the seven days of creation, and indeed, Marcus makes a clear association of his subject matter with the Bible: "in this work are treated the seven principal things in the universe, celestial bodies, the elements, birds, fish, animals, trees and plants, minerals and precious stones, both what they are, and where they are found in divine scriptures."[26] His use of this structure is partly, no doubt, an homage to the work of his great Dominican predecessor, Vincent de Beauvais, but more important, it reveals his attitude towards *ordinatio*.

Marcus operates within a tradition of *distinctiones* and *divisiones,* in which the new Aristotelian learning had made it seem appropriate to divide and subdivide all human experience. We see this idea clearly expressed in Alexander of Hales's *Summa,* where the author notes that "apprehensio veritatis secundum humanum rationem explicatur per divisiones,"[27] and indeed, part of the standard *accessus ad auctores* of the schools was a discussion of the books and chapters of a work.[28] Marcus systematizes his subject matter in accord with these theories of *divisio* so that the searcher can find individual subdivisions through the rubrics, marginal signposts, and two compendious indexes which are a feature of all the manuscripts.

The *compilator* brought a new idea of arrangement to the medieval reference book, and as an ancillary benefit, developed a way to use such a book. This was the alphabetical index usually called *tabula,*[29] which enabled the searcher to find subdivisions within the compilation. A work written about fifty years before the *LM* was the anonymous *Moralia super Evangelia,* which, as its title suggests, is a *compilatio* of moralized gospel passages containing exempla. The indexes accompanying the text are perhaps the earliest we have of this type. One is a topic index to enable a user to locate such subjects as *humilitas* or *ira;* it has no particular order. The other is more a list of key words for a preacher to use in sermons and is arranged A to Z.[30] Marcus's indexes are a considerable advance on the two associated with the *Moralia* and make interesting, if often curious, reading.

One index to the *LM* lists the contents of each *tractatus* analyzed into chapters; the other, called *tabula specialis,* is arranged alphabetically by moral subjects keyed to particular chapters. Accordingly, we find an entry under "Popes and Cardinals, their conditions," which directs the reader to the chapter on elephants. Another entry on Antichrist gives three different *conditiones* of that personage keyed to chapters on puppies, the wolf, and the basilisk. Thus the user of the *LM* may find an item in the work according to the letter or to the spirit.

As we might expect in a preacher's handbook, there is little or no interest in the actual habits or qualities of the hundreds of animals, birds, and plants surveyed. Though occasionally Marcus will add the phrase "experience shows" to "authority says," he still turns to Aristotle or Pliny rather than to personal observation for "the truth of the letter." This, of course, is not at all surprising, since to the compilers of preaching compendia, the ancients recorded actual habits and qualities of living things. Only *fachliteratur* collections or some of the hunting handbooks like that of

Gaston Phoebus recorded genuine experiences with nature. Marcus's moralizations of natural phenomena, on the other hand, are supported "by the true authority of sacred scripture and by the saints, or by the glosses and expositions of the Paris masters."[31]

These "Paris masters" seem to have taught Marcus something of scholastic logic as well, as he shows some acquaintance with the form of the *summa* and uses its techniques of division and distinction. Even his choice of the word *tractatus* to describe the major divisions of his text is solidly rooted in scholastic logic. Jordan of Saxony's commentary on Priscian (c. 1220) uses the word in relation to the new Aristotelian idea of formal cause: "forma tractatus est forma rei tradite que consistit in separatione librorum et capitulorum et ordine eorundem."[32] In a Munich manuscript of Aristotle, Nicholas of Paris (c. 1250) speaks again of the "tractatus que est ordinatio librorum partialium et capitulorum."[33] The *tractatus* on elements is subdivided into four subsections, and the chapters on creatures are divided into a number of *distinctiones* "according to properties or conditions," indicated by Roman numerals and paragraph signs.

It is interesting that Marcus, unlike some of his contemporaries, had not yet come upon the Arabic numeral as a reference aid, though these numbers had been available in Italy in a variety of mathematical and astrological works since about 1200.[34] In the Vatican manuscript of *LM,* additional aids to subdivision have been provided, possibly by a first owner, as they are in a hand contemporary with the rest of the work. For example, each passage of Scripture quoted in the text column has a flourished bracket to its left in the margin, and each patristic author cited or saint mentioned has a marginal notation through a system of initials: G for Gregory the Great, A for St. Augustine, or, in some cases, the full name itself. Thus a glance down the margin helps the reader to identify the presence of material not directly connected with the natural history content of the work.

A typical chapter beginning is this one for the peacock:[35] "The peacock has properties according to authorities." Then follow citations from Isidore of Seville and Augustine, giving, in the case of the latter, book and chapter references in the *City of God* for peacock lore. This material is followed in turn by allegorizations of various aspects or qualities of the peacock, its bright plumage, its vanity, and the like. The *moralitates,* as well, contain texts from the Fathers and from Scripture.

The ornithological information, if I may so describe it, is derived from the thirty-second chapter of Bartholomew's twelfth book, on birds, which offers twelve major points about the peacock's appearance and habits.

Marcus uses only eight of these and does not follow Bartholomew's order, preferring to arrange his material according to a kind of exegetical logic. He also widens considerably the range of authorities both for the properties and for the *moralitates,* adding more Aristotle, citing Augustine's experiments with peacock flesh, and quoting from the *Confessions,* the *Ecclesiastical Hierarchies* of Pseudo-Dionysius, the *Ecclesiastical Histories* of Eusebius, the *Dialogues* of Gregory the Great, the commentary of St. Bernard on Canticles, and the *Vita* of St. Edmund. From the Bible come a variety of references to Job, Ecclesiasticus, Proverbs, Psalms, Luke, II Corinthians, and the Acts of the Apostles. How much of this material he knew directly and how much he got at second hand is hard to say, but he does quote Scripture verbatim, whereas some of the material from Pseudo-Dionysius and others is paraphrased as though it may have come from florilegia.[36] We can see from Marcus's use of Bartholomew that it is incorrect to think of him as a mere applier of *moralitates* to the work of the earlier Franciscan; he reorganizes and expands his original according to his own needs and library resources.

In most cases, Marcus shows himself a fairly subtle moralizer of natural history, with a feeling for extended metaphor. The *moralitates* are apt and develop organically from the *conditiones* or *proprietates* with which he is working. To open his chapter on the peacock, for example, the author relates St. Augustine's own tale of how, when in Carthage, he tried to eat the flesh of the peacock, and found that it was hard and did not putrify or smell even after a long while. Nor, as Isidore noted, was it easily cooked.[37] "This signifies," says Marcus, "those men firm and rooted in the virtues of evangelical chastity and the odor of good reputation." Two passages from II Corinthians are then employed to gloss the idea: "for we are a sweet odor to Christ," and "thanks be to God who allows us to triumph in Christ and makes manifest to us the sweet smell of his knowledge in all places." Thus both the moralization and his supportive passages from Scripture develop the idea of smell implicit in the notion that the bird's flesh does not rot. Apparently drawing upon the old idea of the peacock's flesh as a symbol of resurrection, which made the bird a popular image in the art of the catacombs, Marcus then gives a loose rendition of a passage in the *Ecclesiastical Hierarchies* of Pseudo-Dionysius to the effect that God makes not only the soul but the body precious in the holy life of the saints after death.[38]

Typically, a detail of natural history leads into a *moralitas* which introduces a generally relevant scriptural or patristic citation, followed by a specific application which Marcus calls an *exemplum,*[39] an illustration from

Scripture or a saint's legend involving a particular person. Thus the peacock's beautiful blue breast feathers, as mentioned by Isidore, lead to the following moralization.

> These feathers signify the various and most deceptive vanities of the devil and his ministers, who transfigure themselves into angels of light and apostles of Christ. 2 Corinthians 11: "For such are false apostles, deceitful workers, transfiguring themselves into the apostles of Christ. And this is no marvel for Satan himself was transformed into an angel of light. Therefore it is no great thing if his ministers should also be transformed as the ministers of righteousness, whose end shall be according to their works." And here is an *exemplum,* in the story of the devil, who crowned with a diadem and dressed in purple appeared to St. Martin and said he was Jesus. Martin, however, disputed with him, saying that it was not in this form that Jesus would come, as he himself foretold.

In some cases the biblical passage is presented in opposition to a particular sin or vice, so that the preacher could have a ready-made pairing. An example of this technique appears in the eighth and last "condition" of peacocks. Among the curious lore about this bird offered by Pliny and presented by Bartholomew is the belief that the bird swallows its own dung, which is exceedingly valuable for its medicinal properties, because of the envy the peacock bears mankind. For this reason, peacock dung is never found. Marcus moralized this information, seeing in it avaricious and envious men, citing Ecclesiasticus: "Help a pauper according to his need and do not send him away hungry. Lose thy money for a brother and a friend and do not hide it under a stone to rust." Following out the implications of the envious peacock who would not give of its substance to man, Marcus compares two antithetical sorts of men. He briefly recounts the story of St. Edmund, who would never deny any beggar alms, and whose right arm, which he extended to them, is to this day preserved intact and uncorrupted. He compares Edmund the generous alms-giver to the Emperor Decius and Julian the Apostate, who hated beggars; both perished damnably. "And we have," he concludes, "an *exemplum* of all this in Luke's account of the rich man who would not give crumbs from his feast to Lazarus the beggar and was buried in hell."

The connection of Lazarus to Decius, Julian, and St. Edmund may seem a bit forced by present-day standards, but to someone seeking exempla of generosity and miserliness, the juxtaposition of these stories served a very useful function. Marcus of Orvieto's purpose here was to provide a reference work of sorts, like the modern concordance or Bartlett's *Dictionary of Quotations,* gathering together facts and quotations on various moral and doctrinal points which could then be easily worked into a sermon. Such books flourished with the increasing interest in preaching and pastoral activity during the thirteenth century, and they continued to be popular well into the age of print, for we find sixteenth-century editions of John Bromyard's *Summa praedicantium,* seventeenth-century editions of Pierre Bersuire's *Repertorium biblicum,* and eighteenth-century editions of Thomas of Ireland's *Manipulus florum.*

Marcus's collection developed from earlier preachers' aids like the alphabetically arranged collection of biblical *distinctiones,* such as that made in the twelfth century by Alan of Lille,[40] where we find various meanings of a biblical word *in bono* or *in malo.* These collections gradually acquired exempla and supporting passages from the Fathers, and outgrew their simple alphabetical format, requiring subdivision into several parts and the addition of analytic tables to help their readers find subjects, or *auctoritates* to illustrate or support points made in a sermon. As the university sermon developed in the thirteenth century, its many parts called for an increased number of exempla and citations, and the preacher's pastoral need to deal with ethical problems made collections arranged by various moral categories desirable.

The *LM*'s indexes made such categories quickly available. It should be noted, however, that alphabetization was not universally or rapidly accepted, as Lloyd Daly has shown in several interesting studies.[41] It went against the belief in a divinely ordained universe where Deus came before Angelus no matter what the order the first letters of these words might have in the alphabet. Alphabetization seemed to defy the rationally derived systematic organization of the philosopher and theologian from substances to things. This tension may be seen in the organization of Marcus's source, the *De proprietatibus rerum* of Bartholomew. The first eleven books are arranged systematically. For example, in Book 1, the first chapter is titled "De Deo" and the last "de nominibus que conveniunt Christo et homini." The fifth book on the human body arranges its sixty-six chapters with a general introduction followed by the properties of the head down through the soles of the feet in fifty-five chapters, the last eleven dealing with large categories like bones and nerves. Only in Book 12 on birds, where there is no natural or artificial order, do we find alphabetization from Aquila to Vespertilione. Mountains in Book 14 are treated similarly, from Ararat to Ziph; so are countries in the following book and metals, herbs, animals, and so on. The differing degrees of efficacy between the systematic and the alphabetic forms of organization may be quickly determined by a search for a foreknown topic in the *tabulae* which precede each of the books of the *De proprietatibus*. Alphabetization in *tabulae* substantially speeded up the process of searching a work and gave rise to the distinction I made earlier between works meant to be read and works made to be used and searched.[42]

The *LM* is an interesting combination of old and new elements. The hexameral format belongs to a tradition in which, as Vincent de Beauvais tells us, objects are dealt with in the order in which they are created,[43] or as they went from God to the material world, as they were in the structure of the first two-thirds of Bartholomew's encyclopedia. This format has no particular utility to Marcus except as a way of breaking up his material, since he is not dealing with theology in the manner of Bartholomew, who begins with God, angels, and so on, and then moves to the created world. Adapted to the hexameral format is an elaborate and newly fashionable system of subdivision and analysis. We have already noted in the Vatican manuscript the reader's aids present in the margins. Thus the preacher in need of a citation from Scripture or the Fathers on plants or animals or elements could simply cast his eye down the left-hand margin looking for B for Bernard, G for Gregory, and the like. The paragraph signs in alternating red and blue further catch the user's eye; they highlight the individual "conditions and properties" of an item. They are also an aid to subdivision within the text and allow the reader to pick out divisions within the chapter quickly, while in the margins the large Roman numerals make it easy to locate the individual chapters within the *tractatus,* signaled by running heads in red and blue.

Although the *LM* was created by a member of a preaching order for the use of persons like himself,[44] its utility was far wider, as the epilogue suggests. We can well imagine those men of sense—astrologers, physicians, philosophers, and theologians—who at various times leafed through its indexes in search of useful information for a poem, or a legal case, or a letter, or quodlibet, in short, for any purpose in which a large body of curious lore, well-analyzed and quickly available to a busy searcher, was of use.

## Appendix

### Transcription of Marcus of Orvieto, *Liber de moralitatibus*, Vat. lat. MS 5935, Tractatus III, c. 30, unfoliated

#### De Pavo

Pavo proprietates habet secundum auctores. ⟨ Primo enim ut dicit Isidorus et Augustinus XXI *De Civitate Dei,* c. iiii dicit se expertum fuisse apud Hipponem carnem habet tam duram ut non putrescat vel olfactum inficiat. Durata per annum, nec facile coquitur. Significat firmos et radicatos in virtutes evangelice castitatis conservantes in se odorem fame et invincibilitatem constantie et longanimitatem perseverantie. 2 Cor. ii: "ipsi bonus odor summus Deo." "Deo autem gratias, qui semper triumphat nos in Christo Jesu, et odorem noticie sue manifestat per nos in omni loco." Dionysius de *Ecclesiastica Hierarchia:* Sancta vita non solum animam sed et corpus facit preciosum ibidem Deus acceptat amari a mundis. (VII.1.i) ⟦

**D.**

Secundo ut experimentum probat et auctor dicit vocem habere terribilem et quasi demonis. Significat detractores et blasphemos. Ecclesiasticus 27.14,15: "Loquela multum jurans horripilationem capiti statuet et irreverentia ipsius obturatio aurium. Narratio peccantium odiosa et risus illorum in delicatis peccatio." Exemplum in Simone Mago disputante cum Petro ut habetur itinerario (Actus 8.9–24). ⟦ III ut ponit Aristotle vivit xx annis et pullificat in fine trium annorum, deinde colorantur eius ale. Significat bonum perseverantem sive successivum perfectum de bono in meliorem, in actibus, et moribus. Juxta illud, Psalmus "Ibunt de virtute in virtutem donec videatur Deus deorum in Syon." (83.8) Gregorius et B[ernardus] in pluribus locis. In via Dei non semper perficere deficere est. Dionysius: virtutis est semper et continue perficere. ⟦ IIII ut dicit idem eicit plumas suas cum prima arbore eiciente folia sua et tunc primo nascitur pluma eius, cum arbores incipiunt pullulare. Significat renovationes bonorum exemplo maiorum semper ad melius. 2 Cor. 4.16: "qui foris noster est homo corrumpatur tamen is, qui intus, est renovatur de die in diem." Exemplum in discipulis sanctorum patrum. De quibus narrat Ieronimus in libro de vitis eorum, qui semper conabantur renovari in Christo extra magiorum suorum. Exemplum et in beatis Mauro, et Placido sub patre Benedicto sicut narrat Gregorius magis in libris II.7 *Dialogis.* ⟦

**D.**

**J.**

**G.**

V ut dicit Isidorus est avis non diligens fetum suum. Sequitur enim masculus feminam et ova femine investigat ut frangat ea, ut sic magis luxurie sue vacet. Quod timens femina abscondit ea ne ab eo valeant inveniri de facili. Significat ipsos prelatos impedientes bonum sive propter motionem in subditis suis. Quod avertens ecclesia martyr per videt rei publice dampno. Proverbia 28.15–16: "Dux indigens prudentia: multos opprimet per calumniam. Leo rugiens et ursus esuriens. Princeps ipius super populum pauperem." Quod contra B[ernardus] super Canticum (sermo 23.2) "discite prelati subditorum vos debere esse matres. Non dominos mansuescite, ponite feritatem. Et si interdum correctione opus est, paterna sit, non tyrannica, suspendite verbera; producite ubera." Huc usque Bernardus. ⟦ VI ut dicit Isidorus habet capud infirmum et deforme quasi ser-

**B.**

pentium et tamen cristatum incessum simplicem et occultum. Collum modicum et erectum, pectus saphyreum, caudem oculatum mira pulchri formitate distinctam et ornatam, pedes deformissimos et rugosos. Significat conditiones varias diaboli et ministrorum eius callidissime et diversimode transfigurantum se in angelos lucis et apostolos Christi. 2 Cor. 11 "nam eiusmodi pseudoapostoli subdoli operarii sunt, transfigurantes se in apostolos Christi. Et non mirum ipse enim Sathanas transfigurat se in angelum lucis." Non ergo mirum se ministri eius transfigurantur velud ministri justicie quorum finis erit secundum opera ipsorum. Exemplum in demone qui diademate coronatus purpura ad ornatus beato Martino decipiendo apparuit cum dicens Jesum Christum se esse quem beatus Martinus confutatum decens quod non in tali forma dominus Jesus venturum se esse predixit. ℂ VII ut dicit idem pennarum suarum admirans pulchritudinem erigit eas et admodum rote sive circuli pergium capiti circum ponit. Videns autem pedum suorum deformitatem erubescit et velut oblitus predicte pennarum pulchritudinis, eas subito deprimit ac submittit. Significat vanagloriosos de sua pulchritudine et mundi gloria se jactantes et ostentantes qui tamen suam fragilitatem et feditatem maiorem bene considerantes et studiose suum virtutem attendentes humilianter et a veritatis ostentatione resiliunt. Job 5.24: "visitans speciem tuam, non peccabis." Augustinus in libro *Confessionum* "O si cognoscant se homines! et qui gloriatur in domino glorietur. Quisquis autem enuntiat tibi merita sua domine Deus meus quid tibi enuntiat nisi numina tua?" ℂ Octavo ut dicit Plinius in libro XXIX c. xxxviii pavo resorbet fimum suum invidens utilitati hominum. Valde enim medicinale est sed iam invenitur. Significant avaros et invidos et vilia sua et superflua indigentibus non solum denegantes sed et abscondentes atque celantes. Quo contra Ecclesiasticus 29.12: "propter mandatum assume pauper inopiam illi eius ne dimittas illum. Perde pecuniam propter fratrem et amicum tuum et non abscondas illam sub lapide in perditionem." Scribitur de beato et sancto Edmundo quondam rege Anglie non negante alicui pauperi elymosinam, quod suum brachium dextrum quo pauperibus elymosinas porrigebat, perseverat usque hodie incorruptum et integrum. Scribitur e converso de Decio Cesare et Juliano apostatam in *Historia ecclesiastica* et *Tripartita* quod in odio habebunt pauperes et damnabiliter perierunt. Exemplum etiam et habemus. Lucam 16.19 in divitie epulone impio circa Lazarum mendicum qui sepultus est in inferno.

*A shorter version of this paper was presented at the Eighteenth International Congress on Medieval Studies, Kalamazoo, Michigan, May 1983. I am grateful to Professors R. E. Kaske, Franco Preparata, and Michael Twomey for advice and information.*

## Notes

1. His name, for example, does not appear in connection with any sermons in J. B. Schneyer's monumental *Repertorium der lateinischen Sermones des Mittelalters,* 9 vols. (Münster: Aschendorff, 1969–1972).

2. Morton Bloomfield, et al., *Incipits of Latin Works on the Virtues and Vices, 1100–1500 A.D.* (Cambridge, Massachusetts: Medieval Academy, 1979), p. 430, #5027.

3. The fundamental study on this subject is that of Richard H. and Mary A. Rouse, *Preachers, Florilegia and Sermons: Studies in the Manipulus Florum of Thomas of Ireland* (Toronto:.Pontifical Institute, 1979).

4. The best general study of the subject discussed here is that of Richard H. and Mary A. Rouse, "*Statim invenire:* Schools, Preachers, and New Attitudes to the Page," in Robert L. Benson and Giles Constable, eds., *Renaissance and Renewal in the Twelfth Century* (Cambridge, Massachusetts: Harvard University Press, 1982), pp. 201–225.

5. Pierre Bersuire, *Opera omnia* (Mainz: Antonii Herati, 1609), I, p. 3. See also Charles Samaran, "Pierre Bersuire," *Histoire littéraire de la France,* 39 (Paris: Impr. Nationale, 1962), pp. 317–318, and J. Engels, "Berchoriana I" and "Berchoriana I: Suite," *Vivarium,* 2 (1964), 117.

6. See Léopold Delisle, "Traités divers sur les propriétés des choses," *Histoire littéraire de la France,* 30 (Paris: Impr. Nationale, 1888), pp. 343ff.; Vittorio Cian, *Vivaldo Belcazer e l'enciclopedismo italiano delle origine* (Turin: Loescher, 1902); Anton Schoenbach, "Des Bartholomaeus Anglicus Beschreibung Deutschlands gegen 1240," *Mitteilungen des Institutes für österreichische Geschichtsforschung,* 27 (1906), 54–90; Edmund Voigt, "Bartholomaeus Anglicus, *De proprietatibus rerum,* Literarhistorisches und bibliographisches," *Englische Studien,* 41 (1910), 337–359; H. Matrod, "Fr. Roger Bacon et Fr. Barthélemy d'Angleterre," *Etudes franciscaines,* 28 (1912), 468–483; Thomas Plassman, "Bartholomaeus Anglicus," *Archivum franciscanum historicum,* 12 (1919), 68–109; Gerald E. Se Boyar, "Bartholomaeus Anglicus and His Encyclopedia," *The Journal of English and Germanic Philology,* 19 (1920), 168–189; Robert L. Collison, *Encyclopaedias: Their History Throughout the Ages* (New York: Hafner, 1964); Robert James Long, ed., *Bartholomaeus Anglicus, On the Properties of the Body and Soul* (Toronto: Pontifical Institute, 1979); D. C. Greetham, "The Concept of Nature in Bartholomaeus Anglicus (fl. 1230)," *The Journal of the History of Ideas,* 41 (1980), 663–677; and most recently A. S. G. Edwards, "Bartholomaeus Anglicus' *De proprietatibus rerum* and Medieval English Literature," *Archiv für das Studium der neueren Sprachen und Literaturen,* 222 (1985), 121–128.

7. Salimbene de Adam, *Cronica,* ed. G. Scalia (Bari: Laterza, 1966), 245d, p. 134.

8. This passage is modernized from the Middle English translation of Bartholomew by John of Trevisa, M. C. Seymour, et al., eds., *On the Properties of Things* (Oxford: Oxford University Press, 1975), vol. I, pp. 41, 43.

9. A critical text of the prologue to the *Speculum majus* has been made by Anna-Dorothee von den Brincken, "Geschichtsbetrachtung bei Vincenz von Beauvais," *Deutsches Archiv für Erforschung des Mittelalters,* 34 (1978), 465. See also Serge Lusignan, *Préface au Speculum majus* (Montreal: Institut d'études médiévales, 1979); Jean Schneider, "Recherches sur une encyclopedie du xiii<sup>e</sup> siècle: Le *Speculum majus* de Vincent of Beauvais," *Contes rendues de l'academie des inscriptions et belles lettres* (1976), 174–189; Monique Paulmier-Foucart, "L'Atelier Vincent de Beauvais," *Le moyen âge,* 85 (1979), 87–99; and *Spicae, Cahiers de l'atelier Vincent de Beauvais,* I (1978), II (1980), and III (1981).

10. Books 3 and 6 of the *LM,* "De avibus" and "De arboribus sive plantis," have been published from the Paris MS by J. B. Pitra in *Spicilegium Solesmense* (Paris: Didot frères, 1855), 2: 347–467 and 470–519.

11. See above, n. 3.

12. P. Glorieux, *Répertoire des maîtres en théologie de Paris au xiii<sup>e</sup> siècle* (Paris: J. Vrin, 1934), II, 305, places it among the works of Pseudo-Giles of Rome.

13. See above, n. 5.

14. R. E. Kaske, Arthur Groos, and Michael Twomey, *Medieval Christian Literary Imagery: A Guide to Interpretation* (Toronto: Toronto University Press, 1988), 45–46.

15. Op. cit. pp. 334–353.

16. Engels, "Berchoriana I: Suite," p. 117.

17. Assisi Bib. Communale 243: "Juxta quod inductus, ductus et informatus sum multipliciter et frequenter a venerabili patre et domino meo singulari domino Benedictus Sancti Nicholas in carcere tulliano, diaconis cardinalis," fol. 7.

18. See T. S. R. Boase, *Boniface VIII* (London: Constable, 1933).

19. Maurice Faucon, *La Librairie des papes d'Avignon, sa formation, sa composition, ses catalogues (1316–1420)* (Paris: E. Thorin, 1886–1887), vol. 2, item 777, p. 128, and item 690, II.121.

20. "Si cui autem sano viro, astrologo, philosopho, theologo, physico vel quacumque facultate perito in opere prefato aliquid fuerit visum addendum, minuendum aut eciam corrigendum vel declarandum, obsecro ego frater Marcus urbis veteri fratrum minorum ordinis pauperculus compilator huius operis ut addat, minuat, corrigat, et declaret: sine prejudicio enim hec scripsi ad saniorum hominum seu virorum emendationem et correctionem votivam," fol. 130<sup>v</sup>.

21. "Explicit liber de proprietatibus rerum, post quae, non vetustate sed malitia, deleta sunt aliqua verba, procul dubio nomen Auctoris vel saltem scriptoris reuelantia." Henry Narducci, *Catalogus codicum manuscriptorum . . . in Bibliotheca Angelica* (Rome: Ludovichi Cecchini, 1893), p. 311.

22. This phrase is that of Richard Rouse, *Preachers, Florilegia,* p. 13.

23. The best study of this subject is that of Malcolm B. Parkes, "The Influence of the Concepts of *Ordinatio* and *Compilatio* on the Development of the Book," in J. J. G. Alexander and M. T. Gibson, eds., *Medieval Learning and Literature: Essays Presented to Richard William Hunt* (Oxford: Oxford University Press, 1976), 115–141. See also for later examples, Alastair Minnis, "Late-Medieval Discussions of *Compilatio* and the Role of the *Compilator,*" *Beiträge zur Geschichte der deutschen Sprache und Literatur,* 101 (1979), 385–421.

24. Bonaventure, *In primum librum sententiarum*, pro. qu. iv in *Opera omnia* (Quaracchi: Typ. Coll. S. Bonaventurae, 1882–1903), i. 14.2.

25. Quoted from Rouse, *Preachers, Florilegia*, appendix 2, p. 236.

26. "Ideo scripturus per ordinem de corporibus celestibus, et elementis, avibus, piscibus, animalibus, arboribus, herbis et lapidibus preciosis, qui et que in veneranda pagine autentice . . . describuntur," fol. 7ᵛ.

27. Alexander of Hales, *Summa theologica* (Quaracchi: Typ. Coll. S. Bonaventurae, 1924), tract. introd., qu. i, art. I, cap. 4.

28. See on this subject Edwin A. Quain, "The Medieval *Accessus ad auctores*," *Traditio*, 2 (1944), 319–407.

29. See, for general discussion, D. A. Callus, "The 'Tabulae super originalia patrum' of Robert Kilwardby O. P.," in *Studia mediaevalia in honorum . . . R. J. Martin* (Bruges: de Tempel, 1948), pp. 85–112.

30. See E. J. Dobson, *Moralities on the Gospels: A New Source of 'Ancrene Wisse'* (Oxford: Oxford University Press, 1975).

31. "Per veras scripture sacre auctoritates et per sanctos sive glossas vel etiam magistrorum Parisiensium expositiones," fol. 7ᵛ.

32. For text and discussion, see M. Grabmann, *Mittelalterliches Geistesleben* (Munich: Hueber, 1926–1956), III, 234, and J. Pinborg, "Die Entwicklung der Sprachtheorie im Mittelalters," *Beiträge zur Geschichte der Philosophie und Theologie der Mittelalters*, 42 (1967), 25–26.

33. See B. Sandkühler, *Die frühen Dante kommentare und ihr Verhältnis zur mittelalterlichen Kommentartradition* (Munich: Hueber, 1967), p. 41, and the Letter to Can Grande in M. Barbi, et al., eds., *Le Opere di Dante* (Florence: Bemporad, 1960), *Epist.*, XIII.18.

34. On Leonardo Fibonacci or Leonardo of Pisa, whose *Liber Abaci* (1202) made widespread the use of "Arabic" numerals in Italy and elsewhere in the West, see Karl Menninger, *Number Words and Number Symbols*, tr. Paul Broneer (Cambridge, Massachusetts: MIT Press, 1969), pp. 425–426; and more recently, Alexander Murray, *Reason and Society in the Middle Ages* (Oxford: Oxford University Press, 1978), pp. 190–193.

35. The complete text of this entry will be found in the appendix to the present article.

36. See, for example, the *tabulae* to the works of Augustine, Jerome, Dionysius, and others made by Robert of Paris 1256, B.N. MS lat. 16334.

37. Civ. dei, XXI.4; *Etymologiae*, XII.7.48.

38. See Maurice de Gandillac, ed., *Oeuvres complètes du Pseudo-Denys l'Aréopagite* (Paris: Aubier, 1943), ch. 7, pp. 312–313.

39. See J. Welter, *L'exemplum dans la littérature religieuse et didactique du moyen âge* (Paris: E. H. Guitard, 1927).

40. See on this subject P. S. Moore, *The Works of Peter of Poitiers* (Washington, DC: Catholic University of America, 1936), and R. H. and M. A. Rouse, "Biblical Distinctions in the Thirteenth Century," *Archives d'histoire doctrinale et littéraire du moyen âge*, 41 (1974), 22–37; the 80 books and 9,885 chapters of Vincent de Beauvais' *Speculum* show the full development of this technique by the mid-thirteenth century. A. Wilmart, "*Un répertoire d'exégèse composé en Angleterre vers le début du xiiie siècle*," in P. H. Vincent, ed., *Memorial Lagrange* (Paris:

J. Vrin, 1940), pp. 307–346; and D. A. Callus, "The Contribution to the Study of the Fathers Made by the 13th-Century Oxford Schools," *The Journal of Ecclesiastical History,* 5 (1954), 139–148.

41. See, for example, Lloyd Daly, "Contributions to a History of Alphabetization in Antiquity and the Middle Ages," *Collection Latomus,* 90 (Brussels, 1967).

42. See the statement, for example, of Arnulf of Liège in the prologue to his *Alphabetum narrationum:* "volui divina gratia assistente multa in hoc uno volumine compilare de diversis tamen libris diversas quedam prout mihi magis placuit extraxi et ut querenti facilius occurrant materias diversas cum exemplis sub ordine litterarum alphabeti parare satis ordinate curavi" [B. L. Harley 268] in J. A. Herbert, ed., *The British Museum Catalogue of Romances in the Department of Manuscripts* (London: The British Museum, 1910), vol. 3, p. 429.

43. See J. Zahlten, *Creatio Mundi, Darstellungen der sechs Schöpfungstage und naturwissenschaftliches Weltbild im Mittelalter* (Stuttgart: Klett-Cotta, 1979), for a good account of the ramifications of the hexameral tradition.

44. See A. G. Little, *Liber exemplorum ad usum praedicantium,* British Society of Franciscan Studies 1 (Aberdeen: Typis Academicis, 1908); Homer Pfander, "The Medieval Friars and Some Alphabetical Reference-books for Sermons," *Medium Aevum,* 3 (1934), 19–29; Johannes Baptist Schneyer, *Geschichte der katholischen Predigt* (Freiburg i.Br.: Seelsorge Verlag, 1969), 175–185; Rouse and Rouse, *Preachers, Florilegia,* ch. I, pp. 19–29; and most recently, Christina von Nolcken, "Some Alphabetical Compendia and How Preachers Used Them in Fourteenth-Century England," *Viator,* 12 (1981), 271–288.

# Appendix: Manuscripts of Western Medieval Bestiary Versions

The principal sources of the following citations are: Florence McCulloch, *Mediaeval French and Latin Bestiaries* (Chapel Hill, 1962); Nikolaus Henkel, *Studien zum Physiologus im Mittelalter* (Tübingen, 1976); Max Goldstaub and Richard Wendriner, *Ein Tosco-Venezianischer Bestiarius* (Halle, 1892); Kenneth McKenzie, *PMLA*, 20, n.s. 13 (1905), 380–433; and Michel Salvat, "Notes sur les bestiaires catalans," in *Epopée animale, fable, fabliau. Actes du IV<sup>e</sup> Colloque de la Société Internationale Renardienne (Evreux, 1981)* (Paris: Presses universitaires de France, 1984), pp. 499–508. Additions by the editors are marked with an asterisk (\*).

## Latin Versions

B-Is VERSION (From McCulloch, 1962)
Combines the B *Physiologus* with excerpts from Isidore of Seville, *Etymologiae*. Manuscripts from the tenth to the late thirteenth centuries.

Cambridge, Corpus Christi College 22*
Malibu, Getty Museum Ludwig XV, 3 (formerly Sion College)
Malibu, Getty Museum Ludwig XV, 4 (formerly Dyson Perrins)
Oxford, Bodleian Library Bodley 602
Oxford, Bodleian Library Douce 167
Oxford, Bodleian Library Laud Misc. 247
Vatican, Cod. Palat. lat. 1074

DICTA CHRYSOSTOMI (DC) VERSION (From Henkel, 1976)
Based on the B *Physiologus*, this version has fewer chapters than its model, a division into beasts and birds, and additions to the Eagle chapter from Augustine and Jerome. Manuscripts date from the twelfth to the fifteenth centuries; a small majority are from the fourteenth and fifteenth centuries. Most manuscripts are of German production, although the version probably originated in France.

Bad Windsheim, Ratsbibl. Cod. 28

Brussels, Bibl. Roy. 18421–29*

Epinal, Bibl. Mun. 58 (209)

Göttweg, Stiftsbibl. Cod. ms. 154

Göttweg, Stiftsbibl. Cod. ms. 200

Harvard University, Houghton Library TYP 101

Leningrad, Gos. Publ. Biblioteka Saltykova-Shchedrina lat. Q.v.III,1*
    (see Clark, pp. 27, 32ff.)

Leipzig, Universitätsbibl. Paul. fol. 351

Leipzig, Universitätsbibl. Paul. 4° 1305

Linz, Studienbibl. Cod. ms. Cc.II.15

London, Brit. Library Sloane 278

Munich, Staatsbibl. clm 536

Munich, Staatsbibl. clm 2655

Munich, Staatsbibl. clm 3221

Munich, Staatsbibl. clm 5613

Munich, Staatsbibl. clm 5921

Munich, Staatsbibl. clm 6908

Munich, Staatsbibl. clm 9600

Munich, Staatsbibl. clm 14216

Munich, Staatsbibl. clm 14348

Munich, Staatsbibl. clm 14693

Munich, Staatsbibl. clm 16189

Munich, Staatsbibl. clm 19648

Munich, Staatsbibl. clm 23787

New York, Morgan Library M. 832

Paris, Bibl. de l'Arsenal lat. 394

Paris, Bibl. Nat. lat. 10448

Uppsala, Univ. Bibl. C 145

Vienna, Oesterr. Nat. Bibl. 303

Vienna, Oesterr. Nat. Bibl. 1010

Vienna, Oesterr. Nat. Bibl. 2511

Vienna, Oesterr. Nat. Bibl. 4609

Vienna, Oesterr. Nat. Bibl. 13378

Wolfenbüttel, Landesbibl. 35a Helmst.


H Version (From McCulloch, 1962)

A version of almost certain Parisian origin (see Clark, p. 33), based on the
B-Is version. The manuscripts are more or less contemporary, dating from
the third quarter of the thirteenth century.

Cambridge, Sidney Sussex College 100
Chalon-sur-Saône 14
Paris, Bibl. Nat. lat. 2495A
Paris, Bibl. Nat. lat. 2495B
Paris, Bibl. Nat. lat. 14429
Valenciennes, Bibl. Mun. 101

TRANSITIONAL VERSION (From McCulloch, 1962)
A much expanded bestiary combining B *Physiologus* chapters in the B-Is
order, additional Isidore excerpts and paraphrases, and chapters related to
the Second Family version all now classified under beasts, birds, fish, ser-
pents. Manuscripts from the late twelfth, early thirteenth, and early four-
teenth centuries.
　　Alnwick Castle Bestiary
　　Leningrad, Gos. Pub. Biblioteka Saltykova-Shchedrina lat. Q.v.V,1
　　London, Brit. Library Roy. 12.C.xix
　　Munich, Staatsbibl. gall. 16
　　New York, Morgan Library M. 81

SECOND FAMILY VERSION (From McCulloch, 1962)
The best known version, it is still longer. The contents resemble those of
the Transitional version, but with many more chapters, and further animal
classifications. Manuscripts from the twelfth to sixteenth centuries, but
principally the thirteenth century.
　　Aberdeen Univ. Library 24
　　Brussels, Bibl. Roy. 8340
　　Cambridge, Corpus Christi College 53
　　Cambridge, Fitzwilliam Museum 379*
　　Cambridge, Gonville and Caius College 109
　　Cambridge, Gonville and Caius College 372
　　Cambridge, Gonville and Caius College 384
　　Cambridge, Univ. Library Ii.4.26
　　Canterbury, Cath. Library Lit.D.10
　　Chartres, Bibl. Mun. 63 (125)*
　　Copenhagen, Kongl. Bibl. Gl. Kgl. 1633 4°
　　Douai, Bibl. Mun. 711
　　Le Mans, Bibl. Mun. 84*
　　London, Brit. Library Add. 11283
　　London, Brit. Library Harley 3244
　　London, Brit. Library Harley 4751

London, Brit. Library Roy. 12.F.xiii
London, Brit. Library Sloane 3544
Malibu, Getty Museum, Salvatorberg Bestiary (on loan), (Sotheby
    26.11, 1976, lot 829)*
Nîmes, Bibl. Mun. 82
New York, Morgan Library M. 890
Oxford, Bodleian Library Ashmole 1511
Oxford, Bodleian Library Bodley 533
Oxford, Bodleian Library Bodley 764
Oxford, Bodleian Library Douce 88
Oxford, Bodleian Library Douce 151
Oxford, St. Johns College 61
Oxford, St. Johns College 178
Oxford, Univ. College 120
Paris, Bibl. Nat. lat. 3630
Paris, Bibl. Nat. lat. 11207
Paris, Mazarine Library 742 (1115)*
Vatican, Apostolic Library Reg. 258

THIRD FAMILY VERSION (From McCulloch, 1962)
Even more chapters than the Second Family version. Includes Isidore's
account of fabulous races, extracts from Bernard Silvestris, the Wheel of
Fortune and Wonders of the World, extracts from Seneca and John of
Salisbury. All manuscripts are thirteenth and fourteenth century.
    Cambridge, Fitzwilliam Mus. 254
    Cambridge, Univ. Library Kk.4.25
    Oxford, Bodleian Library, Bodleian e Mus. 136
    Oxford, Bodleian Library Douce 88 E
    Westminster Abbey Library 22

FOURTH FAMILY VERSION (From McCulloch, 1962)
Also very large, and including excerpts from Bartholomaeus Anglicus and
Isidore. One manuscript, fifteenth century.
    Cambridge, Univ. Library Gg.6.5


*French Versions*
BESTIAIRE IN VERSE BY PHILIPPE DE THAON (From McCulloch, 1962)
Written in the early twelfth century for the English court, the text is based

on the B-Is bestiary and contains Latin prologues and rubrics. Classification of the animals. Manuscripts from the twelfth to the fourteenth centuries.

Copenhagen, Kongl. Bibl. 3466
London, Brit. Library Cott. Nero A.v
Oxford, Merton College 249

*BESTIAIRE* OF GERVAISE (From McCulloch, 1962)
Appears to derive from the DC Latin version. May have been written in Normandy in the early thirteenth century. One manuscript.

London, Brit. Library Add. 28260

*BESTIAIRE* OF GUILLAUME LE CLERC (From McCulloch, 1962)
Composed by a Norman cleric, it was one of the most popular French versions. Also called the *Bestiaire divin,* it was written in the early thirteenth century. Based on the B-Is Latin version. Manuscripts mainly thirteenth and fourteenth centuries.

Cambridge, Fitzwilliam McLean 123
Cambridge, Fitzwilliam Mus. J.20
Cambridge, Trinity College o.2.14 (2)
London, Brit. Library Cott. Vesp. A.vii
London, Brit. Library Egerton 613
London, Brit. Library Roy. 16.E.viii (missing)
Lyon, Palais des Arts 78
Oxford, Bodleian Library Douce 132
Oxford, Bodleian Library Douce 912
Paris, Bibl. de l'Arsenal 2691
Paris, Bibl. Nat. fr. 902
Paris, Bibl. Nat. fr. 1444
Paris, Bibl. Nat. fr. 2168
Paris, Bibl. Nat. fr. 14964
Paris, Bibl. Nat. fr. 14969
Paris, Bibl. Nat. fr. 14970
Paris, Bibl. Nat. fr. 20046
Paris, Bibl. Nat. fr. 24428
Paris, Bibl. Nat. fr. 25406
Paris, Bibl. Nat. fr. 25408
Paris, Bibl. Nat. Rothschild IV.2.24
ex-Phillipps Coll. 4156
Vatican, Apostolic Library Reg. 1682

*BESTIAIRE* OF PIERRE DE BEAUVAIS (From McCulloch, 1962)
Written before 1218 by Pierre, also called Le Picard, this is a complicated
version with a long and a short form. It, too, is based on the B-Is Latin
version, with additions from a variety of other sources. Manuscripts from
thirteenth to fifteenth centuries.

LONG FORM:
Montpellier, Fac. de Médicine H.437
Paris, Bibl. de l'Arsenal fr. 3516
ex-Phillipps 6739 (see Mermier, n. 88)
Vatican, Apostolic Library Reg. 1323
SHORT FORM:
Malines, Bibl. du Séminaire 32
Paris, Bibl. Nat. fr. 834
Paris, Bibl. Nat. fr. 944
Paris, Bibl. Nat. nouv. acq. 13251

## Middle English Version

Composed in East Midlands, first half thirteenth century, from the metri-
cal Latin *Physiologus* by Theobaldus (eleventh-century Italian monk). One
manuscript.
London, Brit. Library Arundel 292*

## Italian Versions

(From Goldstaub and Wendriner, 1892, and McKenzie, 1905.)
Appearing first in the fourteenth century, the Italian bestiaries combine an
Italian translation of the *Physiologus* with a variety of new materials, includ-
ing fables.
Florence, Bibl. Laurenziana Cod. plut. LXXXX Inf. Cod. 47 (Bibl.
   Gadd.)
Florence, Bibl. Laurenziana Cod. Ashb. 649
Florence, Bibl. Naz. Cod. Magliabecchiano II.8.33
Florence, Bibl. Naz. cl. XII Cod. Strozz. Magliabecchiano 135
Florence, Bibl. Ricardiana Cod. 1357 P.III.4
Florence, Bibl. Ricardiana Cod. 2183 R.IV 4 Nr. 2260
Florence, Bibl. Ricardiana Cod. 2281

Naples, Bibl. Naz. XII.E.11
Padova, Museo Civico di Padova (Bibl. Comun.) Cod. C.R.M.248
Paris, Bibl. Nat. ital. 450
Rome, Bibl. Corsini 44.G.27


## Catalan Versions

(From Salvat, 1984.)
These manuscripts are all copies of the Tuscan translation of the bestiary.
They date from the fifteenth and sixteenth centuries.

Barcelona, Bibl. Universitaria 75
Barcelona, Bibl. de Cataluña 87
Barcelona, Bibl. de Cataluña 310
Vic, Bibl. Capitular 229
Vic, Bibl. Capitular 1354

# Bibliography of Bestiary Studies Since 1962

This bibliography is a continuation of the one that Florence McCulloch included in the notes of her *Mediaeval Latin and French Bestiaries* as revised in 1962. The works listed below are published studies, mainly in literature and art, which have a direct bearing on the bestiary and related lore. Choices have at times been arbitrary. The time period covered by these studies is primarily that of the Middle Ages.

Albers, H. "Tierillustrationen in einer medizinischen Handschrift des 13. Jh. (Wellcome MS 573)," *Wiener Jahrbuch für Kunstgeschichte*, 26 (1973), 32–45.

Albertus Magnus. *The Book of Secrets of the Virtues of Herbs, Stones, and Certain Beasts*. . . . Ed. M. R. Best and F. H. Brightman. Oxford: Oxford University Press, 1973.

———. *Man and the Beasts*. Tr. J. J. Scanlan. Binghamton, NY: MRTS, 1987.

Armengaud, F., and D. Poirion. "Bestiaires." *Encyclopaedia universalis*, III. Paris: Encyclopaedia Universalis France, 1968. Pages 214–223.

Armstrong, Edward A. *The Folklore of Birds*. New York: Dover, 1970.

Baxter, Roland. "A Baronial Bestiary: Heraldic Evidence for the Patronage of Manuscript Bodley 764." *Journal of the Warburg and Courtauld Institutes*, 50 (1987), 196–200.

Beer, Jeanette. *Master Richard's Bestiary of Love and Response*. Berkeley: University of California Press, 1986.

*Bestiary, Bodleian Library, Oxford, MS Ashmole 1511*. Graz: Akademische Druk- und Verlagsanstalt, 1982

Bianciotto, Gabriel, ed. *Bestiaires du moyen âge*. Paris: Stock, 1980.

———. "Sur le Bestiaire d'amour de Richart de Fournival." In *Epopée animale, fable, fabliau. Actes du IVᵉ Colloque de la Société Internationale Renardienne (Evreux, 1981)*. Ed. G. Bianciotto and Michel Salvat. Paris: Publications de l'Université de Rouen, 1984. Pages 107–119.

———, and M. Salvat, ed. *Epopée animale, fable, fabliau. Actes du IVᵉ Colloque de la Société Internationale Renardienne (Evreux, 1981)*. Paris: Publications de l'Université de Rouen, 1984.

Bibolet, Françoise. "Les portraits d'oiseaux illustrants le De avibus d'Hugues de Fouilloy (ms Troyes 177)." *Mélanges à la mémoire du Père Anselme Dimier*, Pt. II, vol. 4. Ed. Benoît Chauvin. Beernem: De Windroos, 1984. Pages 409–447.

Brunner-Traut, Emma. "Ägyptische Mythen im Physiologus." *Festschrift für Siegfried Schott*. Ed. Wolfgang Helck. Wiesbaden: Harrassowitz, 1968. Pages 13–44.

————. "Altägyptische Mythen im Physiologus." *Antaios,* 10 (1969), 184–198.

————. "Spitzmaus und Ichneumon als Tiere des Sonnengottes." *Nachtr. der Akademie der Wissenschaften in Göttingen,* 7. Göttingen, 1965. Pages 123–163.

Cadart-Ricard, O. "Le thème de l'oiseau . . . chez onze troubadours. . . ." *Cahiers de civilisation médiévale,* 21 (1978), 205–230.

Campbell, T. P. "Thematic Unity in the Old English Physiologus." *Archiv für das Studium der neueren Sprachen und Literaturen,* 215 (1978), 73–79.

Cella, Mariaserena. "Le fonti letterarie della simbologia medievale: i bestiari," *Romanico, Atti del seminario di studi diretto da Piero Sanpaolesi . . . 1973.* Milan: Istituto per la storia del arte Lombarda, 1975.

Clark, Ann. *Beasts and Bawdy.* New York: Taplinger, 1975.

Clark, Willene B. "Three Manuscripts for Clairmarais: A Cistercian Contribution to Early Gothic Figure Style." *Cistercian Art and Architecture,* III. Ed. Meredith P. Lillich. Kalamazoo: Cistercian Publications, 1987. Pages 97–110. (On an aviary manuscript.)

————. "The Illustrated Medieval Aviary and the Lay-Brotherhood," *Gesta,* 21 (1982), 63–74.

Cledat, Jean-Paul. *Bestiaire fabuleux.* Paris: A. Michel, 1971.

Clutton-Brock, Juliet. *Domesticated Animals from Early Times.* Austin: University of Texas Press, 1981.

Cogliati Arano, Luisa. "Approccio metodologico al bestiario medievale." *Atti del I Congreso Nazionale di Storia dell'Arte* (Rome 1978). Rome: Consiglio naz. delle ricerche, 1980.

————. "Bestiari ed erbari dal manoscritto alla stampa." In *Le stampe e la diffusione delle imagini e degli stili* (International Congress of the History of Art, Bologna, 1979). Ed. Henri Zerner. Bologna: CLUEG, 1983. Pages 17–22.

————. "Fonti figurative del 'Bestiario' di Leonardo." *Arte Lombarda,* 62 (1982), 151–160.

————. "Il manoscritto C.246 Inf. della Biblioteca Ambrosiana, Solino." *Miniatura italiana in eta romanica e gotica.* Florence: Olschki, 1979. Pages 239–258.

Crespo, Roberto. *Una versione pisana del* Bestiaire d'amours. Leiden: Collana Romanistica Leidense XVII, 1972.

Dardano, Maurizio. "Note sul bestiario toscano." *Italia dialettale,* 30 (1967), 29–117.

Decembrio, Pier Candido. *The Book of Animals.* Facsimile of the Vatican manuscript. Stuttgart, Paris, New York: Belvedere Press, 1987.

De Clerq, Charles. "La Nature et le sens du De avibus d'Hugues de Fouilloy." *Methoden in Wissenschaft und Kunst des Mittelalters.* Ed. Albert Zimmerman. Berlin: De Gruyter, 1970. Pages 279–302.

De La Breteque, François. "Image d'un animal: le lion. Sa définition et ses 'limites' dans les textes et l'iconographie (XIᵉ–XIVᵉ siècles)." *Le Monde animal et ses représentations au moyen-âge (XIᵉ–XVᵉ siècles).* Actes du XVᵉᵐᵉ Congrès de la Société des Historiens Médiévistes de l'Enseignement Supérieur Public, Toulouse, 25–26 mai 1984. Toulouse: Université de Toulouse-Le-Mirail, 1985. Pages 11–45.

Demus, Otto. "Bemerkungen zum Physiologus von Smyrna." *Jahrbuch der österreichen Byzantinistik,* 25 (1976), 235–257.

Deschamps, N., and R. Bruno. "L'univers des bestiaires: Dossier bibliographique et choix de textes." *Etudes françaises*, 10 (August 1974), 231–282.

Deschaux, R. "Le bestiaire de Guillaume de Machaut." *Cahiers de l'Association internationale des études françaises*, 31 (1979), 7–16.

Dicke, Gerd, and Klaus Grubmueller. *Die Fabeln des Mittelalters und der frühen Neuzeit*. Munich: Wilhelm Fink Verlag, 1987.

Diekstra, F. N. M. "The *Physiologus*, the Bestiaries, and Medieval Animal Lore." *Neophilologus*, 69: 1 (1985), 142–155.

Dixon, Laurinda S. "Music, Medicine, and Morals: The Iconography of an Early Musical Instrument." *Studies in Iconography*, 7/8 (1981–1982), 147–156. (Bestiary subjects.)

Durliat, Marcel. "Le monde animal et ses représentations iconographiques du XIᵉ au XVᵉᵐᵉ siècle." *Le monde animal et ses représentations au moyen-âge*. Actes du XVᵉᵐᵉ Congrès de la Société des Historiens Médiévistes de l'Enseignement Supérieur Publique, Toulouse, 25–26 mai 1984. Toulouse: Université de Toulouse-Le-Mirail, 1985. Pages 73–92.

Einhorn, Jurgen W. "Das Einhorn als Sinnzeichen des Todes: Die Parabel vom Mann im Abgrund." *Frühmittelalterliche Studien*, 6 (1972), 381–417.

———. *Spiritalis unicornis. Das Einhorn als Bedeutungstrager in Literatur und Kunst des Mittelalters*. Munich: Wilhelm Fink Verlag, 1976.

Elliott, Thomas J. *A Medieval Bestiary* [Middle English Bestiary Brit. Library Arundel MS 292]. Boston: Godine, 1971.

Faucheux, Claude. "Remarques sur le bestiaire du Rosarius et sur son auteur." In *XIV Congresso internazionale di linguistica et filologia romanze. Atti, V.* Ed. A. Varvaro. Naples: Macchiardi, 1981. Pages 433–443.

Forbes, Thomas R. "Medical Lore in the Bestiaries." *Medical History*, 12 (1968), 245–253.

Forsyth, Ilene H. "The Theme of Cockfighting in Burgundian Romanesque Sculpture." *Speculum*, 53 (1978), 252–282. (Discusses the cock in the bestiary.)

Freeman, Margaret B. *The Unicorn Tapestries*. New York: Metropolitan Museum of Art, E. P. Dutton, 1976.

Friedman, John B. "The Marvels-of-the-East Tradition in Anglo-Saxon Art." *Sources of Anglo-Saxon Culture*. Ed. P. E. Szarmach and V. D. Oggins. Kalamazoo: Medieval Institute Publications, 1986.

———. *The Monstrous Races in Medieval Art and Thought*. Cambridge, Massachusetts, and London: Harvard University Press, 1981.

Friedmann, Herbert. *A Bestiary for Saint Jerome: Animal Symbolism in European Religious Art*. Washington, DC: Smithsonian Institution Press, 1980.

Fuente, Albert de la. "Tigres y estilos en bestiario." *Explicacion de textos literarios*, 8 (1979–80), 137–143.

Garver, M. E., and Kenneth McKenzie. *Il Bestiario toscano (Spogli elettronici del 'italiano delle origini e del duecento)*. Vol. II, *Forme*. Bologna: Il Mulino, 1971.

Gaxdaru, D. "Vestigios de bestiarios medievales en las literaturas hispanicas e iberoamericanas." *Romanistisches Jahrbuch*, 22 (1971), 259–274.

George, Wilma. "The Bestiary: A Handbook of the Local Archives." *Archives of Natural History*, 10 (1981), 187–203.

————. "The Living World of the Bestiary." *Archives of Natural History*, 12 (1985), 161–164.

————. "The Yale." *Journal of the Warburg and Courtauld Institutes*, 31 (1968), 423–428.

Gerhardt, Mia J. "The Ant-Lion: Nature Study and Interpretation of a Biblical Text from the *Physiologus* to Albert the Great." *Vivarium*, 3 (1965), 1–23.

————. "Zoologie médiévale: préoccupations et procédés." *Miscellanea Mediaevalia*, 7 (1970), 231–248.

Gerlach, Peter. "Physiologus." *Lexikon der christlichen Ikonographie*, III. Ed. Engelbert Kirschbaum, Günter Bandmann, et al. Rome: Herder, 1971. Pages 432–436.

Graham, Victor. "The Pelican as Image and Symbol." *Revue de littérature comparée*, 36 (1962), 235–243.

Gransden, Antonia. "Realistic Observation in Twelfth Century England." *Speculum*, 47 (1972), 29–51. (Includes bestiaries.)

Grilletto, Renato. "I copti e la mummificazione: note agli scavi nella necropoli di Antinoe." *Corso di cultura sull'arte ravennate e bizantina*, 28 (1981), 119–123. (On the phoenix myth.)

Grossinger, Christa. "English Misericords of the Thirteenth and Fourteenth Centuries and Their Relationship to Manuscript Illuminations." *Journal of the Warburg and Courtauld Institutes*, 36 (1975), 97–108. (Bestiary subjects.)

Gruffydd, M. Lloyd. "Seventeenth-century Bestiary Ware from Buckley, Clwyd." *Archaeologia Cambrensis*, 129 (1980), 160–164.

Haring, Nicolas. "Notes on the *Liber Avium* of Hugues de Fouilloy." *Recherches de théologie ancienne et médiévale*, 46 (1979), 53–83.

Hassall, William O. "Bestiares d'Oxford." *Les dossiers de l'archéologie*, 16 (May–June 1976), 71–81.

————. "Medieval Animal Pictures." *British History Illustrated*, 5: 2 (1978), 20–25.

Helsinger, Howard. "Images on the Beatus Page of Some Medieval Psalters." *Art Bulletin*, 53 (1971), 161–176. (Animal iconography.)

Henderson, Arnold Clayton. "Medieval Beasts and Modern Cages: The Making of Meaning in Fables and Bestiaries." *PMLA*, 97: 1 (1982), 40–49.

Henkel, Nikolaus. "Die Begleitverse als Tituli in der *Physiologus*-Überlieferung." *Mittellateinisches Jahrbuch*, 14 (1979), 256–258.

————. *Studien zum Physiologus im Mittelalter*. Tübingen: Max Niemeyer Verlag, 1976.

Heslop, T. A. "Brief in Words but Heavy in the Weight of Its Mysteries." *Art History*, 9 (1986), 1–11. (On hidden animal symbolism.)

*Het dier in de prentkunst: grafiek uit de 15ᵈᵉ tot de 17ᵈᵉ eeuw*. Exhibition catalog, Museum Boymans-van Beuningen, Rotterdam, February–April 1974.

Holmes, Urban Tigner. "The Monster in Medieval Literature." In *Studies in Honour of Alfred G. Engstrom*. Ed. T. Cargo and E. H. Mickel. Chapel Hill: University of North Carolina Press, 1972. Pages 53–62.

Hutchinson, G. Evelyn. "Attitudes Toward Nature in Medieval England: The Alphonso and Bird Psalters." *Isis*, 65 (1974), 5–37.

Igarashi-Takeshita, Midori. "Les lions dans la sculpture romane en Poitou." *Cahiers de civilisation médiévale*, 23: 1 (1980), 37–54.

Jauss, H. R. "Rezeption und Poetisierung des *Physiologus*." *Grundriß der romanischen Literaturen des Mittelalters*. Heidelberg: Carl Winter, 1968. Vol. 6, part 1, pp. 170–

181; vol. 6, part 2, pp. 219–230.

Jean-Nesmy, Claude, ed. *Bestiaire roman: Textes médiévaux*. La Pierre-qui-Vivre: Zodiaque, 1977.

Jones, G. F. "Oswald von Wolkenstein's Animals and Animal Symbolism." *Modern Language Notes*, 94 (1974), 524–540.

Kadar, Zoltan. "Anfänge der zoologischen Buchillustration." *Das Altertum*, 19 (1973), 88–95.

———. *Survivals of Greek Zoological Illuminations in Byzantine Manuscripts*. Budapest: Akademiai Kaido, 1978.

Kaimakis, Dimitris, ed. *Der Physiologus nach der ersten Redaktion*. Beiträge für klassischen Philologie, 63. Meisenheim am Glan: A. Hain, 1974.

Kappler, Claude. *Monstres, démons et merveilles à la fin du moyen âge*. Paris: Payot, 1980.

Kauffmann, C. M. *Romanesque Manuscripts 1066–1190*. A Survey of Manuscripts Illuminated in the British Isles III. London: Harvey Miller, 1975. Nos. 36 and 104–106 are bestiaries.

Kleineidam, Hartmut. "*Li Volucraires*, Edition eines afr. Gedichtes aus dem 13. Jh.," *Zeitschrift für romanische Philologie*, 86 (1970), 1–21.

Klingender, Francis D. *Animals in Art and Thought to the End of the Middle Ages*. London: Routledge and Kegan Paul, 1971.

Kracher, A., ed. *Millstätter Genesis und Physiologus Handschrift*. Facsimile of Klagenfurt, Geschichtsverein für Kärnten . . . MS 619. Graz: Akademische Druck- und Verlagsanstalt, 1967.

Kraus, H. P. *Monumenta codicum manuscriptorum*. New York: H. P. Kraus, 1974. (Includes a bestiary.)

———. *In Retrospect: A Catalogue of 100 Outstanding Manuscripts*. . . . New York: H. P. Kraus, 1978. (Includes a bestiary.)

Kuijper, F. "Ad Theobaldi *Physiologus*." *Mittelateinisches Jahrbuch*, 9 (1973), 122–123.

Lacroix, Jean. "Sur quelques bestiaires moderns." In *Epopée animale, fable, fabliau. Actes du IVᵉ Colloque de la Société Internationale Renardienne (Evreux, 1981)*. Ed. G. Bianciotto and M. Salvat. Paris: Publications de l'Université de Rouen, 1984.

Lefevre, S. "Polymorphisme et métamorphose dans les bestiaires." In *Métamorphose et bestiaire fantastique au moyen âge*. Ed. L. Harf-Lancner. Paris: Ecole Normale Supérieure de Jeunes Filles, 1985. Pages 215–246.

Lewine, Carol F. "*Vulpes fossa habent* or the Miracle of the Bent Woman in the Gospels of St. Augustine, Corpus Christi College, Cambridge, MS 286." *Art Bulletin*, 56 (1974), 489–504. (Motif occurring in bestiaries.)

Lugones, N. A. "El ave fénix en el *Libro de Alexandre*." *Revista de archivos bibliotecas y museos, Madrid*, 79 (1976), 581–586.

———. *Los bestiarios en la literatura medieval española*. In *Dissertation Abstracts International*, 37 (1976), No. 2854A.

Malaxecheverria, Ignacio. *Le bestiaire médiéval et l'archétype de la fémininité*. Paris: Lettres Modernes, 1982.

———. "Castor et lynx médiévaux: leur sénéfiance." *Florilegium: Carleton University Annual Papers on Classical Antiquity and the Middle Ages*, 3 (1981), 228–238.

Marijnissen, Roger H. *Laatmideeleeuwse symboliek en de beeldentaal van Hieronymus Bosch*. Brussels: Paleis der Academien, 1977.

Mateo Gomez, Isabel. *Temas profanos en la escultura gótica española: las sillerías de coro*. Madrid: Consejo Superior de Investigaciones Cientificas, Instituto Diego Velásquez, 1979. (Bestiary motifs.)

Maurer, Friedrich. *Der altdeutsche Physiologus*. Tübingen: Max Niemeyer Verlag, 1967.

McCulloch, Florence. "L'éale et la centicore—deux bêtes fabuleuses." In *Hommages René Crozet*. Poitiers: Centre d'études supérieures de civilisation médiévale, 1966.

————. "Mermicoleon, a Medieval Latin Word for 'Pearl Oyster.'" *Mediaeval Studies*, 27 (1965), 331–334.

————. "Richard de Fournival's *Bestiaire d'amour* and Pierre Gringore's *Menu propos*." *Romance Notes*, 10 (1968), 145–160.

————. "Le tigre et le miroir—la vie d'une image." *Revue des sciences humaines*, 33 (1968), 149–160.

————. "The Waldensian Bestiary and Libellus de natura animalium." *Mediaevalia et Humanistica*, 5 (1963), 15–30.

Menhardt, Hermann. "Die Mandragora im Millstätter Physiologus, bei Honorius Augustodunensis und im St. Trudperter Hohenliede." In *Festschrift Ludwig Wolff*. Neumünster, 1962. Pages 173–194.

Mermier, Guy. "De Pierre de Beauvais et particulièrement de son bestiaire: vers une solution des problèmes." *Romanische Forschungen*, 78 (1966), 338–371.

————, ed. *Le Bestiaire de Pierre de Beauvais, version courte*. Paris: A. G. Nizet, 1977.

Misch, M. *Apis est animal—apis est ecclesia: Ein Beitrag zum Verhältnis von Naturkunde und Theologie in Spämittelalter und mittelalterlicher Literatur*. Bern: Lang, 1974.

Mode, Heinz Adolf. *Fabeltiere und Dämonen in der Kunst: die fantastische Welt der Mischwesen*. Leipzig: Edition Leipzig, 1973; Stuttgart: Kohlhammer, 1974. (Translated as *Fabulous Beasts and Demons*, London and New York: Phaidon, 1975.)

Mokretsova, I. P., and V. L. Romanova. *Les manuscrits enluminés français du XIIIᵉ siècle dans les collections soviétiques 1270–1300*. Moscow: Iskusstvo, 1984. No. X. (Aviary-bestiary manuscript.)

*Monsters, Gargoyles, and Dragons: Animals in the Middle Ages*. Exhibition catalog, Mount Holyoke College. Ed. Joan Esch. South Hadley, Massachusetts: Mount Holyoke College, 1977.

Morgan, Nigel. *Early Gothic Manuscripts (I): 1190–1285*. A Survey of Manuscripts Illuminated in the British Isles IV, 2 vols. London, Oxford, New York: Harvey Miller and Oxford University Press, 1982, 1988. Nos. 11, 13, 17, 19–21, 42, 53–55, 64, 76, 80, 98, 115, 144, 171, and 172 are English bestiaries.

Mota, J. A., R. V. Matos, V. L. Sampaio, and N. Rossi, eds. *Livro des aves (Diccionario da lingua Portuguesa: Texto e Vocabularios)*. Rio de Janeiro: Instituto Nacional do Livro, 1965.

Muratova, Xenia. "Adam donne leur noms aux animaux: L'iconographie de la scène dans l'art du moyen âge et ses traits particuliers dans les manuscrits des bestiaires. . . ." *Nuovi studi medievali*, 18 (1977), 367–394.

————. "L'arte longobarda e il *Physiologus*." *Atti del 6. Congresso internazionale di studi sull'alto medioevo (Milan, 1978)*. Spoleto: Centro Italiano di Studi Sull'Alto Medioevo, 1980. Pages 547–558.

————. "Bestiaries: An Aspect of Medieval Patronage." In *Art and Patronage in the English Romanesque*. Ed. Sarah Macready and F. H. Thompson. The Society of Antiquaries of London, Occasional Paper (New Series) VIII. London: Burlington House/Thames and Hudson, 1986.

————. "The Decorated Manuscripts of the Bestiary of Philippe de Thaon . . . and the Problem of the Illustrations of the Medieval Poetical Bestiary." *Proceedings. Third International Beast Epic, Fable, and Fabliaux Colloquium*. Ed. Jan Goossens and Timothy Sodmann. Cologne and Vienna: Böhlau, 1981.

————. "L'iconografia medievale e l'ambiente storico." *Storia dell arte*, 28 (1978), 171–179.

————. "I manoscritti miniati del bestiario medievale: origine, formazione e sviluppo dei cicli di illustrazioni. I bestiari miniati in Inghilterra nei secoli XII–XIV." *Settimani di studio del centro italiano di studi sull'alto medioevo XXXI: L'uomo di fronte al mondo animale nel alto medioevo*. Spoleto: Panetto and Petrelli, 1985.

————. *The Medieval Bestiary*. Partial facsimile, with commentary, of Leningrad State Public Library Saltykova-Shchedrina MS lat. Q.v.V.1. Moscow: Iskusstvo, 1984.

————. "Les miniatures du manuscrit Fr. 14969 de la Bibliothèque nationale de Paris (le bestiaire de Guillaume le Clerc). . . ." *Marche romane*, 28 (1978), 141–148.

————. "Problèmes de l'origine et des sources des cycles d'illustrations des manuscrits des bestiaires." In *Epopée animale, fable, fabliau. Actes du IVᵉ Colloque de la Société Internationale Renardienne (Evreux, 1981)*. Ed. G. Bianciotto and M. Salvat. Paris: Publications de l'Université de Rouen, 1984.

————. "La production des manuscrits du Physiologus grecs enluminés en Italie aux XVᵉ–XVIᵉ siècles et leur place dans l'histoire de la tradition de l'illustration du Physiologue." *Jahrbuch der oesterreichischen Byzantinistik*, 32: 6 (1982), 327–340.

Muratova, Xenia, D. Poirion, M.-F. Dupuis, and S. Louis. *Bestiarium: Fac-similé du manuscrit du bestiaire Ashmole 1511*. . . . Paris: Club du Livre, 1984.

Neuss, Elmer. *Studien zu den althochdeutschen Tierbezeichnungen der Handschriften Paris lat. 9344, Berlin lat. 8073, Trier R.III.13, und Wolfenbüttel 10.3.Aug.40*. Munich: W. Fink, 1973.

Ohly, Friedrich. "Probleme der mittelalterlichen Bedeutungsforschung und das Taubenbild des Hugo de Folieto." *Frühmittelalterliche Studien*, 2 (1968), 162–201.

Olteanu, Pandele, ed. "N. Milescu-Spătarul: 'Cartea naturii.'" *Manuscriptum*, 13: 2 (1982), 55–66.

Pasti, Stefana. "Un altare ed un'epigrafe medioevali nel duomo di Segni." *Storia dell'arte*, 44 (1982), 57–62. (On birds and dragons.)

Pastoreau, Michel. "Le Bestiaire héraldique au moyen âge." *Revue française d'héraldique et de sigillographie*, 1972, 3–17.

————. "Quel est le roi des animaux?" *Le Monde animal et ses représentations au moyen-âge (XIᵉ–XVᵉ siècles)*. Actes du XVᵉᵐᵉ Congrès de la Société des Historiens Médiévistes de l'Enseignement Supérieur Public, Toulouse, 25–26 mai 1984. Toulouse: Université de Toulouse-Le-Mirail, 1984. Pages 133–142.

Penco, Gregorio. "Il simbolismo animalesco nella letteratura monastica." *Studia Monastica,* 6 (1964), 7–36.

Peters, Heinz. "'Miles Christianus' oder Falke und Taube: Eine ikonographische Skizze." In *Festschrift für Otto von Simson zu 65. Geburtstag.* Ed. L. Griesebach and K. Renger. Berlin: Propyläen, 1977. Pages 53–61. (On the Aviary.)

Pfeffer, Wendy. *The Change of Philomel: The Nightingale in Medieval Literature.* New York: Peter Lang, 1985.

*Physiologus Bernensis.* Facsimile of Bern, Bürgerbibliothek MS 318. Ed. C. von Steiger and O. Homburger. Basel: Alkuin-Verlag, 1964.

Planche, Alice. "La double licorne ou le chasseur chassé." *Marche romane,* 30: 3–4 (1980), 237–246.

Pucko, Vasilij. *"Hudozestvennyj dekor Jur'evskogo Evangelija."* Ars Hungarica, 7: 1 (1979), 7–22. (Animal drawings in a twelfth-century Russian Gospels.)

Randall, Lilian M. C. *Images in the Margins of Gothic Manuscripts.* Berkeley and Los Angeles: University of California Press, 1966. (Bestiary motifs.)

Rebuffi, Claudia. "La redazione rimaneggiata del *Bestiaire* di Pierre de Beauvais: Problemi di cronologia." *In ricordo di Cesare Angelini: Studi di letteratura e filologia.* Ed. Franco Alessio and Angelo Stella. Milan: Saggiatore, 1979. Pages 23–33.

———. "Studi sulla tradizione del bestiaire di Pierre de Beauvais." *Medioevo Romanzo,* 3 (1976), 165–194.

Reinsch, Robert. *Le Bestiaire. Das Tierbuch.* Wiesbaden: M. Sandig, 1967.

Roscoe, Ingrid. "Mimic Without Mind: Singerie in Northern Europe." *Apollo,* 114 (August 1981), 96–103.

Roth, Charles. "Du bestiaire divin au bestiaire d'amour." *Etudes de lettres,* series 3: 2 (1969), 199–216.

Rowland, Beryl. *Animals with Human Faces.* Knoxville: University of Tennessee Press, 1973.

———. *Birds with Human Souls.* Knoxville: University of Tennessee Press, 1978.

———. *Blind Beasts: Chaucer's Animal World.* Kent, OH: Kent State University Press, 1971.

———. "T. H. White and the Notebooks of George C. Druce." *The Serif,* 8 (1972), 7–10.

———. "The Wisdom of the Cock." In *Proceedings, Third International Beast Epic, Fable, and Fabliau Colloquium. Muenster, 1979.* Ed. J. Goossens and T. Sodmann. Cologne and Vienna: Böhlau Verlag, 1981. Pages 340–355.

Salvat, Michel. "Notes sur les bestiaire catalans." In *Epopée animale, fable, fabliau. Actes du IVᵉ Colloque de la Société Internationale Renardienne (Evreux, 1981).* Ed. G. Bianciotto and M. Salvat. Paris: Publications de l'Université de Rouen, 1984. Pages 499–508.

Sandler, Lucy Freeman. *Gothic Manuscripts 1285–1385.* A Survey of Manuscripts Illuminated in the British Isles V. London and Oxford: Harvey Miller/Oxford University Press, 1986. Nos. 20, 23, 39, and 49 are bestiaries.

Sauer, Ekkart. "Tier in der christlichen Kunst." In *Lexikon für Theologie und Kirche,* X. Freiburg: Herder, 1965. Pages 190–191.

Schade, Herbert. *Dämonen und Monstren, Gestaltungen des Bösen in der Kunst des frühen Mittelalters.* Regensburg: Pustet, 1962.

Scheller, R. W. *A Survey of Medieval Model Books.* Haarlem: De Erven F. Bohn, 1963. (Includes bestiaries and bestiary motifs.)

Schmidtke, Dietrich. *Geistliche Tierinterpretation in der deutschsprachigen Literatur des Mittelalters (1100–1500).* 2 Vols. Diss., Freie Universität Berlin, 1968.

———. "Physiologus Theobaldi deutsch." *Beiträge zur Geschichte der deutschen Sprache und Literatur,* 89 (1967), 270–301.

Schwab, Ute, ed. *Das Tier in der Dichtung.* Heidelberg: Carl Winter, 1970.

Shur, Elmer G. "An Interpretation of the Unicorn." *Folklore,* 75 (1964), 91–109.

Silvestre, Hubert. "Le nouveau primitif du *Bruxellensis* 10066-7." In *Miscellanea codicologica F. Masai: dicata MCMLXXIX.* Ed. Pierre Cockshaw, Monique-Cécile Garand, and Pierre Jodogne. Ghent: E. Story-Scientia S.P.R.L., 1979. Pages 131–151. (Manuscript includes a *Physiologus.*)

Stahl, Harvey. "Le bestiaire de Douai." *Revue de l'art,* 8 (1970), 6–15.

Stammler, Wolfgang. "Melker Physiologus." *Spätlese des Mittelalters,* II: Religiöse Schrifttum. Ed. Wolfgang Stammler. Berlin: E. Schmidt, 1965. Pages 103–133.

Steinen, Wolfram von den. "Altchristlich-mittelalterliche Tiersymbolik." *Symbolon,* 4 (1964), 218–243.

———. "Ein 'Moralischer Physiologus' in Reimen." In *Festschrift Josef Quint.* Bonn, 1964. Pages 218–243.

Stock, Brian. *Myth and Science in the Twelfth Century.* Princeton: Princeton University Press, 1972. (General nature study.)

Storm, Melvin. "The Tercelet as Tiger: Bestiary Hypocrisy in the Squire's Tale." *English Language Notes,* 14 (1975/76), 172–174.

Sünger, Marie Therese. *Studien zur Struktur der Wiener und Millstätter Genesis.* Klagenfurt: Kärntner Museumschriften, 1964. (Includes *Physiologus.*)

*Theobaldi Physiologus.* Ed. and tr. P. T. Eden. Leiden: E. J. Brill, 1972.

Threu, Ursula. "Das Wiesel im Physiologus." *Wissenschaftliche Zeitschrift der Universität Rostock, gesellschafts- und sprachwiss. Reihe,* 12: 2 (1963), 275ff.

Tubach, F. C. "Amos VII, 14, Schenute und der Physiologus." *Novum testamentum,* 10 (1968), 234–240.

———. "Zur Datierung des Physiologus." *Zeitschrift für neutestamentliche Wissenschaft,* 57 (1966), 101–104.

———. *Index exemplorum: A Handbook of Medieval Religious Tales.* Helsinki: Suomalainen Tiedeakatemia, 1969. (Includes Bestiary motifs.)

Unterkircher, Franz. *Bestiarium: Die Texte der Handschrift MS Ashmole 1511 der Bodleian Library Oxford in Lateinischer und Deutscher Sprache.* Interpretationes ad codices, Bd. 3. Graz: Akademische Druck- und Verlagsanstalt, 1986.

———. *Tiere, Glaube, Aberglaube: Die schönsten Miniaturen aus dem Bestiarium (Bodleian Library, Oxford, MS Ashmole 1511).* Graz: Akademische Druck- und Verlagsanstalt, 1986.

Vaurie, C. "Birds in the Prayer Book of Bonne of Luxembourg." *The Metropolitan Museum of Art Bulletin,* 19 (1970–71), 279–283.

Vincent-Cassy, Mireille. "Les animaux et les péchés capitaux: de la symbolique à l'emblématique." *Le monde animal et ses représentations au moyen-âge (XIᵉ–XVᵉ siècles).* Actes du XVᵉᵐᵉ Congrès de la Société des Historiens Médiévistes de l'Enseignement Supérieur Public, Toulouse, 24–26 mai 1984. Toulouse: Université de Toulouse-Le-Mirail, 1985.

Wailes, S. L. "The Crane, the Peacock, and the Reading of Walter von der Vogel-
weide 19, 29." *Modern Language Notes,* 88 (1973), 947–955.

Wehrli, Max. "Ruodlieb und die Tiere." In Max Wehrli, *Formen mittelalterlicher
Erzählung.* Zürich: Atlantis, 1969. (Includes *Physiologus.*)

Willemsen, Carl Arnold. *L'Enigma di Otranto: il mosaico pavimentale del presbitero
Pantaleone nella cattedrale.* Tr. R. Disanto. Galantina: Congedo, 1980. (Includes
*Physiologus.*)

Yapp, Brunsdon. "Birds in Bestiaries: Medieval Knowledge of Nature." *The Cambridge Review* (20 November 1984), 183–190.

———. "Birds in Captivity in the Middle Ages." *Archives of Natural History,* 10
(1982), 479–500.

———. *Birds in Medieval Manuscripts.* London: The British Library, 1981.

———. "The Birds and Other Animals of Longthorpe Tower." *Antiquaries Journal,* 8:2 (1978), 355–358.

———. "A New Look at English Bestiaries." *Medium aevum,* 14:1 (1985), 1–19.

Zambon, Francesco. *Il Bestiario di Cambridge.* Parma and Milan: Franco Maria
Ricci, 1974.

———. "*Figura bestialis.* Les fondements théoretiques du bestiaire médiéval." In
*Epopée animale, fable, fabliau. Actes du IV^e Colloque de la Société Internationale
Renardienne (Evreux, 1981).* Ed. G. Bianciotto and M. Salvat. Paris: Publications
de l'Université de Rouen, 1984. Pages 709–719.

Zink, Michel. "Le monde animal et ses représentations dans la littérature au moyen
âge." In *Le monde animal et ses représentations au moyen-âge (XI^e–XV^e siècles).*
Actes du XV^ème Congrès de la Société des Historiens Médiévistes de l'Enseignement Supérieur Public, Toulouse, 25–26 mai 1984. Toulouse: Université de
Toulouse-Le-Mirail, 1985. Pages 45–71.

# Contributors

Beer, Jeanette. Professor of French, Purdue University, West Lafayette, Indiana. Author of eight books including the first English translation of Richard de Fournival's *Bestiaire d'Amour* (Berkeley: University of California Press, 1986).

Clark, Willene B. Professor of Art History, Marlboro College, Marlboro, Vermont. Author of articles on early Gothic illumination, the Aviary, and a forthcoming edition, translation, and manuscript study of Hugh of Fouilloy's Aviary.

Curley, Michael J. Associate Professor of English and Director of the Honors Program, University of Puget Sound, Tacoma, Washington. Author of an English translation of the *Physiologus* (Medieval and Renaissance Text Series, Binghamton, New York, 1984).

Friedman, John B. Professor of English, University of Illinois, Champaign-Urbana, Illinois. Author of *The Monstrous Races in Medieval Art and Thought* (Cambridge: Harvard University Press, 1981) and *Orpheus in the Middle Ages* (Cambridge: Harvard University Press, 1970).

Joslin, Mary Coker. Associate Professor of French and Spanish, St. Augustine's College, Raleigh, North Carolina. Author of *The Heard Word* (Jackson: University of Mississippi Press, 1986).

McMunn, Meradith T. Associate Professor of English, Rhode Island College, Providence, Rhode Island. Author of articles on medieval romance, the interrelation of text and illustration in medieval vernacular manuscripts, and a forthcoming edition of the *Roman de Kanor*.

Mermier, Guy R. Professor of French and Director of the Medieval and Renaissance Collegium, University of Michigan, Ann Arbor, Michigan. Author of numerous articles on the medieval bestiary, including the entry on the bestiary in the *Lexikon des Mittelalters,* and editor of *Le Bestiaire de Pierre de Beauvais, version courte* (Paris: Nizet, 1977).

Muratova, Xenia. Professor of Art History, University of Paris–Nanterre, France. Author of *The Medieval Bestiary,* translated by I. Kitrosskaya (Moscow: Iskusstvo, 1984), and numerous articles on bestiaries.

Pfeffer, Wendy. Associate Professor of French, University of Louisville, Louisville, Kentucky. Author of *The Change of Philomel* (New York: Peter Lang, 1985).

Randall, Lilian M. C. Curator of Manuscripts, Walters Art Gallery, Baltimore, Maryland. Author of *Images in the Margins of Medieval Gothic Manuscripts* (Berkeley: University of California Press, 1966) and a forthcoming catalog of manuscripts in the Walters Art Gallery.

Rowland, Beryl. Research Professor of English, York University, Downsview, Ontario. Author of *Blind Beasts: Chaucer's Animal World* (Kent, Ohio: Kent State University Press, 1971); *Animals with Human Faces* (Knoxville: University of Tennessee Press, 1973); and *Birds with Human Souls* (Knoxville: University of Tennessee Press, 1978).

# Index

References to the illustrations are by figure number in italics.

University of Pennsylvania Press
MIDDLE AGES SERIES
*Edward Peters, General Editor*

Edward Peters, ed. *Christian Society and the Crusades, 1198–1229.* Sources in Translation, including The Capture of Damietta by Oliver of Paderborn. 1971

Edward Peters, ed. *The First Crusade: The Chronicle of Fulcher of Chartres and Other Source Materials.* 1971

Katherine Fischer Drew, trans. *The Burgundian Code: The Book of Constitutions or Law of Gundobad and Additional Enactments.* 1972

G. G. Coulton. *From St. Francis to Dante: Translations from the Chronicle of the Franciscan Salimbene (1221–1288).* 1972

Alan C. Kors and Edward Peters, eds. *Witchcraft in Europe, 1110–1700: A Documentary History.* 1972

Richard C. Dales. *The Scientific Achievement of the Middle Ages.* 1973

Katherine Fischer Drew, trans. *The Lombard Laws.* 1973

Edward Peters, ed. *Monks, Bishops, and Pagans: Christian Culture in Gaul and Italy, 500–700.* 1975

Jeanne Krochalis and Edward Peters, ed. and trans. *The World of Piers Plowman.* 1975

Julius Goebel, Jr. *Felony and Misdemeanor: A Study in the History of Criminal Law.* 1976

Susan Mosher Stuard, ed. *Women in Medieval Society.* 1976

Clifford Peterson. *Saint Erkenwald.* 1977

Robert Somerville and Kenneth Pennington, eds. *Law, Church, and Society: Essays in Honor of Stephan Kuttner.* 1977

Donald E. Queller. *The Fourth Crusade: The Conquest of Constantinople, 1201–1204.* 1977

Pierre Riché (Jo Ann McNamara, trans.). *Daily Life in the World of Charlemagne.* 1978

Edward Peters, ed. *Heresy and Authority in Medieval Europe.* 1980

Suzanne Fonay Wemple. *Women in Frankish Society: Marriage and the Cloister, 500–900.* 1981

Edward Peters. *The Magician, the Witch, and the Law.* 1982

Barbara H. Rosenwein. *Rhinoceros Bound: Cluny in the Tenth Century.* 1982

Steven D. Sargent, ed. and trans. *On the Threshold of Exact Science: Selected Writings of Anneliese Maier on Late Medieval Natural Philosophy.* 1982

Benedicta Ward. *Miracles and the Medieval Mind: Theory, Record, and Event, 1000–1215.* 1982

Harry Turtledove, trans. *The Chronicle of Theophanes: An English Translation of* anni mundi *6095–6305 (A.D. 602–813).* 1982

Leonard Cantor, ed. *The English Medieval Landscape.* 1982

Charles T. Davis. *Dante's Italy and Other Essays.* 1984

George T. Dennis, trans. *Maurice's Strategikon: Handbook of Byzantine Military Strategy.* 1984

Thomas F. X. Noble. *The Republic of St. Peter: The Birth of the Papal State, 680–825.* 1984

Kenneth Pennington. *Pope and Bishops: The Papal Monarchy in the Twelfth and Thirteenth Centuries.* 1984

Patrick J. Geary. *Aristocracy in Provence: The Rhône Basin at the Dawn of the Carolingian Age.* 1985

C. Stephen Jaeger. *The Origins of Courtliness: Civilizing Trends and the Formation of Courtly Ideals, 939–1210.* 1985

J. N. Hillgarth, ed. *Christianity and Paganism, 350–750: The Conversion of Western Europe.* 1986

William Chester Jordan. *From Servitude to Freedom: Manumission in the Sénonais in the Thirteenth Century.* 1986

James William Brodman. *Ransoming Captives in Crusader Spain: The Order of Merced on the Christian-Islamic Frontier.* 1986

Frank Tobin. *Meister Eckhart: Thought and Language.* 1986

Daniel Bornstein, trans. *Dino Compagni's Chronicle of Florence.* 1986

James M. Powell. *Anatomy of a Crusade, 1213–1221.* 1986

Jonathan Riley-Smith. *The First Crusade and the Idea of Crusading.* 1986

Susan Mosher Stuard, ed. *Women in Medieval History and Historiography.* 1987

Avril Henry, ed. *The Mirour of Mans Saluacioune.* 1987

María Rosa Menocal. *The Arabic Role in Medieval Literary History.* 1987

Margaret J. Ehrhart. *The Judgment of the Trojan Prince Paris in Medieval Literature.* 1987

Betsy Bowden. *Chaucer Aloud: The Varieties of Textual Interpretation.* 1987

Felipe Fernández-Armesto. *Before Columbus: Exploration and Colonization from the Mediterranean to the Atlantic, 1229–1492.* 1987

Michael Resler, trans. *EREC by Hartmann von Aue.* 1987

A. J. Minnis. *Medieval Theory of Authorship.* 1988

Uta-Renate Blumenthal. *The Investiture Controversy: Church and Monarchy from the Ninth to the Twelfth Century.* 1988

Robert Hollander. *Boccaccio's Last Fiction: "Il Corbaccio."* 1988

Ralph Turner. *Men Raised from the Dust: Administrative Service and Upward Mobility in Angevin England.* 1988

David Anderson. *Before the Knight's Tale: Imitation of Classical Epic in Boccaccio's "Teseida."* 1988

Charlotte A. Newman. *The Anglo-Norman Nobility in the Reign of Henry I: The Second Generation.* 1988

Joseph F. O'Callaghan. *The Cortes of Castile-León, 1188–1350.* 1989

William D. Paden. *The Voice of the Trobairitz: Essays on the Women Troubadours.* 1989

William Chester Jordan. *The French Monarchy and the Jews: From Philip Augustus to the Last Capetians.* 1989

Edward B. Irving, Jr. *Rereading "Beowulf."* 1989

David Burr. *Olivi and Franciscan Poverty: The Origins of the* Usus Pauper *Controversy.* 1989

Willene B. Clark and Meradith T. McMunn, eds. *Beasts and Birds of the Middle Ages: The Bestiary and Its Legacy.* 1989